AF324259

IT'S FOREVER STRICTLY PERSONAL

A FINAL NOSTALGIC MOVIE MEMOIR OF 1992–1999
OR: WHY DINOSAURS, A BOX OF CHOCOLATES, THE TITANIC AND
EVEN MORE BRITISH SPIES FOREVER MATTER TO GEN X'ERS LIKE ME!

Eric Friedmann

Copyright © 2023 Eric Friedmann
All rights reserved
First Edition

NEWMAN SPRINGS PUBLISHING
320 Broad Street
Red Bank, NJ 07701

First originally published by Newman Springs Publishing 2023

This is entirely a work of non-fiction, taken from the deepest roots of my personal adult memories. However, in cases of specific information and facts, particularly television premiere broadcast dates, I'm grateful for the use of public internet sources as Merriam-Webster, Wikipedia and YouTube.

My thoughts, feelings, opinions and personal interpretations of the selected motion pictures in this book are my own. Any similarity to thoughts, feelings, opinions and personal interpretations of others, living or deceased, regarding the same motion pictures, whether published or not, is purely coincidental.

ISBN 978-1-68498-211-0 (Paperback)
ISBN 978-1-68498-212-7 (Digital)

Printed in the United States of America

For my son Sam,
whose own love of film *forever*
inspires and encourages me.

Praise for *It's Still Strictly Personal:*
A Continuing Nostalgic Movie Memoir of 1983–1991

"*It's Still Strictly Personal* is different from the first volume in some important ways and I think those differences matter to a large degree. We come to identify with Eric Friedmann who is struggling to find himself as a person, and the thing that makes this story relevant to us is how he manages to use the movies to accomplish that. Eric ties events in his life to the movies. Sometimes they are moments of revelation, such as discovering a foreign language film that moves you when you have not been immersed in that world before. Even if you are indifferent to Eric as a person, you will still find merit in the story he tells about the times. We get a glimpse into how others live, and it is often very different from the way we live ourselves. That's the value of a book like this, and I understand it because movies allow us to share references and feelings, and the ability to empathize them is enhanced as a result."

—Richard Kirkham, Author of *Kirkham A Movie a Day* and host of the *Lambcast* Podcast

"I absolutely loved this book, and especially loved going on Eric Friedmann's journey along with him. I highly suggest it for all movie buffs."

—Stephanie Larkin, Host of *Between the Covers* and *Author Corner*, and publisher at Red Penguin Books

CHAPTER CONTENTS

1998

1999

Here we are together again, for the last time.

<hr>

I will forever love movies!

Movies will forever be history. History will forever be movies. Movies will forever be life. Life will forever be movies. Like history and life, movies will forever change, and our thoughts, feelings, and memories will forever change with them.

As previously described in *It's Strictly Personal* and *It's Still Strictly Personal*, the movies of my childhood and youth defined who I was, not only in meeting the everyday challenges of life and the world, but in relating to others as well. Movies saw me through my parents' divorce, changes in my education, friendships, and dealing with the joys and pains of love. Even as I developed into manhood beyond my college years, my interpretation of the movies never changed. *Movies comfort us, teach us, and hopefully try to answer some of the big questions of why in life.*

By the time I was twenty-two years old, I'd finally graduated that college pit of hell known as Pratt Institute in Brooklyn, New York. Whatever fun I'd had at school was over, and I'd have to take the next step into responsible adult employment during the early 1990s and its recession. My college girlfriend *Daniela B.* and I were officially broken up, but that didn't stop us from practicing our ongoing "friends with benefits" relationship. Oh yeah, and I was *still* carrying a romantic torch for *Caren L.* (sad as that was).

The '90s was underway, and I felt like a man alone. My parents were split for good, my father lived alone in Queens, my younger brother, Kevin, lived in Chicago, my friends were scattered around, and my mother…well, she was left alone in the big house in Great Neck, which she finally put on the real estate market (again, during a recession). Interest in the house was low, so in a strange twist, she moved out and into a rented Manhattan apartment, while I moved back home to an empty house. I lived alone, and that didn't bother me so much, but I was also responsible for coordinating with real estate agents whenever a perspective buyer wanted to see the house.

Being alone presented a further challenge when it came to movies. Even as I continuously searched for a full-time architect's position while (temporarily) earning my income at a local Great Neck bookstore, my exploration of new and different movies was expanded not only by the fact that I alone answered for my time, but also that I was free to venture into Manhattan at will, where independent, revival, and foreign films were at my disposal at various art houses. Sometimes I went to these movies alone, other times Daniela met me in the city or even drove from her parent's home in Connecticut to spend some time with me at my house. Her intellectual company at the movies was still welcomed, even as it seemed movies didn't change much during this new decade: there were blockbusters, independents, and the usual low-budget trash. Cinematic options seemed endless. With all this freedom and flexibility, you could say the '90s was my personal "golden age" of moviegoing.

One thing that never changed was my ongoing art of movie collecting. VHS tapes were still the form of home video in the early '90s, and one's card-carrying membership at the local Blockbuster store was a great commodity. I still had no additional TV options beyond the standard thirteen channels, so I often relied on whatever movies I occasionally taped off TV and committed myself to editing commercials out of my recording. But I had *some* money, so purchasing brand-new store-bought copies of my favorite movies wasn't a demanding challenge anymore as it was when I was younger.

Throughout it all, though, I never ceased to explore the possibilities of how movies potentially affected my life and my existence. As we entered the age of CGI, what sort of movies would speak to me and enable me to *feel* them, rather than just watch them? What sort of movies would arouse my potential and drive me to grow and evolve as a person? While men like Oliver Stone had recently astounded me with *JFK*, and

Barbra Streisand demonstrated that she could go beyond the music I didn't care for and direct a dramatic piece of work like *The Prince of Tides*, men I depended on like Steven Spielberg had previously disappointed me with films like *Indiana Jones and the Temple of Doom* and *Hook*. But with the potential of a new era always came the possibilities that I could not only be surprised, but also be inspired by anyone or anything.

*****

Beginning with the year 1992 and moving forward through the year 1999, I shall, for the third and final time, discuss, critique, and analyze selected movies as they pertained to my personal life, feelings, and memories as a grown man who experienced them between the ages of twenty-five and thirty-two. Like two times before, these aren't necessarily the *best* or most award-winning movies of each respective year, but rather, what's personally meaningful to me. Like two times before, I won't go into great depths of what the movie is about and what I think of it, but rather about how the movie and its cultural impact (if any) affected my life at the time I saw it as the younger man I once was.

Like the last times, I continue to be a different person as time and movies evolve. How I feel about a movie from the first time I saw it on screen or rented tape is still fairly dead-on in how I continue to feel about it today. As before, the *now* and the *then* are a thing of the past, and they remain one and the same. I'm also past the point in which I had naive expectations of movies which turned out to be letdowns. My movie intuitions seemed far better perceived now, and it was rare that they were ever wrong.

So now, if you'll permit me more of your valuable reading time one last time, allow me to take you along on the final journey back to the wonderful and weird years of 1992–1999, when the new theatrical motion picture releases of the time continued to turn the life of a grown man into the die-hard movie fanatic he'd always be, with his own stories to tell, his feelings to share, and his memories to reflect upon. It will forever be my hope that you'll continue to remember a time that *"takes you back"* and will forever *"put you in that special place"* of movie comfort…because let's never forget, *it's forever strictly personal.*

THE YEAR WAS 1992...

- United States president George Bush and Russian president Boris Yeltsin meet at Camp David to officially declare the end of the Cold War.
- International armed conflict in Bosnia and Herzegovina begins the Bosnian War.
- At Wembley Stadium in London, the televised Freddie Mercury Tribute Concert raises millions of dollars for AIDS research.
- The acquittal of the four police officers in the Rodney King beating triggers massive riots in Los Angeles.
- On *Saturday Night Live*, Sinéad O'Connor causes a huge controversy when she tears up a photo of Pope John Paul II.
- In the presidential election, Governor Bill Clinton defeats George Bush and independent candidate Ross Perot.

...AND THERE WERE MOVIES!

When 1992 began, I was into my last semester at Pratt Institute, and for the first three months of that year, Daniela and I were still a couple. The breakup was oncoming for some time and erupted one night into an unpleasant scene. But after a cool-down period, we were in bed together, though we didn't get back together. Perhaps ours was a true test of that old bullshit line at the end of many break-ups, "I hope we can still be friends." I suppose whether or not we passed such a test is subject to many perspectives, but we made a go of it. We were civil, friendly, still hot for each other, and still went to the movies together.

Like winters and springs before, before May kicked off the summer blockbuster season, movies often didn't leave much to mark our memories. There was always something good, something bad, and something easily forgettable. Any of these three categories easily described releases like *The Hand that Rocks the Cradle*, *Freejack*, *Shining Through*, and even *Wayne's World* (Daniela and I saw all of them).

Every once in a while, there *was* something noteworthy that caught everyone's attention; perhaps it was the outrageous courtroom comedy of Joe Pesci and Marisa Tomei (bless her priceless rant about the prancing deer who loses part of his head to a fuckin' bullet— LOL) in *My Cousin Vinny* or the sexual heat and sweat from Michael Douglas and Sharon Stone in *Basic Instinct*. *Vinny* was a good example of a rare springtime release that came along to not only carry its own weight alongside others, but to also carry itself into the summer season to stand tall against many popular blockbusters of that year.

Regardless of how I personally felt about titles like *Alien 3*, *Batman Returns*, *Lethal Weapon 3*, and *Patriot Games*, *Vinny* was still going strong enough for those of us who not only loved the film, but also wanted to see it again (I saw it twice). But even as I was no exception to those who loved that film, I suppose at that age back then, comedies were nothing more than what they were meant to be: pure escapist laughter, with little-to-nothing new to inspire one's impressionable mind. *Basic Instinct*, of course, offered much to the senses and one's horny imagination (I'll get into that shortly).

Even as the summer offered little by way of anything noteworthy (in my opinion), there was an exceptional evening in front of the screen that stays with me forever. A trip to Southampton over Memorial Day weekend to see the opening of *Alien 3* was itself a wasted effort. It was only when I unexpectedly walked into another theater to watch the Italian film *Mediterraneo* by Gabriele Salvatores that I was happily awestruck. This World War II comedy-drama which followed the life and pleasures of a group of misfit Italian soldiers was not only a shining example of life's pure joy at the movies, but it also reminded me of why I continued to explore the magic of Italian cinema, which began for me with *Cinema Paradiso* two years earlier. Turns out *Mediterraneo* had been in general release for nearly a year already, and I'd somehow managed to miss it. Who would've thought it would require two hours of a pointless sci-fi sequel featuring Sigourney Weaver with a shaved head for me to finally discover this priceless Italian gem?

But let's not knock sci-fi. As it turned out, what kicked off the year for me was a small (and dismissed by many) sci-fi action film offering the possibilities of a future that took our minds and senses to a whole new form of existence—a concept I'd never heard of before called *virtual reality*.

The Lawnmower Man
Directed by Brett Leonard
(March 6, 1992, U.S. Release Date)

It's amazing how timely a motion picture seems at the time of its release and how dated it becomes a short time later. When originally released in March 1992, the reality of electronic mail and the internet were still years away, so the bold concept of virtual reality as the new normal seemed the gateway to a probable future. Looking back on it now, as compared to the digital world we live in today, *The Lawnmower Man* may be the most dated computer technology-related film since *Wargames* in 1983.

My initial interest in seeing this movie had little to do with computer technology. Its original marketing scheme attached Stephen King's name to the title. That was short-lived, as King sued the film's producers for attaching his name to a film that had virtually (no pun intended) nothing to do with his own short story originally published in his 1978 collection, *Night Shift*. Still, I didn't know this at the time, so I thought I was going to see a new King screen adaptation. From the moment the opening title card over black appeared with these words, I knew better:

> *By the turn of the millennium a technology known as* VIRTUAL REALITY *will be in widespread use. It will allow you to enter computer generated artificial worlds as unlimited as the imagination itself.*

*Its creators foresee millions of positive uses—while
others fear it as a new form of mind control…*

Reading that back in '92, I was awestruck with imagination and with questions if such a thing were truly possible in our time. This was the possibility of reality, yet I couldn't ignore the fact that I was watching a fantasy film in which a scientist Dr. Lawrence Angelo (played by Pierce Brosnan, whom I'd never heard of before) worked for a powerful company called VSI, or "The Shop," conducting experiments in virtual reality and psychoactive drugs to enhance cognitive performance in his chimpanzee subject. While Dr. Angelo's intentions were for the greater good of mankind, VSI had financial and military intentions in mind. The experimental chimp, using his trained aggressive warfare tactics, escaped from his cage and killed several VSI guards before being killed himself.

Frustrated, Dr. Angelo continued his work underground by recruiting the local mentally challenged gardener named Jobe Smith (played by Jeff Fahey) to willfully participate in his experiments, promising that they'd make him smarter. With the aggression factors eliminated, the intelligence-boosting treatments and games Jobe participated in made him smarter at an accelerated rate. The new program was so successful that Jobe eventually developed his own means of telepathy and psychokinesis.

Meanwhile, the project's director kept constant tabs on the experiment's progress and secretly switched Dr. Angelo's new medications with the aggressive ones. The first casualty was the accidental erasing of Jobe's lover Marnie's mind during a session of cybersex at the simulation lab. As Jobe continued the aggressive treatments on his own, he sought revenge against those who mistreated him in the past, including the local town bully, the sadistic priest who raised him, and the abusive father of his teenage friend Peter.

Upon learning the medications were switched, Dr. Angelo confronted Jobe, who captured the doctor and announced the ultimate plan to achieve his final stage of evolution by transforming himself into pure energy in the VSI computer mainframe, in which he'd eventually reach into all the systems of the world with a *"birth cry"* of every telephone on Earth ringing simultaneously (the thought of such an event peaked my curiosity). When men from "The Shop" attempted to capture Jobe, he turned his power on them and scattered their molecules.

Upon returning to the VSI lab, Jobe entered the mainframe to "evolve" into a complete virtual being, leaving his physical body forever. Dr. Angelo wasn't far behind, as he encrypted links to the outside world, trapping Jobe in the mainframe. Furious, Jobe searched for an unencrypted network connection to free himself, repeatedly hearing, *"Access denied."*

Outside the lab, multiple bombs planted by Dr. Angelo were timed to go off, but not before he attempted to save Jobe by joining him in the virtual world to try and reason with him. His attempts failed, and Jobe freed him when he learned that Peter, the one person he still cared about, was in the building that would be destroyed by multiple explosions. Before the film ended, we were reminded about man's wisdom versus his madness, as Jobe's prophecy was fulfilled with the global ringing of telephones.

I'd seen actor Jeff Fahey before in two very bad horror films, *Psycho III* in 1986 and *Body Parts* in 1991. In *The Lawnmower Man*, he nails his role and his slow transformation perfectly. As the idiot, his character's pure innocence, both in voice and physical stature, evokes nothing but childlike sympathy from us. As the transformation begins, so does Fahey's voice and stature, giving off not only his newfound intelligence and confidence, but also his dangerous arrogance and evil, making the concept of man in his before and after stage very clear and thought-provoking. Like Daniel Keyes 1959 novel *Flowers for Algernon*, the story also deals with a mentally disabled man whose intelligence is technologically boosted to levels of genius. Like Mary Shelley's 1818 novel *Frankenstein*, the simpleton is dangerously boosted to levels of evil. I can't help but feel a sense of frightened awe when I hear Jobe speak these words:

> *I realize that nothing we've been doing is new. We*
> *haven't been tapping into new areas of the brain—*
> *we've just been awakening the most ancient. This*

> *technology is simply a route to powers that conjurers and alchemists used centuries ago. The human race lost that knowledge and now I'm reclaiming it through virtual reality.*

More frighteningly real is the response Dr. Angelo gives him in which he says, *"You're moving too fast. Even with all these new abilities, there are dangers. Man may be able to evolve a thousand-fold through this technology, but the rush must be tempered with wisdom"* (this so-called *wisdom*, in my opinion, still doesn't exist even in today's world).

While *The Lawnmower Man* may be an outdated topic, even in sci-fi, its story, and computer effects are no less fun and entertaining to watch. Even in the twenty-first-century world of digital 3D CGI that's thrown in your face at every movie theater you go to today, the effects here still aren't too shabby, and they're fun to watch, in a 1982 *Tron*-sort-of-way. Beyond the effects and the thrills, this is still what I'd consider to be an intelligent high-concept tale of man's wisdom, ignorance, and madness in the hands of unexplored technological advances. Since the creation of fire, our first true technology, man's achievements haven't ceased to evolve itself through its technology. But as Khan said in the episode "Space Seed" of *Star Trek: The Original Series, "How little man himself has changed,"* and is likely to ever change. While there are arguments for both sides, I can't help but wonder how many horrific events of crime and terrorism might never have happened had technology like the internet been invented (on the other hand, how else would I buy my concert tickets?).

More than thirty years later, whatever happened to virtual reality? Oh, I'm sure it's still out there somewhere, buried underground in secret worlds of computer technology that I don't pretend to understand. Back in '92, I'm sure such possibilities seemed like the reality of the future. But the world saw instead the creation and emergence of the internet, emailing, iPhones, and computer social networks. It's probably safe to say that the concept, hopes, and dreams of virtual reality took a major back seat to all that and eventually became as obsolete as the VCR and the cassette player. But remember, I'm no computer expert or geek, so perhaps I don't have all the facts (perhaps I never will).

Let me conclude with a personal story. While I saw *The Lawnmower Man* with Daniela at the time of its release, the real story comes months later when I acquired my own VHS copy of the director's cut. It was Labor Day weekend of '92, and I had a group of friends staying with me at the family beach house in Westhampton Beach, Long Island. One night, we all watched the movie and enjoyed it a bit more when we all had a few extra drinks in our system. By the time of the film's climax, when Jobe tries to permanently absorb himself into the computer mainframe and repeatedly hits the walls of Access Denied, we were all cracking up. In particular, the girls who were staying with me began closing their bare legs real tight and said, "Access denied," leaving all horny young men to only fantasize about what might have been, had access been granted.

Perhaps you had to be there, but take my word for it—it was funny at the time, and the memory is still with me. Thank you, ladies.

Basic Instinct

Directed by Paul Verhoeven
(March 20, 1992, U.S. Release Date)

It was because of *Basic Instinct* that I learned the following: if you're offended by the contents and implied messages of a movie and you don't want people to see it, the last thing you should do is create a wave of controversy surrounding it. This will only fuel people's desire to quickly get to the theater to see what all the hubbub is about. It mattered little to me and Daniela that the film was protested by gay and lesbian rights activists, claiming it followed a pattern of negative depictions of lesbians and bisexuals as twisted, evil murderers, because we saw it the weekend it opened. In other words, if you really don't want people to see a controversial film, then keep your mouth shut, because controversy fuels box office sales.

Without having seen the movie yet, I was already fully aware of its strong sexual themes and circumstances, and two thoughts kept racing through my head. The first was that seeing it with my sexually charged girlfriend (we were still together then) only heightened my enjoyment. The second was a consideration of actor Michael Douglas and his work with women like Glenn Close in *Fatal Attraction* and Kathleen Turner in *The War of the Roses*. Add Sharon Stone to the mix, and there was no doubt the man got more ass than a car rental (you *had* to love the guy). This would also be the second time Douglas played a cop on screen, the first time in Ridley Scott's 1989 film *Black Rain*.

Douglas played San Francisco homicide detective Nick Curran, investigating the murder of a retired rock star brutally stabbed to death with an ice pick during sex with his blonde lover, face unseen. The immediate suspect was the victim's bisexual girlfriend Catherine Tramell (Stone) who also wrote a crime novel mirroring the actual crime. We were meant to believe that either Catherine was the actual murderer or that someone else was attempting to frame her by copying the killing exactly as she wrote it in her novel. I loved Catherine immediately. She was beautiful, hot, seductive, talked dirty, and had no hesitation about exposing her vagina during a police interrogation, stating, *"It's nice."*

Despite having an alibi for the night in question, as well as passing a lie detector test, Nick refused to eliminate her as a suspect. He discovered she had a history of befriending female murderers, including her girlfriend Roxy and old lady Hazel Dobkins. Regardless of his suspicions of Catherine, it didn't stop him from getting closer to her, having the greatest sex of his life with her (*"I think she's the fuck of the century!"*), and eventually falling in love with her, even while he was still sleeping with his on again-off again lover and current psychologist Dr. Beth Garner. Even when Nick discovered that Catherine was writing her latest novel with the main character based on *him*, and that she was also bribing Internal Affairs for information on his psychiatric file, he still refused to back away from her (goes to show you that men have two brains, and we tend to think with only the one between our legs).

As their torrid, cat-and-mouse love affair continued, there was a scene at a dance club in which Catherine danced and made out with Roxy in front of Nick. I don't have to tell you what a traditional heterosexual male like me thought of *that* scene, or the scene of violent sex between Nick and Catherine that followed (even with my girlfriend sitting next to me). When Catherine tied Nick to the headboard with a white silk scarf (just like the film's opening murder), we all couldn't help but think for a moment that Nick was about to get it the same way. He didn't, but he was nearly killed when Roxy tried to run him down with Catherine's car, but ended up dying herself when the car crashed. Bereaved, Catherine confessed to Nick about a lesbian encounter at college that didn't go well. It was later revealed that Catherine's brief female college lover was Dr. Beth Garner, who apparently developed a serious and dangerous fixation on Catherine, though Beth claimed it was the other way around when Nick confronted her about it.

As Catherine's new book came to an end, she coldly and abruptly broke off the affair with Nick. Realizing her book contained a moment when the detective discovers his partner's dead body in an elevator, Nick raced against time while his partner Gus was stabbed to death with an ice pick in an elevator in the same manner described in the book. Beth turned up at that exact moment and was shot to death by Nick, believing her to be the murderer. He appeared to be right, because mounting evidence revealed Beth to be the killer of just about every victim. In the final moment between Catherine and Nick, they were together again and (of course) had wild sex. As they discussed their possible future, the camera panned downward to reveal an ice pick under the bed, leaving us all in the theater with a feeling of "What the fuck!"

With regard to that moment that kept us all guessing, let's try and clear this up right now. It's my humble opinion that that final shot of the ice pick under the bed at the end of the film did *not* reveal Catherine Tramell to be the killer. Here's my conclusion of what that shot means—if you take a look at the film at the fifty-four minute mark, you'll notice a close-up shot of Nick Curran's keys on a table with a Bart Simpson keychain on it. His ex-lover, Beth, attempts to return them to him. In their heated argument, he picks up the keys and hands them back to her. So Beth *still* has the keys to his apartment. I believe that before she was killed at the end of the film, she'd gone (unseen) to Nick's place, planted the ice pick under his bed, and planned to kill him later on, had she gotten the chance. I believe that when Catherine lowered her arm over the side of the bed, she *didn't know* the ice pick was there (that's my conclusion. Take it or leave it).

As a motion picture, were it not for the impressive performances by Michael Douglas and Sharon Stone, *Basic Instinct* would pass for almost nothing more than late-night softcore porn on Cinemax or Showtime. While the intense sexuality of Stone's character cannot be denied by any red-blooded heterosexual male (or lesbian) with an active libido, there's deception and diabolical motives behind just about everything she says and does. It's in her eyes and voice, and it pierces both the brain in your head and the one between your legs (the one most men think with). It keeps you guessing and wondering what's coming 'round the bend, which is what any effective psychological thriller should do. It also proves undeniably that men are weak and easily controlled when it comes to the promise of great sex. Look at how Douglas is almost willing to allow himself to be murdered by the hands of the woman who's just given him the greatest and most satisfying fuck of his life. Look at how all the policemen during her interrogation go completely limp with stupidity during the iconic open legs beaver shot that made Stone famous overnight, because she represented every sexual fantasy we could imagine in a beautiful and desirable woman (I appreciate those fantasies).

Daniela and I not only loved the movie, but within a couple of weeks, I'd purchased an illegal bootleg VHS copy of it on the streets of Manhattan (someone had actually pointed a video camera at the movie screen to record it). Without going into any indiscreet detail, *Basic Instinct* became *our* movie. How much did it become *our* movie? Let's just say we were both dumb enough to pay to see Phillip Noyce's 1993 film *Sliver* and Verhoeven's 1995 flop *Showgirls* together in the years that followed. Still, she and I were definitely on a sexual movie kick of sorts. It was one of those things that continued to define who we were back then. We had good times, we had bad times, but we had *times*. Like it or not, those are the times all memories are made of.

Thank you, Daniela.

The Player
Directed by Robert Altman
(April 10, 1992, U.S. Release Date)

The Player was released at a time when my college education for architecture was coming to an end, and I was also just starting to come into my own in terms of my screenwriting abilities. With these abilities, I was also learned about what it took to pitch and sell a screenplay in Hollywood, at least in how books, classes and even the movies were explaining it to me. Everyone has their own opinion and theory about how things should be done in the movie business. Different authors of different "how to" books will tell you different things, and different professors and instructors of different classes will also tell you different things. So what's the end result? It's that it's all bullshit and more about who you know and how much luck you can achieve. This is why, thirty years later, I ended up a miserable architect and not a professional screenwriter, as I'd once dreamed.

As part of my informal education into Hollywood through the movies, *The Player* showed me a character in the form of Griffin Mill (played by Tim Robbins), a Hollywood studio executive whose job it was to listen to pitches of stories from screenwriters and decide whether or not they'd make good movies and get green-lit into production. Before this film, I had no idea that such a position existed in the movie business, and I couldn't help but wonder if it was a useless justification of one's high paycheck. At the same time, I couldn't help but consider how easy the concept sounded in theory—pitch a story, pitch it well, and the executive listening to you would (hopefully) like it and you'd get your movie made. Sure, that's what the ignorant New York architect-to-be thought at that time because he didn't have a clue just how cold, cruel and even corrupt things were out there in "La-La" movieland.

As a film viewer, however, it was easy to recognize the parody of cynicism Robert Altman brought to his story based on his own career in dealing with the Hollywood system and working outside of it for many years. However, rather than overpreach the injustices of the Hollywood community, he chose to invoke satire with not only cameo appearances of popular movie stars and celebrities, but also in the naughty cat-and-mouse fun involved with murder, and getting away with that murder. Griffin was a seemingly all-around nice guy in his business, but that business also unavoidably made him an asshole at times, and he managed to make some enemies along the way by repeatedly telling screenwriters he'd *get back to them,* though he almost never did. Those in the movie business likely know that such a line was crap and simply a polite disguise for "forget it" and "no chance in hell."

One writer, however, retaliated against such industry lies and repeatedly sent Griffin death threats on post cards. Fearing for his life and trying to resolve the situation, Griffin tracked down the writer in Pasadena, California at an art house movie theater showing Vittorio De Sica's *The Bicycle Thief,* which I felt was thrown into the story to combat the onslaught of mainstream Hollywood crap the public was constantly exposed to, and to also remind us of the art house film essentials we should never forget. Griffin encountered David Kahane at the theater, a screenwriter who was also pissed off at Griffin (for the same reasons explained already) and was also, by strange chance, *not* the one who'd sent Griffin the post cards. Heated words led to a physical confrontation that inevitably caused Kahane's accidental murder. Accident or not, however, Griffin fled the scene after making it look like a botched robbery. We knew he was guilty, but the question now was, would he get caught? Perhaps because of his occasional (and more frequent) asshole nature, I *wanted* him to get caught. But I also remembered this was Hollywood, where corruption and cover-ups were just as common as in big corporate business and the Mafia.

Like Alfred Hitchcock and many of the crime classics of the age (I took notice of the symbolic black-and-white film noir movie posters that occupied Griffin's office), Griffin went to great lengths to cover up his crime. And as matters progressed, I couldn't help but feel that same desire for his acquittal and freedom from suspicion. It seemed obvious that Altman, while having a great deal of fun with this story, was also implying how ugly Hollywood was in fiction and in reality. From that ugliness, I knew and even accepted that Griffin Mill would not only get away with murder, but would also gladly step on any toes and graves to achieve what he wanted in the movie business. Even as he preached the good work of producing mean-ingful films by the new John Hustons, Orson Welleses, and Frank Capras of the 1990s, in the end, he knew only too well how to sell his soul for the typical upbeat, happy Hollywood ending of his lat-est project to achieve the much-needed Hollywood bucks and keep things running peacefully and smoothly within the studio structure he long embraced—and survived.

Returning to the aspirations I once had as a screenwriter, I can only say that as someone from New York, I've seen and experienced my own small share of inside-industry crap that's made Hollywood so infamous. I've pitched stories, I've written countless letters to movie agents according to the exact rules all these bullshit books insist you follow, and I even attended a weekend Hollywood Pitch Festival back in August 2000 in which I was also repeatedly told, "I'll get back to you." Not that I ever believed that line for a minute, but for one weekend of my life, I had a lot of fun and made some new friends. Still, looking at things the way they are today, in which only those who write and direct stories of comic book action heroes capable of generating endless franchises are the ones who are ever going to get their movies made—well, perhaps the unavoidable conclusion is that someone like *me*, someone who once tried to write simpler and more meaningful stories, will *never* find a place in the movie business.

Well, at least I *tried*, dammit, and my dreams of writing today are now successfully realized through my books instead.

Unlawful Entry

Directed by Jonathan Kaplan
(June 26, 1992, U.S. Release Date)

Timing was everything for what could've easily been dismissed as just another psychological thriller during the '92 summer blockbuster season. *Unlawful Entry*, and its premise of a Los Angeles couple who befriend a lonely and psychopathic cop was intriguing enough as an echo of *Fatal Attraction*, particularly when you added an impressive cast like Kurt Russell, Ray Liotta, and Madeleine Stowe to the mix.

But it was impossible to ignore the fact that just a couple of months prior, the L.A. riots and civil disturbances took place for six days following the shocking acquittal of the four officers who used excessive force in the arrest and beating of Rodney King, which was secretly videotaped and aired on TV. The police force, and its reputation of corruption and injustice, were impossible to ignore at the time (they still are today), and it was Liotta's portrayal of such a cop that made the film more intriguing, if not timely. Whether such timing was highly insensitive or dead-on depended on those watching it, I suppose.

The film wasted no time in showing how quickly the lives of an upscale married couple, Michael and Karen Carr (Russell and Stowe) could become unglued in one night by the invasion of an intruder through an open skylight. The intruder got ahold of Karen and put a knife to her throat to escape the house. From the moment the police arrived, officer Pete Davis (Liotta) was immediately attracted to Karen and extended his friendship to the couple by cutting through the red tape to expedite the installation of their new security system (for which Michael was stupid enough to reveal his new password to Pete).

As the new friendship between Michael and Pete developed, Michael wasn't shy about admitting his desire for brutal revenge against the intruder who took his wife hostage. Days later, on a police "ride along" with Pete's partner, Michael was surprised to learn that Pete had not only arrested the intruder, but also offered Michael the opportunity to fulfill his violent revenge by offering him his nightstick to beat the intruder. Like so many of us, though, what we think we'd like to do, and what we're actually willing to do in real life are often two different things. Michael refused, but Pete administered his own vicious beating to the intruder after he tried to escape custody. Disturbed, Michael sensed Pete's mental instability and decided to keep him far away from him and Karen. Not possible.

Pete was obsessed with Karen and stalked the couple, even showing up at the couple's bedroom one night while they were making love, claiming he and his partner responded to their security alarm. Other matters, like a boot on the tire of his car, and cancelled credit cards, followed Michael like a predator. When Michael filed a formal complaint against Pete, Pete used his police connection to sabotage Michael's business reputation in the middle of a big deal for the opening of a new night club. The only sympathy Michael got was from Pete's partner, who ordered Pete to give up his obsession of Karen and seek psychiatric help or face suspension. The result of that threat got the partner killed when Pete set him up to look like he was murdered by a known criminal. The final move was when Pete framed Michael on false drug charges by planting a large supply of cocaine in his house, leaving the path clear for him to move in on the distraught Karen. Michael managed to get out of jail on bail, but needed to take matters into his own hands.

At the Carr's house, Karen played along with Pete to delude him into thinking she would be his, but only until she got ahold of a gun and ordered him to leave. Distraught and enraged, Pete attempted to rape her but was subdued when Michael showed up and attacked him. The men fought, and it looked like Michael would lose, until

Karen attacked Pete, sending him down the stairs, and bleeding unconscious. But like any of those horror movie serial killers of the 1980s, Peter awoke to taunt his victims one last time, before he was finally shot dead by Michael.

I mentioned *Fatal Attraction* earlier, and I think there are many similarities in how we interpret the so-called "good people" and "bad people" of a film like this. As brilliantly psychotic as Ray Liotta is in his role, there are moments when we not only side with his actions as a police officer, but even *condemn* some of Kurt Russell's actions. Let's remember that the trouble starts when Michael freaks out watching Pete beat his arrested criminal, and concludes that Pete is unstable. However, this instability, in my opinion, is more about the *man* rather than the cop. As a cop, he's forced to do whatever it takes to subdue his man and avoid his own injury or death. As a man, he's still at the point where he considers himself a friend of Michael and Karen and would love to watch Michael extract justice by taking revenge against the man who held a knife to his wife's throat. Michael sees only a senseless beating of a black man by a white cop, and it's impossible for us not to feel the sensitivity behind that action at that particular time in 1992.

As a man, Michael may not be of a reasonable frame of mind, either. When he's faced with telling Pete how he feels about their new relationship, he insults Pete, screams at him, and orders him out of his club. Is that the best way to handle an already delicate situation with someone, especially a cop? One can't help but feel that Michael's lack of tact and sensitivity invites trouble against him. You can't help but want to shout at the screen, "Oh geez, man, don't handle it that way. Be nice about it, or that crazy cop will kill you."

Beyond being a great thriller in a summer filled with heroes like Batman, Jack Ryan, and the partnership of Martin Riggs and Roger Murtaugh, there's serious and unrestrained realism involved in what is a socially relevant drama when faced with the harshness and delusions of police authority and power. This power takes place in the face of social and class structure, and the potential for complex police figures like Ray Liotta to become unhinged in such violent urban settings as in the big city of Los Angeles. Credibility of such premises (or accusations) may be debatable even in today's world. But back in the summer of '92, when Americans were still feeling frail and vulnerable about the security and stability of the police force, a film like *Unlawful Entry* may have been what we needed to confirm our worst fears and uncertainties, and remind us that, like it or not, it simply isn't a pretty world out there.

Twin Peaks: Fire Walk with Me
Directed by David Lynch
(August 28, 1992, U.S. Release Date)

Did you watch *Twin Peaks* back in the early '90s? If you didn't, and you know nothing about the show, my writing for this particular film may go over your head. Just the same, give it a shot. If nothing else, you may be inspired to start streaming the show from the beginning.

When David Lynch's groundbreaking TV show premiered on ABC on April 8, 1990, I didn't tune in to see the two-hour pilot that immediately grabbed the world's attention. It was a week later when I met a girl named *Cathy M.* in my dormitory. I was instantly attracted to her and wasted almost no time in trying to get a date with her. She shot me down quickly, but to her credit, she was very sweet about it. We agreed to be friends instead (we actually *meant* it). I asked her if she wanted to hang out, but she told me she was committed to watching *Twin Peaks* that night. She was surprised at my ignorance of this new and popular show, and invited me to her room to watch it with her. I'd missed the pilot, but I was immediately hooked on this new TV phenomenon trying to solve the mystery of *"who killed Laura Palmer?"*

Those who followed the show more than thirty years ago know that while it started off with a bang, it died a quick death after Laura Palmer's murderer (spoiler alert—*it was her father*) was revealed and was cancelled after wrapping things up at the end of just two seasons. Still, David Lynch couldn't get his head and heart away from the world of *Twin Peaks* and wanted to make a film to further explore the material of Laura Palmer and the contradictions of her character—lovely and radiant on the outside, but dying on the inside. Actress Sheryl Lee, who played Laura, never got to live her character's torment as the victim of incest, as she was already dead when the series began (only flashbacks of Laura were filmed). There was also the torment of her father Leland Palmer and the dark side of Bob that raged within his soul.

The final result was the R-rated prequel film *Twin Peaks: Fire Walk with Me* more than a year after the series was cancelled. It was released without marketing or fanfare on Labor Day weekend of '92, which also turned out to be one of the best weekends I ever had with friends at the family beach house in Westhampton Beach. In attendance besides myself was Daniela, Cathy, and Chris T. (remember him from my writing of David Lynch's *Blue Velvet* in *It's Still Strictly Personal?*). Besides graduating from the same college, what we also had in common was our undeniable love of *Twin Peaks*. During that weekend, the sun didn't shine once, but it also didn't rain. So while we nonchalantly went about our days without planning much in advance, one thing that was certain was a drive to Southampton on Sunday night to attend the late night showing of *Fire Walk with Me*.

The theater was practically empty. Except for my group of friends, there were two or three other people, and they sat in the back. So for all practical purposes, my friends and I had the theater to ourselves. This was *our* theater, *our* night, and *our* love of *Twin Peaks* bringing us together. As far as we were concerned, David Lynch made this prequel for *us*. This private arrogance wasn't without merit, because it was immediately obvious when the film began and the floating corpse of Teresa Banks was identified on screen, that understanding of this film, its characters and its circumstances were highly predicated on having watched the TV series. That was fine with us.

Beginning one year before the murder of Laura Palmer, FBI agents Chester Desmond and Sam Stanley were assigned to investigate the murder of teenage drifter and prostitute Teresa Banks in the town of Deer Meadow, Washington. The weirdness of David Lynch wasted no time with a woman named Lil, whose physical appearance and actions revealed information about their assignment, including an artificial blue rose pinned to her dress. While examining Teresa's corpse in the morgue, they discovered a small piece of paper inserted under her fingernail with the letter *T* printed on it (you may recall that Laura had the same kind of paper with the letter *R* printed on it). Later, while retrieving Teresa's missing ring, the camera froze, as if to suggest Desmond had been taken by an unseen force.

At the FBI headquarters in Philadelphia, Special Agent Dale Cooper (Kyle MacLachlan returning to the role) and his boss Gordon Cole (David Lynch himself) experienced a vision of their long-lost colleague Phillip Jeffries, played by David Bowie. Cathy practically screamed with joy when he appeared on screen (she *worships* Bowie). He told them of a meeting he witnessed of mysterious spirits above a convenience store, including the Man from Another Place and the killer Bob. Bob, we already knew to be the evil spirit inhabiting the body of Leland Palmer when he killed his victims.

One year later, and we were once again in the town of Twin Peaks. Laura was alive, addicted to cocaine, and seeing James Hurley behind her biker boyfriend Bobby Briggs's back. In her bedroom, she discovered pages torn out of her secret diary, whom she entrusted with her friend Harold Smith. Heeding a mysterious warning from an old woman and her grandson, Laura raced home to discover Bob in her bedroom. Fleeing her house in terror, she hid and watched her father exit the house, deducing that he and Bob were one and the same. Leland was abusive with her that night, and then lovingly tender with her later. Her dream of being in the Black Lodge with Cooper and the Man from Another Place was creepy and visually haunting, as only Lynch could deliver. Cooper warned Laura not to take Teresa's ring, but it was in her hand, nonetheless. When she awoke, the ring was gone.

Throughout the film, I'd occasionally look at the faces of my friends. Like myself, they were either fixated on every frame or overcome with the urge to smile, as if suggesting that everything on screen made sense to us. We understood every scene, hint, and innuendo, including the brief appearance of a bloodied Annie Blackburn in Laura's bed, who told her *"the good Dale is in the Lodge and can't leave"* and to write it in her diary. It took me a moment to catch on, but her words referenced Dale's actions in the final episode of the show's final season.

The scene that followed in the Roadhouse was an example of everything Lynch couldn't get away with on TV, including drug use, nudity, and acts of sex. We also learned that Laura and Ronette Pulaski knew Teresa Banks. In a private moment with Laura and her father in the car, they were verbally assaulted by Philip Gerard (aka the one-armed man) who was possessed by the demon known as Mike, when he tried to warn Laura about her father and Bob. Teresa's ring was on his finger, and the film flashbacked to a potential foursome with her and Leland. This didn't happen when he was shocked to discover that one of the girls was his own daughter and fled the scene. We were reminded again that we were watching an R-rated movie instead of censored TV show, because the incestuous nature of Laura's torment was not only visual, but physical, when Bob came through her window and raped her, only to reveal himself as Leland for a brief moment, sending Laura into terror.

Finally, on the night we all knew was coming, Laura met Leo Johnson, Jacques Renault, and Ronette at the cabin in the woods. Leland followed her there, and made his evil existence known when he attacked the men, and took the girls to an abandoned train car. Transforming into Bob, he beat Ronette unconscious and viciously murdered Laura, but not before she put Teresa's ring on her finger, which prevented Bob from possessing her. Wrapped in plastic, Laura was placed in the lake until she washed up ashore the next morning, which is where the TV pilot began more than two years earlier. In the Black Lodge, Cooper was there to comfort her spirit. When she saw the angel of goodness, she laughed and cried, and we all believed that Laura Palmer would find peace in a happier place.

The night wasn't over. When we returned to the beach house, everything around us was pitch black. The street lamps weren't functioning and the light on my front deck was out. There were no lights on inside the house. The walk from the car to the front door felt like an eternity. Daniela and Cathy were freaked out of their minds, especially having just sat through more than two hours of David Lynch's psychological horror show. Naturally, being guys, Chris and I did everything we could to scare the hell out of them. Once we were safe inside the house, we broke out the beers, the munchies, and continued the night the best way we knew how: by watching the *Twin Peaks* pilot I owned on videotape, picking up where *Fire Walk with Me* concluded.

This prequel was doomed before it ever hit the screen, because if you didn't follow the TV show, the film's content would mean nothing to you, and probably just piss you off. This was a time before streaming, and not even the complete videotape series of the show was available yet. So it's no wonder *Fire Walk with Me* bombed at both the box office and with critics. Those who "didn't get it" likely felt the character of Laura Palmer to be uninteresting and noncompelling, in a tale that simply went beyond the standards of TV to feature language, violence, nudity, and sex. I can appreciate all that, so it's from the perspective of one who followed the show, and enjoys following Lynch's bizarre art form, that I can offer all the personal love and praise I bestow on this film.

Like the Italian director Federico Fellini, Lynch takes the opportunity to be as self-indulgent as he wishes to be with material he's loved for much of his career. He's brave in taking the small American town from TV and showing a darker, more horrific side of it in the life of a beautiful young woman we know is going to die in the end. It's this knowledge of Laura Palmer's pending death that instills a psychological edge in our thoughts, in knowing there's nothing that can save her. Laura *will* die by the hands of her own father, and we know it's coming with every terrifying minute that passes because we understand what it's like to be in her shoes as she horribly suffers.

Despite its negative backlash (even by some die-hard fans of the show), *Fire Walk with Me* has enjoyed some positive critical reevaluation and cult status. But like it or not, for better or worse, the film is every bit as weird and twisted as anything David Lynch has offered us before with films like *Blue Velvet* and *Wild at Heart*. I mean, it's *Twin Peaks*, for crying out loud, and in the end, it may be all but critic-proof because of the love and support that comes from people who understand the artist—people like myself, Daniela, Cathy and Chris.

Thank you, my friends, for one of the most personal weekends in the Hamptons I've ever experienced and will never forget.

Husbands and Wives
Directed by Woody Allen
(September 18, 1992, U.S. Release Date)

I miss Woody Allen. Let me rephrase that…I miss the Woody Allen *I* knew and loved. He's not dead (yet), and (as of this writing) he still makes movies regularly, but in my opinion, they haven't been the same for over two decades. I miss the neurotic, narcissistic Woody of Manhattan who worried about his health and couldn't make his love life work. I miss the beautifully furnished apartments, the scenes of Central Park captured at just the right time of the year, and the quiet, intimate, candle-lit restaurants. The Woody Allen films of Paris, Rome, England and Europe, I just can't get into. I suppose, whether I like it or not, that's just the way things are as the man ages.

Strangely, the release of *Husbands and Wives* was perfectly timed. In my personal life, it was around the time my mother and I were getting closer to each other by meeting more frequently in Manhattan at the movies, which were of the independent and artful nature, and Woody Allen films fit perfectly into either of those categories. It was also released at the time the world discovered that Woody and his longtime companion of twelve years, Mia Farrow, were coming to a horrible end because Mr. Allen decided to start screwing his adopted daughter, Soon-Yi Previn. Since we all know nothing helps a film's box office receipts like some good, juicy controversy or scandal, *Husbands and Wives* piqued my interest and did much better than it likely would've were it just another release during the director's career. When you think about it, the timing is even better than I could've imagined: a film about troubled marriages starring Woody and Mia just as their own real relationship comes crumbling down. It also coincidentally featured Woody's character seducing a young, twenty-year-old college girl. I still remember Woody saying on TV, *"The heart wants what it wants."* True, but perhaps I couldn't see *wanting* Soon-Yi Previn.

I didn't know it at the time, but *Husbands and Wives* is inspired by Swedish director Ingmar Bergman's 1973 TV miniseries *Scenes from a Marriage.* The film told the story a two married couples. Gabe and Judy (Woody and Mia) were seemingly happy together after many years of marriage. Jack and Sally (played by director Sydney Pollack and Judy Davis) announced one night before dinner that they were splitting up after many years together and they were both supposedly fine with it. Gabe was shocked, but Judy took the bad news personally and felt hurt by it.

Weeks later, Sally discovered that Jack was seeing someone else, and was enraged to learn he was already having the affair during their marriage. Gabe and Judy met Jack's new girlfriend named Samantha, an aerobics trainer, during a chance meeting on the city streets. Gabe was puzzled, unable to comprehend why Jack would leave a fine woman like Sally for what he described as a *"cocktail waitress."* According to Jack, though, Sally was a cold woman, who always made him feel like he was constantly auditioning every part of his life for her. The word *auditioning* caught my attention. Sitting in my theater seat next to my mother, I recalled my father's similar feelings toward her when they were together. I couldn't help but wonder what my mother was thinking and feeling at that moment.

In an effort to move on with her life, Sally began seeing Michael, a work colleague of Judy's whom she introduced to Sally, despite the fact that she was interested in Michael herself. Michael was taken with Sally, but she seemed dissatisfied with the new relationship, or *cold* as Jack described her. But even as Jack's relationship with his new young girlfriend moved forward, he was jealous when learned Sally was dating Michael. It wasn't long before he inevitably asked Sally to give their marriage another chance. My mother couldn't help but freely express her awe and amazement at Jack's nerve, as if she knew *exactly* what was happening on screen (she *did* because my father did the same thing in 1980 when they split for the second time).

Meanwhile, Gabe developed a friendship with one of his female college writing students named Rain (played by Juliette Lewis, whom I remembered well from *Cape Fear*). In what I considered an unexpected and foolish move, he allowed this young girl to read the only copy of the novel he was working on. When she came back to comment on it, she praised its brilliant writing, but was highly critical of its character flaws, to which Gabe reacted defensively. As if that weren't enough, she accidentally left his only copy in the back seat of a taxi cab. They got it back, but I couldn't decide where Gabe's foolishness was greatest—was it the fact that he was willing to be criticized by a schoolgirl twit, or the fact that he'd given her his *only copy* and almost lost it? Geez, I wanted to shout at the screen, "Make a copy first, you idiot!"

Time was interesting in this film. Despite how things began with these two couples, it was Jack and Sally who ended up back together, while Gabe and Judy finally called it quits. Judy inevitably married Michael. Our final look at these marriages was a tense situation between a reunited Jack and Sally, in which they told their interviewer that they still had their unresolved marital problems, though they accepted them as the price paid to remain and grow old together. Gabe lived alone and chose not to date for fear he might hurt someone. When he asked the unseen documentary crew, *"Can I go? Is this over?"* I couldn't help but want to reply to the screen, "Yes, Woody, it's over, in more ways than you know."

One doesn't have to actually be married to know that marriage is a complicated mess. I knew it because I watched my parent's journey to marital hell and back more than once. Woody Allen knew it, and showed us that break-ups could be just as complicated. People move on to other partners. Sometimes they're bright, educated, sophisticated, old fashioned men for Judy like Michael (played by Liam Neeson), and sometimes they're uneducated, ditzy health food-obsessed, astrology-committed, yet fun and sexually exciting women for Jack, like Samantha. With Jack and Sally, we learn that despite a difficult marriage, and despite futile attempts to move on with others, two people who have shared too many years and experiences, and have very deep roots with each other are likely destined to be together forever, one way or another (in the *movies*, anyway). The marriage of Gabe and Judy is the opposite. The shocking announcement of Jack and Sally's break-up at the beginning of the film provokes Judy's hidden desires to be free from a marriage she doesn't feel passion for anymore, proving that in the end, even her seemingly fine marriage isn't durable.

Husbands and Wives isn't Woody's funniest film. In fact, its vividly shot and documentary-style filmmaking hardly makes it funny at all, but it's still undeniably classic Woody Allen like his others, because it deals with many of the self-analyzing issues of drama, intelligence and truth of life for those living in New York City. As a married man myself now, I've often felt the ultimate goal of marriage is to keep our partner happy, despite the need to cry out for ourselves (like a child) for what will make *us* happy on our own terms. These are terms I've done my best to try and achieve within my own marital union. Whether or not I've achieved this successfully is something I still struggle with, and I don't suppose I'll ever get a truly viable answer. What I *am* sure of, if nothing else, is that I've (hopefully) done a better job than my parents did, even after three times at bat. I've always tried to learn from *other people's* mistakes, and my parents surely made enough of them to constitute some of my own helpful life lessons.

In the end, perhaps we all write our own story of *Husbands and Wives*, whether we lived it ourselves or watched it as children from the sidelines. Some of us may even ask the question at the end, "Can I go? Is this over?"

Singles

Directed by Cameron Crowe
(September 18, 1992, U.S. Release Date)

In 2014, CNN began their annual summer documentary series of each decade with *The Sixties*. By the time they got to *The Nineties* in 2017, it was impossible for me not to reflect on what that decade meant to me, both personally and in popular culture. Keeping that decade fresh in my mind and memories means recalling two of its most popular TV shows, *Melrose Place* and *Friends*. Surprisingly, it's easy to forget, or to simply not acknowledge, that neither of those shows would've likely existed had it not been for Cameron Crowe's film *Singles*.

From my perspective, the film had no connection or prerequisite status to any TV shows of the future when I went to see in back in '92. For me, it was an experience of postcollege youth perfectly timed to coincide with my own recent college graduation. The story centered on the social and romantic lives of a group of young people of the Generation X era (*my* era), living in Seattle, Washington during the phenomenon of grunge music at the start of the '90s. Many of them lived in the same apartment complex (like in *Melrose Place*) and often hung out together at the local coffee shop (like in *Friends*). While the film divided itself into chapters of their multiple lives, we focused our attention on Steve Dunne and Linda Power (played by Campbell Scott and Kyra Sedgwick) from the moment they met at a popular grunge club straight on through their rocky relationship, with moments including an unexpected pregnancy and a car accident that inevitably took the baby from her.

I could see how crazy each of them were about each other from the time they met, yet neither of them seemed capable of a true commitment, even when they agreed to get married because of the pregnancy. Rocky or not, their relationship was built on love, and that of course, almost always triumphed in the end. And if we weren't entirely sure of how to keep up with things, we had the benefit of on-screen narration by its principal character that echoed Woody Allen in *Annie Hall* or even Ferris Bueller himself speaking to us on his day off.

Although not given equal screen time, we couldn't ignore the relationship between Cliff (played by Matt Dillon), a grunge rock musician playing in a fictional band called Citizen Dick with bandmates played by the actual members of Pearl Jam, and Janet (played by Bridget Fonda), a waitress at the popular coffee shop who wanted to be an architect (poor choice of careers). She loved him, while he only *liked* her (sounds like me and Caren back then). She was committed to him, while he saw other women. She eventually came to her senses and dumped him, while he regretted his aloofness with her and tried to win her back.

This was all part of what supposedly constituted real life, real world relationships and their irresistible moments of happiness, setback, pain, sorrow and stupidity. But more than these clichés, I felt the film made a successful attempt at pointing out the vulnerability and insecurities people like myself experienced during our post-college years. Not only were we faced with the prospect of finding our first place to live (not me: I moved back home, and my mother moved out) and securing our first real job (in my case, during a recession), but also how to get past the ongoing grind of dealing with the opposite sex without all the bullshit games involved with dating, sex, relationships, etc. This was my own life in the fall of '92, and for the next six years, I didn't have a single serious relationship until I met the woman that would one day become my wife. Those years prior to meeting that woman comprised of *many* first dates, a continued "friends with benefits" relationship with Daniela, and an equally continued-held torch for Caren. In short, the '90s was a real bitch for me as a single man.

As a filmmaker, I think Cameron Crowe has managed to repeatedly capture the hearts and minds of young people since he wrote the screenplay for *Fast Times at Ridgemont High* in 1982. He continued in 1989 with *Say Anything* and went straight on through to *Almost Famous* in 2000. Through it all, he's also reminded us of the music representing the soundtrack of our lives, regardless of what the era was. High school was never without its rock music, love wasn't without Peter Gabriel and the boom box held high above our heads, fun wasn't without the live rock concerts we loved, and as singles (like myself) trying to figure out where we belonged, the grunge rock music took what we previously knew as heavy metal hair music in the '80s and turned into something completely wild and different.

Unfortunately, true rock may have very well ended in the '90s during the grunge period. Honestly, what sort of music can the entire twenty-first century (so far) claim for itself with any pride? Lady GaGa and Taylor Swift (geez, it's enough to make me sick)? Perhaps Matt Dillon says it best when he loudly protests, *"Where are the anthems for our youth? What happened to music that meant something? The Who at the Kingdome, or Kiss at the Coliseum? Where is the* Misty Mountain Hop? *Where is the* Smoke on the Water? *Where is the* Iron Man *of today?"*

I hear you, Matt, and I feel for you.

A River Runs Through It
Directed by Robert Redford
(October 9, 1992, U.S. Release Date)

I've always believed there are specific moments of your life in which you truly believe you're experiencing peace and contentment. That hasn't happened a lot in my life, but when it has, I never forget it. These moments have almost always occurred in the town of Westhampton Beach, and the one associated with this film is no different.

It was a cold Saturday in December '92, and Daniela and I decided to spend the day together driving to check my family's beach house, which was something I did several times during the off-season. Everything around us, both among the houses and in town, was very quiet. Having no further tasks or plans after checking the house, we decided to catch *A River Runs Through It* at the Hampton Arts Theater in town, where it was still going strong after more than two months since its release. From the moment it began, it was obvious this wouldn't be a film filled with excitement or speed, but rather the perfect way to cap off an afternoon in a small, quiet beach town with a good friend (I'll take *that* kind of day anytime).

The peaceful serenity of Robert Redford's film and the way it beautifully captured the waters and the mountains of Montana were exemplary of the picturesque serenity of a simpler life at the turn of the century. Narrated by Redford himself, this was a coming-of-age tale of two Montana brothers. One of them studious, Norman Maclean (played by Craig Sheffer), of whose family the film was based on, and the other rebellious, Paul MacLean (played by Brad Pitt), both of them sons of the local town Presbyterian minister (played by Tom Skerritt). It was a life where the religion of church and the passion for fly fishing were practically one and the same, and we watched how fishing impacted their lives. As the boys matured into manhood, they evolved into their own lives, loves and passions, while still never losing their love of fishing. Norman went off to college in the east to study and teach literature, while Paul remained at home to become a journalist for the local town newspaper. Being the always rebellious one who was never afraid of a confrontation, he found it easy (and fun) to stand up to the issues of the era, including racism against the American Indian, and the violent troubles that Prohibition, illegal liquor and gambling brought.

It was impossible for me not to wonder when and where Paul was going to meet his fate if he didn't quit pushing his luck with certain people (by the end of the film, we were told he'd been beaten to death). Norman, on the other hand, played it safe and fell in love with the first beautiful girl he laid his eyes on at the local town dance, Jesse Burns (played by Emily Lloyd). Despite the great personality differences between both brothers, it was the art of fishing, and the love of the land and the waters of Montana that made their relationship strong. This seemed one of those rare movies in which two brothers were also best friends (doesn't happen too often, in my opinion).

The film ended beautifully with the last scene of Norman Maclean as an old man back at the river of Montana where he used to fish with his family many years ago. My immediate thought was that this was the real Norman himself, but I eventually learned that the real man died in 1990, two years before the film was released. Although it *was* Norman's actual words from 1976 that closed the film, as Redford narrated:

> *When I'm alone in the half light of the canyon,*
> *all existence seems to fade to a being with my soul*
> *and memories, and the sounds of the Big Blackfoot*
> *River, and the four-count rhythm, and a hope that*
> *a fish will rise. Eventually all things merge into one,*
> *and a river runs through it. The river was cut by*

the world's great flood, and runs over rocks from the basement of time. On some of the rocks are timeless raindrops. Under the rocks are the words, and some of the words are theirs. I am haunted by waters.

While the performances in this film are strong enough, particularly that of Brad Pitt in a groundbreaking role, the film is more of a visual experience in the heart and beauty of America's landscape, as well as Redford's best directorial work since *Ordinary People* in 1980, I think. One can't help feel enthralled by the power of the rivers and the life in and around them. We feel closer to nature and her possibilities while, perhaps, reaching down into our own souls to find meaning with the visual beauty around us. It's just fishing, yes, but it's the pure simplicity of life's pleasures that takes us to another place in our minds and hearts.

This was how I felt walking out of that small Hamptons movie theater, surrounded by the peaceful town of my childhood and youth that already went dark by day's end. I remember telling Daniela how good I felt at that moment, not only from experiencing an extraordinary film like *A River Runs Through It* with her, but also in the knowledge of knowing all was well with the home I loved and treasured, as well as knowing it would be there to greet me again when the new beach season began again next spring. The year was coming to an end, and the promises of the new-year-to-come seemed hopeful in my mind because of a quiet, little film by Robert Redford that opened my eyes to the beauty of life, and the possibilities of how we chose to live it.

As it turned out, that didn't happen. Less than two weeks after our day's visit, the ongoing years of beach erosion finally broke through and flooded the main road leading to my house. The entire community was cut off by the Atlantic Ocean, thus preventing me from accessing the house for the next several years. This was the end of an era for me, and like Norman Maclean, I'd spend many years of my life haunted by my own waters.

Malcom X

Directed by Spike Lee
(November 18, 1992, U.S. Release Date)

Just like *Basic Instinct* earlier in '92, Spike Lee's film of *Malcom X* was deeply marred in controversy even before filming began. I'd followed Spike Lee closely since *Do the Right Thing* and all the controversy and outrage just fueled the fire of my resolve to get in line to see the film as early as possible (with Daniela, as it turned out). The crux of it was Malcom X's inflammatory and angry denunciation of white people before he undertook his sacred pilgrimage to Mecca, or his *haji*, as it's called. He was, arguably, not well regarded among white citizens of American, by and large. Nonetheless, he rose to become a national hero in the black community and a symbol of black's struggles, particularly during the civil rights movement of the 1960s.

Like other film biopics of well-known figures, Lee began the film showing us the character (born Malcom Little) in his earliest years with flashbacks to a rough childhood in rural Michigan in which he was separated from his family after his father, an activist for black rights, was murdered by the Ku Klux Klan, and his mother was deemed unfit to raise him and his siblings on her own. She later suffered mental deterioration and was committed to an institution. Malcom faced his young life with racial prejudice from all sides of the white person's world who sought to keep him down and not allow him to chase his true potential. As a child in foster care, when he said he wanted to be a lawyer, he was shot down by his (white) teacher, claiming that such a career for a n——— (I won't say it) was unrealistic and that a carpenter would be better suited for him (I remember looking over at Daniela with an expression on my face suggesting I wanted to reach out to the screen and pulverize that teacher for being such an asshole).

Manhood brought on thievery, hustling, and running numbers for the local crime boss called West Indian Archie. Interestingly, when Malcom and his partner in crime, Shorty (played by Spike Lee himself) were arrested for burglary, it was the crime of sleeping with white women that landed them extra jail time. While incarcerated, Malcom met Baines, a member of the Nation of Islam, who directed him to the teachings of the group's leader Elijah Muhammad. Resistant to these teachings at first, cliché dictated that prison life would eventually allow Malcom to come to terms with himself and change his outlook and actions toward life. As he embraced the practices and faith of the Muslim religion, he resented white people for their mistreatment of his race.

Upon his release from prison, Malcom was delegated a speaker and representative to the people of the Nation of Islam. Here, I might add, was where the stellar performance of Denzel Washington as Malcom truly unleashed itself, not only through his powerful preaching messages, but also as a simple man who fell in love with and married nurse Betty Sanders (played by Angela Bassett), eventually having four daughters together.

Following the assassination of JFK in November 1963, Malcom commented that his death was the product of the white violence present in America since its founding, comparing the killing to *the chickens coming home to roost.* That statement damaged his reputation and credibility, and he was suspended as the Nation's representative for ninety days. During this time of exile, Malcom learned that Elijah Muhammad had fathered several children out of wedlock, which directly contradicted his own teachings of Islam. Considered an act of betrayal, Malcom lost his faith in the organization. During his pilgrimage to Mecca, where he conjugated with Muslims from all of the world's cultures (including white), he came to view his own beliefs in a different light. Returning to America, he publicly announced that he'd no longer preach African-American separation and instead advocate tolerance instead of protest. He was publicly exiled from the Nation of Islam and sent many death threats by its members, who also firebombed his house.

Like *Gandhi* in 1982, I knew the death of Malcom X was inevitable. As he prepared to speak before a crowd in Harlem, New York, in February 1965, he was repeatedly shot by disciples of the Nation of Islam. Malcom was dead on arrival to the hospital, and the film concluded with a series of real-life clips featuring the aftermath of Malcom's death, including a eulogy by Martin Luther King and a lengthy and spirited speech spoken by actor Ossie Davis's voiceover. I think when we left the Manhattan movie theater on that November day in '92, Daniela and I were both just a little emotionally exhausted—not only from the length of the film, but also in the length of such an extraordinary life as was that of Malcom X, whom we both still felt we knew little about.

In any film that relies on stirring dialogue through repeated speeches during a time of struggle, it's impossible to feel any boredom or impatience when you're listening to a man like Denzel Washington speak the words of his cause and purpose. Unlike Martin Luther King, though, Malcom X wasn't a believer in passive or nonviolent resistance. For a black person not to exercise his or her right to defend themselves when faced with aggression or violence, he deemed unintelligent, and I think he was *right*. Like all great men who dared to stir the shit storm of society's balance, Malcom X ended up gunned down in a brutal assassination by his own people. Like all great men, history often doesn't fully appreciate and understand their greatness until after they're dead (perhaps that's just how history works).

As a nonprejudice white man who knows only a small share of American history, I can claim that my knowledge and experience of who Malcom X was comes only from Spike Lee's epic film. How much was accurate? Who can say? There are people on both sides of history who'll likely argue two different sides of what's historically correct or not. Knowing Lee's true passion to have this film made, and the fact that it's based on Malcom's own words as told to author Alex Haley, I'd like to think we're watching the story of a man's life in its accurate form. If that's true, then it's painfully obvious just how sick America was with racial hatred during the years before I was born. Has anything improved? Lee didn't think so at the time of making this film. Just watch the opening credits accompanied by the amateur video footage of the L.A. police beating Rodney King only a year and a half before the release of *Malcom X.*

This film has, and continues to be, the acting triumph of Denzel Washington's long career; one I feel he deserved the Oscar for best actor even more than the one he inevitably achieved for *Training Day* eight years later. In my opinion, none of his other film roles will ever measure up to the obviously difficult task of portraying a man who helped to change the course of America and its attitudes toward the oppression of black citizens in our society. We'd probably all agree there's still a very long way to go. Malcom X would've agreed, too, had he lived this long.

The Crying Game
Directed by Neil Jordan
(November 25, 1992, U.S. Release Date)

Every once in a while, when we go to the movies, or watch one on TV, we may experience moments that I like to refer to as the, "Holy shit! What the fuck just happened!" moment. Every generation knows what I'm talking about. Imagine how movie audiences freaked out in 1960 when they witnessed actress Janet Leigh stabbed to death midway through Alfred Hitchcock's *Psycho*. Imagine how shocked you and I were when we learned that actor Kevin Spacey was actually Keyser Söze in Bryan Singer's 1995 film *The Usual Suspects*, or that Bruce Willis was actually dead in M. Night Shyamalan's 1999 film *The Sixth Sense*. You get what I mean, right?

While I consider the above-mentioned scene in *Psycho* probably the greatest film shocker of all time, I won't call it *my* greatest film shocker because by the time I finally saw the movie for the first time on TV, I already knew that Leigh was going to get it when she did. For me, the greatest "Holy shit! What the fuck just happened?" moment in film definitely occurred when I experienced for the first time, the 1992 independent film from Miramax that was supposed to be all the rage, *The Crying Game*.

But first, let me tell you a little bit about the movie theater in which Daniela and I saw it. In Manhattan, there exists at the corner of Houston and Mercer Street, the Angelica Film Center. It originally opened in September 1989, and audiences continue to embrace the theater today. When you walk inside at ground level, you're greeted by a large and welcoming café, and then you take escalators down to the theater level. Architecturally, the theater is uninteresting, and while its underground screens cannot compare in size to many of the more impersonal multiplex screens throughout many of the cities in the United States, it's famous, nonetheless, for helping to make independent and foreign films a vibrant part of the motion picture industry. Many of the best independent films of the past decades have debuted at the Angelica during many of the film festivals held there. It was at this theater that we went to see *The Crying Game*.

When the film opened with a long, continuous shot of a rural fairground in Northern Ireland to the tune of Percy Sledge's *"When a Man Loves a Woman,"* my immediate reaction was boredom. This shot was too long to have to endure during just the opening credits. Yet I told myself, "Eric, you're at the Angelica. These are intelligent, important films. Just bear with it and wait to see what happens." On the surface, the film seemed a psychological thriller set against the backdrop of the IRA (Irish Republican Army) and their kidnapping of a black British soldier named Jody after a tempting blonde woman named Jude lured him to a secluded area with the promise of sex. She and her group of IRA members, including Fergus, ransomed Jody for the release of an imprisoned IRA member, threatening to shoot him in three days if their demands weren't met. While Fergus guarded over Jody, the two of them were unwittingly bonding, much to the dismay of the other IRA members.

Jody eventually got Fergus to promise to seek out Jody's girl-friend Dil in London should Jody be killed. The deadline for their demands was eventually unmet, and Fergus was ordered to take Jody to the woods and kill him. Jody attempted to escape by running, but Fergus couldn't bring himself to shoot. This proved pointless, because Jody was killed when he ran into the road and was struck by a British military armored carrier truck as it attacked the IRA safe house.

With his comrades seemingly killed in the raid, Fergus fled to London, where he took a job as a construction laborer, now living under the name Jimmy. He kept his promise to Jody and found Dil, a lovely black woman, working at a hair salon. They often met at the local pub, the Metro, where Dil sometimes performed. Their relationship progressed, but Fergus was guilt-ridden over Jody's death, despite the fact that he was falling in love with Dil. When the two finally decided to have sex at Dil's apartment, the movie shocker of my life occurred when all of us in the theater learned that she was really a *HE* (Holy shit! What the fuck just happened?). Wait a second—did I just see what I *thought* I saw? This beautiful woman has a penis? She's a *man*?? Revealed, it finally was, the great truth of *The Crying Game*—*"the movie everyone was talking about, but no one's giving away its secret,"* and now Daniela and I were part of the big revelation along with the rest of the independent-loving audiences of cinema. As for Fergus, he was initially sickened at first about what he'd just seen (what straight man wouldn't be?). As time progressed, though, he found that his genuine love and affection for Dil knew no boundaries or limitations, though he could seemingly never bring himself to have sex with her…sorry, *him.*

Jude unexpectedly reappeared and found Fergus, forcing him to help assassinate a British judge. If he didn't cooperate, she and the IRA would kill Dil. To protect Dil, he asked her to cut her long hair short and wear Jody's old cricket uniform to disguise herself as a man. This seemed a simple, yet brilliant idea to "throw off the dogs." But the night before the assassination, Dil got drunk and Fergus took her home, where he confessed his role in Jody's death. Drunk, Dil didn't understand Fergus's confession. In the morning, though, Dil tied Fergus's arms and legs to the bed with stockings, leaving him unable to complete his role in the assassination. Holding him at gunpoint, Dil demanded that Fergus love him and never leave him. Fergus complied, though we couldn't be sure if it was because he meant it, or he just wanted to be freed.

The judge was killed by the IRA without Fergus, but Jude returned to Dil's apartment to seek revenge. Dil shot Jude to death, repeating her belief that Jude used *"those tits and that ass to get my Jody!"* He then pointed the gun at Fergus, but couldn't shoot, because Jody wouldn't allow it. Fergus stopped Dil from shooting himself and told him to go into hiding, as he was prepared to be arrested for Jude's murder. Some months later, Dil (having grown her hair out again) went to visit Fergus in jail, forever touched by his willingness to take the fall for her…sorry, *him.*

I realized when it was over that Daniela and I could've easily attended *The Crying Game* simply because it was the big independent movie with the big secret gaining a lot of Oscar buzz at the time. But it was impossible to deny we'd become deeply involved in a story that started off as one thing, and then turned into something else altogether (not too unlike *Psycho*). I was also forced to consider Fergus's commitment to loving and protecting Dil after learning who and what he/she really was. Perhaps it's the old cliché of love knowing no boundaries, and that we as decent human beings are obliged to commit ourselves to those we care about. Yet I'm also the first to admit that I'm not a perfect human being. While I believe that everyone has the right to be who and what they truly are, I can't deny my initial distaste toward transgenderism, despite its overall unchallenged acceptance in the current social norm. I don't understand it, and I'm not entirely sure I'd know how to accept it if I ever came into contact with it. If I fell in love with someone I honestly believed to be a woman, could that love remain untainted if I found out that person was *man*? I don't think I'll ever know the answer to that question because the one I love was, is and will always definitely be a *woman…* last time I checked, anyway.

*****

This is the last film of 1992 I shall discuss in any great detail.

When the year ended, I felt like a different man than the one I was at the start of it. I was now a college graduate with about as much ambition as Dustin Hoffman in *The Graduate*. I was living alone at home, and my immediate employment prospects seemed no better than working at the local book store.

The family beach house in Westhampton Beach was in serious trouble from years of ongoing beach erosion which brought the Atlantic Ocean closer and closer to the main road of the inlet. Then finally, in December 1992, two back-to-back nor'easters sealed the lid on the coffin by breaking the barrier of the inlet, resulting in the ocean and the bay meeting at both ends, thus cutting off all residents from their homes, including ours. This was a tragic end to a life at the beach that defined the best part of myself since first purchased in 1978. All I could do was painfully walk away and curse Mother Nature's wrath, wondering if she'd inevitably sink our house, like so many others.

My personal life fared no better. Daniela and I were split, though we still maintained our "friends with benefits" relationship. Dating other women was challenging, as I felt impatient in getting to know anyone new, and Caren continued to be a distant and difficult dream. In fact, by the end of the year, I'd spent very little time with her. She was still a college girl in Massachusetts and also spent the summer working there. I saw her only here and there whenever she returned for brief visits with her family. In fact, I'd say the longest time we'd spent together was a summer night at the Elton John/Eric Clapton concert at the former Shea Stadium and an all-night diner afterwards.

Oddly, I spent New Year's Eve with her in Massachusetts, just the two of us. I wish I could tell you that night inevitably led to us sleeping together and reconciling, but I'm afraid it ended up no better than both of us waiting what seemed like forever for the delivery of a Domino's pizza and watching Alan Alda's 1981 comedy *The Four Seasons* on videotape. And despite the fact that she and I discussed how we both hoped we would one day share lives with good friends as in the movie, I couldn't help but get the sick feeling that as we entered the new year of 1993, things between myself and Caren were going to slowly deteriorate.

And that, my friends, was the year 1992 for me.

THE YEAR WAS 1993...

- At the World Trade Center in New York City, a van with a bomb parked below the North tower explodes, injuring over a thousand people and killing six.
- In Waco, Texas, at the Branch Davidian compound, a fifty-one-day stand-off ends with a fire killing seventy-six people, including cult leader David Koresh.
- U.S. president Bill Clinton orders a cruise missile attack on Iraqi intelligence headquarter in response to a plot to assassinate former U.S. president George Bush during his April visit to Kuwait.
- Michael Jackson is accused of sexually abusing thirteen year-old Jordan Chandler.
- Israeli Prime Minister Yitzhak Rabin and PLO leader Yasser Arafat sign a peace accord, shaking hands with Bill Clinton in attendance.
- On the Long Island Railroad, six people are murdered when Colin Ferguson, a black Jamaican immigrant, opens fire in a racially motivated shooting.

...AND THERE WERE MOVIES!

On March 13, 1993, the eastern United States was hit with a record two-day blizzard (which I later learned killed one hundred eighty-four people). During those two days, I was stranded inside my mother's house in Great Neck, unable to drive to work. Thankfully, I'd prepared myself in advance with a well-stocked kitchen and I was also lucky to have not lost power, thus allowing me to spend my time watching lots of movies on tape and TV. During my isolation, as I listened to the wrath of the snow blowing outside, I couldn't help feeling truly alone for the first time in my life. My immediate family was scattered in different directions, my friends weren't so accessible now that college was over, and I felt the pain of not having anyone romantic in my life. As I stood over the stove cooking pasta one night, I wished that Caren was with me so I could instead cook for two. Sad wish, I know, but the heart isn't always logical when it's hurting.

On Valentine's Day, I decided not to feel sorry for myself about being alone and asked Cathy (also single) to join me for dinner and a movie in Manhattan. We went to see Louis Malle's *Damage* (it was just okay) and then indulged ourselves in those mile-high Jewish delicatessen sandwiches at the *Stage Deli* on Seventh Avenue (it closed in 2012). It may not have been a Valentine's Day of love and romance in the traditional sense, but the movie, food, and platonic love we both shared was just what our lonely souls needed that day.

I also became aware that the summer was just a couple of months away, and for the first time in my life, the family beach house was no longer an option. How would I spend my summer? The thought of driving to public beaches was sickening, and I had no intention of joining a public pool. It was only by chance that I looked at the back portion of the Village Voice and discovered ads for share house participations in Westhampton Beach. Wait—were share houses happening the whole time I spent my summers in the privacy of my own house? Apparently so. Suddenly, things looked brighter with the thought of spending the summer in what would inevitably be an ongoing party scene.

As it turned out, I joined a house that wasn't on the beach, but rather a short walking distance from the Westhampton Beach train station, which was convenient, despite my having a car. To make matters better, I joined the house with my cousin *Danny T.*, who, by then, was more than family, but one of my best friends, if not my brother. From Memorial Day to Labor Day, he and I would party like there was no tomorrow, and I could take full advantage of the fact that I wasn't attached to anyone in a committed relationship (despite my *wanting* to be in such with Caren) and could readily and easily sleep with any girl who was willing.

Frankly, with all this social excitement on the way, I barely thought of the summer blockbuster fun on the way. The anticipation of movies like *Jurassic Park*, *The Firm*, *In the Line of Fire* and *The Fugitive* took a backseat to the promise of sun, surf, suds and sex. But first, I needed to *laugh*.

Groundhog Day
Directed by Harold Ramis
(February 12, 1993, U.S. Release Date)

By this time, I would not have seen *anything* that starred Bill Murray. The man who made me laugh in *Caddyshack*, *Stripes*, *Ghostbusters*, and *What About Bob?* didn't exactly rock my world with *Ghostbusters II* and *Quick Change*. In my opinion, his material needed to be approached with some hesitation, if not caution. But at the same time, this was a time in my life where the pains of love and loneliness got the better of me, and the need to laugh all the more necessary, making the trailer for *Groundhog Day* look like just the ticket.

Bill's character of Pittsburgh TV meteorologist Phil Connors seemed just my kinda guy. He was self-centered, impatient, cynical, got nearly physically sick when strange people were overly nice to him, and generally held the opinion that *all* people were morons (what's *not* to love about the guy, right?). The movie's lesson was that he was doomed to relive the same day in February, Groundhog Day, over and over again until he got it right and became a more decent human being. The concept seemed about as cliché as changes in human characteristics could possibly get, and I suppose it was necessary for the right message to come across for the movie to be successful. But for a guy like me, I didn't necessarily *want* Bill Murray to change, because it was his unpleasant persona that made me laugh.

I needed to take a close look at the day in question. Having to wake up at 6:00 a.m. anywhere in the world was bad enough. Having to wake up at 6:00 a.m. and listen to Sonny and Cher sing *"I Got*

You, Babe" didn't make things any better. Having to repeatedly do a stupid, fluff news story about a Pennsylvania town getting together to pay tribute to a large groundhog known as "Punxsutawney Phil" might just as well have been one's death sentence.

But there were some possibilities taking place here too. This endless day could allow one to do whatever they wanted without any consequences because the next day would start over the same way all over again. So go ahead, Phil—drive recklessly, eat all the crap you want, and commit whatever deceptions are necessary to get yourself laid by Nancy Taylor. You're also free (and more than happy) to act and react the appropriate way to the obnoxious likes of Ned Ryerson who insisted he remembered you from high school and wouldn't shut his damn mouth. A man like this was everyone's worst nightmare on a long plane ride, let alone just a few moments on the sidewalk, so it's no wonder the entire theater laughed and cheered when you finally belted him a good one in the face.

If there was one thing a man like Phil proved to me (and others in the theater) was that sometimes one's anger and frustrations can become contagious because inside we may be thinking and feeling the same thing, and long to lash out against others because of it. How could I not feel good inside when Phil finally had enough of all the bullshit and ranted these words into the TV camera:

> *This is pitiful! A thousand people freezin' their butts off waiting to worship a rat! What a hype! Groundhog Day used to mean somethin' in this town! They used to pull the hog out and they used to eat it! You're all hypocrites, all of ya!*

On a sensitive side, though, this sort of day afforded Phil the opportunity to repeatedly try to win over his colleague Rita (played by Andie MacDowell) even though many of his attempts ended with her slapping his face day after day. In the end, however, that cliché I mentioned before won over the situation, and Phil learned to use his "daily" powers to selflessly help others, win the girl he was in love with, and learn to be an all-around nice guy. This is what we expected from the story, but as long as we were laughing along the way, we didn't mind. And in my case, I learned a little something, because until then, I presumed that not only was Punxsutawney a fictional town in Pennsylvania, but that the entire groundhog worshipping event of the day itself was also fiction. Imagine my surprise (and my disappointment) when I later learned from NBC's Al Roker that not only was the town real, but the moronic events themselves too. Seriously?

The day I saw *Groundhog Day* was a day of laughter I needed to try and heal my depression. At a time when I'd discovered how easy it was to "movie hop" from one multiplex theater to another without hassle, I immediately followed Bill Murray's antics by watching the parody *Loaded Weapon I* with Emilio Estevez and Samuel L. Jackson. Compared to the likes of *Airplane!* and *The Naked Gun*, it was terrible. But it was perfectly timed, nonetheless, because it was just the insanity I needed that day. I also contemplated which day of *my* life I'd want to repeat over and over again. Well, I hadn't gotten married yet, so my wedding day was out. I wasn't a father yet, so the birth of my child was out. I hadn't sold an award-winning screenplay yet, so accepting the Oscar was out. Perhaps I could only fantasize of the kind of day Phil spoke about that he wished he could live over and over again instead of Groundhog Day—a day that involved drinking Piña coladas, eating lobster and making love like sea otters.

Yeah, I think I'd just borrow that kind of day for a while.

Like Water for Chocolate
Directed by Alfonso Arau
(February 17, 1993, U.S. Release Date)

By the early '90s, two things happened to my life at the movies. The first was that I discovered and attended more independent and foreign films in Manhattan's smaller theaters. The second was that I attended many of these films with my mother, enabling us to become closer on terms I could most relate to. Although I hadn't read the popular novel in which *Like Water for Chocolate* was based, I knew through working at the local Great Neck book store in '92 that it was a story that used food as its main theme, often including the actual recipes of the dishes described in the novel. In retrospect, this was the perfect film to experience with my mother because it's her side of the family that's provided me with some of my most personal memories and connections with food and their sacred recipes.

The film followed a young, pretty girl named Tita who was forbidden to ever marry or have children because of a longstanding (and ridiculous) tradition which said the youngest daughter was responsible for caring for her mother until she (the mother) died. So when young Pedro (I recognized him from the Italian film *Cinema Paradiso*), whom she was in love with, came calling to ask for Tita's hand in marriage, her mother Mama Elena (a cruel and ruthless bitch who made Norman Bates' mother look like a saint) refused, citing the reason I just explained. She instead offered her middle daughter Rosaura, and Pedro accepted just to be near Tita, whom he'd always love. It was at this moment in the film we learned of its true story, in which its governing forces were food and the magical realism combined with the ordinary. The first sign of food combined with some supernatural magic was when Tita baked her sister's wedding cake with her own tears of sadness falling into the batter. At the ceremony, the cake caused the guests to cry and vomit in sadness and sickness, as they all longed for their true love.

Later, Tita's heated passion for Pedro transferred to the oldest sister Gertrudis upon eating another meal. Gertrudis attempted to cool down by taking a shower but was overcome with intense lust and ran off naked with a group of Mexican revolutionary soldiers (oh sure, we all do *that* in extreme moments of horniness). This moment was well filmed, because despite the fact that Gertrudis (who bore a striking American resemblance to Julia Louis-Dreyfuss of *Seinfeld* and Tina Yothers of *Family Ties*) wasn't particularly beautiful and somewhat chunky, there was still something undeniably desirable about her, nonetheless (maybe it was just because she was naked).

Year after year, Tita continued to express her emotions through her talents in the kitchen and the dishes she prepared. Food was, indeed, the great solace for a family never quite at peace with itself. I couldn't help but feel this dysfunctional family was probably very lucky to possess the passion they had for the food in their lives because there seemed almost nothing happy about them. Tita, her mother, her sisters, her servants, and her doctor friend (who was also in love with Tita) all seemed sad, depressed, confused, or troubled about something. The only relief this family (and the audience) could feel at all was when Mama Elena finally died. Yes, we all felt *happy* when this bitch died because in the entire time she was alive, her sole purpose in life was to make Tita miserable.

By the time the film moved forward twenty years later, we learned of Rosaura's death of *"sever digestive problems."* Pedro confessed to Tita that he still loved her and wanted to marry her. Tita and Pedro made love and ignited the supernatural *"matches"* of their lustful passion too quickly, resulting in Pedro's death just as he experienced an incredibly sensuous orgasm. In her immediate grief, Tita swallowed matches, igniting her entire family's ranch in a blazing inferno. Rosaura's daughter returned to the ranch and found only her Aunt Tita's cookbook, containing her recipes and telling the tale of her and Pedro's love story. It ended as it began, with one of Tita's descendants narrating the history of her family and what the inexplicable magic behind the food they created meant to her and what it would mean to future generations.

In the many years that have passed since I first saw *Like Water for Chocolate*, there's one distinct personal feeling I've never lost sight of, and that's this: life for many of us may not have any magic in it, but I'm willing to bet that we (myself included) take a great deal of joy in the foods we eat and look forward to eating. How many of us, perhaps, had mothers, grandmothers, or aunts who could make their kitchen come alive with the smells, the joys, the wisdom, the values, and the love of good, traditional family cooking (I really miss my Aunt Lillian's cooking)? In fact, when my son was very small, while I cooked him scrambled eggs for breakfast, he asked me, "Daddy, do you make my breakfast with love?" I replied, "Sam, I always cook your food with love." Despite the fact that I felt a bit stupid saying something so corny, it felt obvious that I was recalling a film *Like Water for Chocolate* when I said it.

Food is love, and it always will be, and it's through the cooking of sacred recipes that we'll continue to keep those we've lost and loved alive forever.

Jurassic Park
Directed by Steven Spielberg
(June 11, 1993, U.S. Release Date)

During the five-year period Caren and I were in each other's lives, on and off as friends and romantically, we went to less than ten movies together. Cinematically, our tastes didn't always click. Like many couples, the traditional romantic comedy was often the safest bet (*Sleepless in Seattle* the best example that year), because unlike myself, Caren didn't go much for arthouse cinema and she had no interest in some of the most popular franchise action movies of our time like *Star Wars*, *Star Trek*, and James Bond. Steven Spielberg's adaptation of Michael Crichton's book *Jurassic Park* was the only summer blockbuster action movie we ever went to see together. Whether she had the same interest in it that I did, or she was simply going along to make me happy, I never knew. At the time of its release, though, we were a couple again, and couples often make concessions for each other when going to the movies.

Even as I spent the summer of '93 at a Westhampton Beach share house with my cousin Danny and other young adults my age, my weekend concentration was on wild partying and not the movies—those were left for week nights now. During that time, I'd never seen such fever, excitement and mania for a new summer adventure blockbuster since Spielberg's own *E.T.* back in '82. Key words here were *brand-new*—not a sequel or a remake. That summer I also worked at the local Great Neck book store, and with the new film came a dinosaur craze like I hadn't seen before. The paperback version of Crichton's original novel sold like hotcakes and parents were buying any and all books on dinosaurs for their children to read. Even before Crichton's book was originally published, many Hollywood studios were bidding to acquire the movie rights. It seemed that even if *Jurassic Park* had sucked, it still would've been a record-breaking, high-grossing summer movie sensation.

Before its release, I'd started reading the paperback book. I recall when Dr. Grant first arrived at the park, the text simplified his first look at its awesome wonder with six simple words, *He was looking at a dinosaur.* Spielberg, however, knew how to take the first glimpse of things and turn it into a spectacle of wonder and excitement by carefully blending it with the music of John Williams at just the right moment. For me, it was a moment of fascination that must've been obvious on my face and in my eyes. Had I bothered to look at Caren's face, I doubt I would've seen the same thing. She didn't take the movies as personally as I did (many people don't).

Although it was tempting to classify *Jurassic Park* as a traditional monster movie, this tale of the fictional island of Isla Nublar near Costa Rica's Pacific Coast, where billionaire philanthropist of the InGen Corporation John Hammond (played by Richard Attenborough, who directed *Gandhi*, among other films) and a small team of genetic scientists were in the process of creating a theme park of actual cloned dinosaurs, authentically depicted not only the real possibilities of the cloning procedures, but also explored the dangerous powers of bringing back dinosaurs in the twentieth century to live amongst mankind. As mathematician and chaos theorist Dr. Ian Malcom (played by Jeff Goldblum, whom I was convinced played the perfect scientist, as he also did in *The Fly*) clearly put it, *"God creates dinosaurs. God destroys dinosaurs. God creates man. Man destroys God. Man creates dinosaurs."*

Also on this island for the weekend were paleontologists Dr. Alan Grant and his female partner Dr. Ellie Sattler, brought there in the hopes that they'd professionally endorse John Hammond's new theme park to get the lawyers and investors off his back, and to get the construction schedule moving again. Hammond's two grandchildren Tim and Lex (short for Lexi or Alexa, perhaps) were also there.

As in many cliché tales of terror, all seemed fine and normal in this little unknown and awesome world of science and dinosaurs…until something went wrong.

The first thing to go wrong was Jurassic Park's lead computer programmer Dennis Nedry and his betrayal by stealing fertilized dinosaur embryos to sell to a rival corporation. Through his deactivation of the park's security system to gain access to the embryo storage facility, all power was temporarily cut off, and that included the electrified fences which kept the dinosaurs away from the park's mainstream population. This was when we were introduced to the mighty power of the park's Tyrannosaurus rex when it finally arrived to make its presence known and attack its prey. Dr. Grant, Lex, and Tim escaped the attack, while Dr. Malcom escaped with injury and the accompanying lawyer was eaten by the T. rex while sitting on the toilet (hey, it's a *lawyer*, so no great loss, right?). Nedry himself was killed by a Dilophosaurus when he got lost during a tropical storm on his way to deliver the stolen embryos.

Taking shelter in a treetop, Grant and the two kids waited for morning and then discovered the broken shells of dinosaur eggs. Grant concluded the dinosaurs were breeding because of the frog DNA the scientists used to fill the holes of the gene strands. Some West African frogs were capable of changing their sex in a single-sex environment, therefore allowing the dinosaurs to do the same. As Malcom clearly put it earlier in the film, *"Life finds a way,"* and it did.

As a final solution, Hammond and the group retreated to an emergency bunker and attempted to shut down and reboot the park's computer grid system, allowing the power and phones to return. They also discovered that during the park's shutdown, the remaining electrical fences were deactivated, allowing the Velociraptors to escape and attack at will. These were meat-eating predators without mercy, and their movements and vicious attacks were admittedly frightening to watch. At the film's climax, just before it looked like Dr. Grant, Ellie and the two kids were going to be devoured by the two attacking raptors, the T. rex conveniently (*too* convenient, I think) appeared out of nowhere to kill the raptors, thus allowing the group to escape and flee the island by helicopter. No endorsement would be given, and it looked as though the park would never become a reality.

My initial reaction to the end of *Jurassic Park* was disappointing, in that the simple escape from the island by helicopter seemed anticlimactic and unresolved to the dinosaur's fate. This, I suppose, would later be accounted for with four sequels that followed over time, but it took a second viewing on screen that summer to allow me to simply sit back and enjoy the great adventure without harping too much on the little things like an ambiguous ending. I loved the movie (Caren, I think, only *liked* it), and I was there the day it was released on VHS tape to purchase my own copy (today it looks totally awesome on high-definition Blu-Ray disc).

Over time, it's occurred to me that once the viewer of *Jurassic Park* gets past the technical and educational facts of dinosaurs and how they can be (fictitiously) created, the real fun begins. Like *Jaws*, it's nearly an hour before the action of survival against the great beast begins, and it's absolutely terrifying that it begins with the simple thump of the approaching menace. One can feel the sheer terror of what's coming by watching all of the park's electrical fences fail, as well as watching a plastic cup of water ripple as the monster's footsteps get closer and louder. Like the arrival of King Kong himself, the first time we see the great T. rex, we know things are going to happen and people are going to get killed. This is a scary action sequence that doesn't even require any of John Williams's' brilliant score to help it along. It's this particular scene that's also reminds me that sometimes even a gentle soul like Steven Spielberg has often put children in the most horrifying situations of fear, peril, and survival.

Consider Alex Kintner killed by the great white shark in *Jaws*, the Freeling children scared out of their wits in *Poltergeist*, the abused slave children of *Indiana Jones and the Temple of Doom*, young Celie raped and abused in *The Color Purple*, young Jamie Graham taken as a prisoner of war by the Japanese in *Empire of the Sun*, and the Panning children kidnapped by pirates in *Hook*. You see what I mean? When my son was a small child, I wouldn't have let him anywhere near *Jurassic Park* because the sight of two children being attacked by a ferocious meat-eating dinosaur would've surely kept him up for a few nights.

Through the film's groundbreaking CGI effects and life-like animatronics, we're witnessing the miracle of a species of animal long-since extinct coming back to life again on screen. As I previously mentioned, this isn't delivered as some cheap monster movie like we grew up with on TV. This is a convincing fictional tale of man and beast, the scientific realities of what's possible, and what can go horribly wrong when the power of such possibilities is unleashed on the world. Like many Spielberg efforts before it, *Jurassic Park* is the perfect eye-popping, mind-bending, kick-out-the-jams thrill ride of the summer blockbuster genre. It delivers on its promise to show us all the dinosaurs, and to show them early and often with a sense of awe and wonderment. As a backdrop to the mighty monsters, characters are not necessarily weak, but are almost a little less of a valid point, though we can't deny the story makes use of the fact that a man like Dr. Alan Grant needs to discover his hidden parental instincts by protecting Hammond's grandchildren, despite his initial distaste for children.

I'll conclude by saying that although I thought the 1997 follow-up *The Lost World: Jurassic Park* was a worthy successor, if for no other reason than Spielberg directing another novel by Michael Crichton, the four unfortunate sequels that followed simply prove that once a successful blockbuster film launches what inevitably becomes an uncontrollable franchise, you only end up craving and appreciating the vehicle that originally launched it, and the reasons why you crave something new and fresh on the big screen. These are *my* reasons, and I cherish them.

By the way, it wasn't too long after seeing *Jurassic Park* together that Caren broke up with me *again* for her own bullshit reasons. I was crushed, of course, but I found immediate solace in a summer share house filled with young women in bikinis. I took my revenge by sleeping with one of them immediately after being dumped. That may sound harsh, but the loyalty I give is only as good as the loyalty I *get*.

The Fugitive

Directed by Andrew Davis
(August 6, 1993, U.S. Release Date)

By August '93, I'd lost myself in the fun of my summer share house. This was a new period of social interaction, after having spent so much of my life in the private confines of my own family's beach house. But even as I allowed myself to get sucked into the insanity of it all, I still recognized the importance and pleasure of every once in a while settling down to a Saturday night at the movies preceded by a great dinner at one of those Hamptons seafood restaurants right on the waters of the marina.

The film version of the popular 1960's TV show *The Fugitive* was, I think, the one and only movie I went to that summer at the Westhampton Beach Theater I'd grown up at since I was ten years old. I recall seeing it with three friends of mine—my friend *Stuart S.* (whom I briefly described in the *Cape Fear* chapter of *It's Still Strictly Personal*), his girlfriend at the time, and his sister (for whom I was sexually attracted to, and would eventually sleep with years later). I'd never seen the TV show, but any thriller starring Harrison Ford was always high on my list of movies to see.

From the moment the film began, it grabbed us. In less than fifteen minutes during the opening credits, we witnessed the murder of prominent Chicago vascular surgeon Dr. Richard Kimble's (Ford) wife Helen, his arrest, his trial, his wrongful conviction, and his subsequent death sentence. Because of our minor knowledge of television history, we knew Kimble was innocent, that the murder was actually committed by a one-armed man, and that Kimble would escape his prison sentence only to be chased everywhere as he desperately tried to clear his name and find his wife's true killer.

While transported by bus to death row with other prisoners, an escape attempt took place without Kimble's involvement. The ensuing chaos resulted in the death of two prisoners and the bus driver, which sent the bus into a ravine and into the path of an oncoming train. Kimble saved a guard and escaped the bus himself, just as the train violently derailed and collided with the bus. I remember the entire theater audience cheering following that collision, as if we'd just handed out the people's choice award for the all-time best train crash on screen (it *was*). Kimble was free and on the run. The chase had begun.

Within hours of the accident, U.S. marshal Samuel Gerard (played by Tommy Lee Jones, whom I only knew from the 1992 Steven Segal thriller *Under Siege*) and his team arrived at the crash site to begin their search for their fugitive. I immediately liked Gerard's no nonsense character, as he bluntly demanded a *"hard target search of every gas station, residence, warehouse, farmhouse, henhouse, outhouse, and doghouse in that area,"* also insisting his colleague *"think me up a cup of coffee and a chocolate doughnut with some of those little sprinkles on top, while you're thinking"* (you *had* to love this guy). No doubt, this chase would not only be thrilling, but a whole lot of fun too.

Kimble snuck into a hospital to treat his accident wounds and change his appearance. He then stole an ambulance and disappeared. Gerard caught up to him in a storm drain some miles away, but dropped his gun when he slipped and fell. Kimble picked up the gun and pointed it. But rather than shoot, he declared, *"I didn't kill my wife,"* to which Gerard only replied, *"I don't care."* After cornering Kimble at the edge of the storm drain over a dam, Kimble shocked us by leaping into the water below, escaping again. Eventually returning to Chicago to continue his hunt, Kimble got some money from his friend and colleague Dr. Charles Nichols. While impersonating a janitor at Cook County Hospital's prosthetic department, he obtained a list of men who had prosthetic arms repaired in the time after his wife's murder. But even during his infiltration, Kimble didn't forget he was a doctor, and managed to save a young boy's life when he forged doctor's orders for an emergency surgery.

As the hunt continued at both ends, Gerard speculated that Kimble was searching for the one-armed man. He and Kimble caught up with each other again at a local courthouse at Chicago City Hall, and Kimble escaped again, losing himself among the crowd of the St. Patrick's Day Parade. When he later broke into the home of police officer Fredrick Sykes, he not only realized he'd found the one-armed man who killed his wife, but also that a major pharmaceutical company called Devlin MacGregor and his friend Dr. Nichols were ultimately behind the plot that ended up in Helen's murder and his being framed for that murder.

Aboard an elevated train, Kimble and Sykes confronted each other, resulting in Kimble overpowering Sykes and handcuffing him to a train pole. At a pharmaceutical conference at a Chicago hotel, Kimble interrupted Dr. Nichol's speech, confronting and accusing him of falsifying medical research and orchestrating Helen's murder. They fought on the hotel roof before Gerard finally showed up, declaring his belief that Kimble *was* innocent and that it was time for him to stop running. Dr. Nichols was stopped, Sykes was arrested, and Kimble finally surrendered to Gerard, presumably to be exonerated of all that had happened to him.

Not having watched the original TV show, I have no basis of comparison to judge this Harrison Ford thriller, so my eyes were (and still are) wide open, and my mind is very fresh. Ford, as in most of his roles, fills the spot perfectly with a combination of determined strength and a desperate vulnerability. Tommy Lee Jones as Deputy Gerard represents a clear definition of obsessed commitment to finding and catching his prey. As he clearly states, he doesn't care whether Kimble killed his wife or not. He's the cat, and it's his job to catch the mouse under any and all circumstances. That sounds pretty solid on paper, but somewhere along the way, Gerard is inevitably apt to become more of a human being and realize that Kimble is not only innocent, but that the one-armed man does, indeed, exist and he'll pay for the crime he committed. Even the end resolution isn't in any way cheap or limited, as the corruption and deception behind a monster pharmaceutical company determined to get their new drug passed and approved by the Food and Drug Administration (FDA), is ultimately responsible for the death of Richard Kimble's wife.

Leaving the theater that night in '93, I couldn't help but reflect on how much the evening meant to me. I'd watched a really great movie worthy of Oscar nominations at what was probably my favorite movie theater. Before that, the shrimp and scallops I'd eaten were delectable and delicious, and it was a genuine pleasure to be among really good friends during a summer in the Hamptons. For that brief moment in time, my ongoing romantic troubles with Caren were hardly a thought in my head. This is the place *The Fugitive* occupies in my personal history, and despite the domination of Steven Spielberg's infamous dinosaurs, it was my favorite film of that summer blockbuster season, and also one of the best action thrillers of the 1990s.

Manhattan Murder Mystery
Directed by Woody Allen
(August 18, 1993, U.S. Release Date)

Woody's Allen's *Manhattan Murder Mystery* was a big deal for me for three reasons. First, it continued a trend of intelligent films my mom and I could share together in an effort to get closer. Second, it proved that despite Woody's tabloid troubles between himself and Mia Farrow at the time, his career didn't suffer with his loyal fans. Third, it marked the reteaming of Woody and Diane Keaton for the first time since *Manhattan* in 1979 (though she did have a brief singing cameo in *Radio Days*), and *that* was the biggest deal for someone like me who loved the chemistry of these two ever since I saw them in the 1972 film *Play It Again, Sam*. It must've also looked very financially promising to TriStar Pictures, because at the time, it was the only Woody Allen film to be released during the summer blockbuster season. I also noticed it was the return of writer Marshall Brickman, who also wrote the Allen hits *Sleeper*, *Annie Hall*, and *Manhattan*.

Allen and Keaton played Manhattan couple Larry and Carol Lipton who met their neighbors Paul and Lilian House for the first time after returning home from a New York Rangers hockey game at Madison Square Garden. Their encounter started off pleasant enough when they joined them for coffee and conversation, but things changed the next day when they learned that Lilian had died from an apparent heart attack. The death was surprising because Lilian appeared to be in good health. Suspicion set in when Carol caught Paul in a lie, having discovered an urn in his kitchen filled with Lilian's cremated ashes after he'd already claimed that his wife had been buried. Immediately I noticed certain similarities, if not an homage, to Alfred Hitchcock's *Rear Window* whereas one neighbor suspected another of foul play, and the one closest to the suspicious one couldn't get on board with the possibility of them having invented a mystery.

Paul's cheerfulness did nothing to ease Carol's mounting suspicions, and Larry continued to downplay or disregard the entire idea of murder in that infamous Woody Allen style of nervous, paranoid and neurotic behavior. Marital jealousy developed when Carol's best friend Ted (played by Alan Alda) not only supported her suspicious theories of murder and mayhem, but also tried to help her solve the mystery. Larry suspected that Ted was attracted to his wife, which he actually wasn't wrong about. On the other hand, Larry got closer to one of his female clients, author Marcia Fox (played by Angelica Houston). She was not only attractive and highly sexual, but also intelligent and keen on trying to catch a potential murderer herself, hence the eventual jealousy from Carol.

By a point in the film, all four key members finally worked together to try and trap Paul into falling victim to his own guilty crimes. They had no proof whatsoever, so they could only rely on strategic bluffing and carefully constructed tape recordings to set the trap. One scene in particular was reminiscent of early classic Woody Allen comedies of the '70s when the group's plan with the telephone and the tape recordings went wrong and Larry desperately and very sloppily tried putting the tape ribbon back together again. Watching him go at it with such frenzy took me back to the great memories of him in *Sleeper* and *Love and Death* (also with Keaton). It was funny, it was classic, and I wished I could see more of *that* on screen. By the time plans were set into motion and ultimately backfired, the film climaxed with the murdering neighbor caught and killed, and the ultimate plot behind the crime revealed to all of us through not only the backdrop of Orson Welles's' 1947 film noir classic *The Lady from Shanghai*, but also through Marcia's verbal recap of the events to Ted. And as I watched this bit of farfetchedness alongside Orson Welles' classic, I couldn't help but take Larry's thought on it to heart when he stated that he'd never say that life didn't imitate art again. On the screen, though, it was often life and art in the style of Woody Allen.

For this fan of Woody's films, *Manhattan Murder Mystery* was a return to the "mother's milk" of on-screen film chemistry, because in my opinion, Woody has never worked better with any other costar than Diane Keaton. On screen, they have always been made for each other in the way they seem to know exactly when to feed off of each other's verbal and physical personas, and in this film, they prove they can still strike wonderful sparks of pure ditziness and insanity. Even in a brief moment when Larry tries to prevent Carol from leaving the apartment and declares, *"No, no, I forbid you, I forbid you to go! Is...I...I'm forbidding! Is that what you do when I forbid you? If...if that's what you...? I'm not gonna be forbidding you a lot, if you do..."* we know full well that Woody knows just who he's up against when it's his long-time sidekick, Diane Keaton.

By the time of the film release, the world and the press were still reeling from the crazed family scandal between Allen, Mia Farrow and Soon Yi-Previn. Fans faced forgetting their personal woes over the artist and his immoral actions in life, and embracing the art as it was to give it its fair shot. The whole thing may come off as no more than a dated detective story, but it manages to achieve a gentle, nostalgic grace and a hint of un-self-conscious wisdom in its story and performance. One can also claim that Allen and Keaton are essentially playing their characters of Alvy Singer and Annie Hall all over again, only later in their middle-aged years. Even if such a claim is true, in my opinion, it's still a priceless on-screen chemistry, no matter what the interpretation. I only wish it hadn't ended with *Manhattan Murder Mystery*. Perhaps there's still hope for one more film, as long as the two of them are willing (and manage to stay alive a little longer).

The Remains of the Day
Directed by James Ivory
(November 5, 1993, U.S. Release Date)

I can't help but wonder how many of today's generation of movie-goers know that Anthony Hopkins made a *lot* of movies before his breakout role in *The Silence of the Lambs*? It's uncanny how the star of films like *Magic, The Elephant Man* and *The Bounty* played a psychotic, flesh-eating monster like Dr. Hannibal Lecter before he was infamously put on the Hollywood map (such is show business). At the same time, there was something poetically charming about the idea of him playing a gentle soul when I first saw the trailer for the Merchant/Ivory film of Kazuo Ishiguro's 1989 novel *The Remains of the Day* only two years after that iconic role. While I no longer remember what movie I attended when I saw that trailer, I *do* remember that Daniela was with me, so it seemed a mutual understanding that we'd see it together when it was released.

As James Stevens, the head butler at Darlington Hall in Great Britain during the 1930s, Hopkins seemed the perfect epitome of the true and proper English gentleman; a man taking great pride in being of the utmost service to his wealthy employer Lord Darlington. For a man like Stevens, life was about routine, order and perfection. This wasn't merely his job, but also his perception of the world around him, even if it was limited to the surroundings of the house he served and the staff hc maintained. When he employed the new head housekeeper Miss Kenton (played by Emma Thompson), she immediately challenged him and his inability to express his true feelings. While her frankness and forwardness was, on the surface, irritating and unacceptable to him, it was clear to us that she was, in her own fashion, a breath of fresh air to him and his life of routine and order, though Stevens wouldn't dare show it.

As a true Englishman, Stevens couldn't fathom breaking away from his role as head butler for his Lord for even a moment. Upon hearing that his father (also a butler at the Hall) had passed away after suffering a stroke, his reaction was almost stoic. It wasn't that he didn't love his father, it was just that his death occurred at the worst time possible, when Stevens was in the process of performing his duties for his Lord and his most important political guests. To have broken his professional concentration, or to appear as if he were listening to their conversations and had formed his own opinion would've been considered rude, unprofessional and unacceptable to the etiquette of the proper English butler. Miss Kenton, as professional and effective at her job as she was, repeatedly failed to understand Stevens's personality and inability to express any feelings, and although she made her frustrations clear to him, it was a futile effort.

The film had a political and historical theme present at Darlington Hall, which I considered important. It was the time prior to Hitler's invasion of Europe and Lord Darlington, being also the fine and proper Englishman, had an unfortunate and naïve faith in attempting to form an alliance of peace with German heads of state. While he didn't blatantly appear to believe in Germany's position against Jews, he didn't want to be seen as uncooperative or politically incorrect, so he would sooner unfairly dismiss two young Jewish maids rather than ask for trouble. Stevens and Miss Kenton witnessed this act, and while Miss Kenton clearly expressed her outrage, Stevens insisted on keeping the faith in his Lord, who he still believed to be a fine and honorable man. While all of Darlington Hall's political guests appeared to (falsely) believe that Germany was an ally to the rest of the world, it was only a single American congressman (played by Christopher Reeve) who believed that putting trust in the Germans was a horrible and regrettable mistake (history proving him correct).

One of the challenging (if not confusing) aspects of the film was trying to figure out if throughout all of their years together, Stevens and Miss Kenton were falling in love or not. If they were, both of them refused to openly express it. By the end of her employment at the Hall, Miss Kenton seemingly tried to provoke Mr. Stevens by announcing her engagement to another man (whom we presumed she wasn't in love with) to see what sort of reaction she'd get from him. While his face suggested sorrow and regret over losing the woman he'd be lost without, all he could offer her was his *"warmest congratulations."*

However, there was a single moment in the film that suggested otherwise. When Miss Kenton tried to discover the nature of the book Mr. Stevens was reading, she approached him to remove the book from his hand. The moment she did this, Stevens nervously raised his hand to his forehead and his face expressed a tenderness we'd not seen before (to this day, this is the moment that stays with me the most). It's a simple gesture, but I believe the act of putting his hand to his forehead the way he does, even briefly, is a powerful visual moment that immediately (and temporarily) tears down the emotional wall he's kept around himself. In that moment, we clearly see how much he loves her and how this proper English gentleman has weakened when she gets too close to him. Tragically, he would never tell her this and his potential for true happiness would go unrealized.

Still, when everyone in the theater watched this, we knew how things really were. It's almost frustrating that we couldn't do anything about it because it was only a movie…and in the movies, endings aren't always happy ones. Stevens and Miss Kenton would never come together (watch the slow motion shot when their hands part for the last time, suggesting they'll never see each other again) and even worse is the fact that Stevens would likely not learn anything from his experience with her. Life would continue as it always had for him—orderly, structured, and oh-so properly English.

Since that day with Daniela in 1993, I've seen my small share of British films that date back as early as Alfred Hitchcock's work of the 1930s. In the '90s, I discovered the works of Merchant/Ivory that included *A Room with a View* and *Howard's End* in an attempt to broaden my cinematic horizons (some I liked, some I didn't). As a truly British film, *The Remains of the Day* is one of the best I've seen since *Chariots of Fire*, in its style, purity, simplicity, subtlety and thoughtfulness. The performances are first rate (Hugh Grant, the exception, his character being of a silly nature in a role I don't believe is meant to be funny), particularly by Anthony Hopkins in what I consider to be the best role of his extensive career (sorry Hannibal). I also think the late Christopher Reeve finally breaks away from Superman and gives an extraordinary performance of his own as Congressman Jack Lewis (two years before his tragic paralysis). He made a few more films before and after his accident (and eventual death), but I honestly wish he hadn't. His appearance in *The Remains of the Day* would've been the perfect swan song to his career and his life. His role is perhaps best summed up when he speaks these harsh and critical words to a room full of political statesman who are on the verge of a serous historical mistake:

> *You are, all of you, amateurs. And international affairs should never be run by gentlemen amateurs. Do you have any idea of what sort of place the world is becoming all around you? The days when you could just act out of your noble instincts, are over. Europe has become the arena of realpolitik, the politics of reality. If you like, real politics. What you need is not gentlemen politicians, but real ones. You need professionals to run your affairs, or you're headed for disaster.*

I'd like to personally dedicate that bit of dialogue to all American voters out there who were tragically stupid (and insane) enough to vote for a sociopathic clown like *Donald Trump* into the White House in 2016. Thank goodness those same voters failed in 2020.

Mrs. Doubtfire

Directed by Chris Columbus
(November 24, 1993, U.S. Release Date)

As a general rule, I've never cared for Disney musical films (even when I was a kid), particularly the animated ones. In fact, I remember feeling outraged when a kiddie cartoon like Disney's *Beauty and the Beast* was nominated for Best Picture of 1991 (seriously, *this* is what they chose to go up against quality Oscar contenders like *JFK* and *The Prince of Tides*?). On the other hand, I enthusiastically went to see Disney's *Aladdin* in 1992 because I knew the voice of Robin Williams as the Genie would be a hilarious experience (I wasn't wrong).

One year later, the release of *Mrs. Doubtfire* by the same director as the first two *Home Alone* movies was high on my list, and I made a strict point of seeing the film with my father (I'll explain that later). I knew men in drag was generally considered an effective formula in comic cinema. For myself, it was an acquired taste depending on who was doing the female dress-up. While men like Tony Curtis and Jack Lemmon in *Some Like It Hot* and Dustin Hoffman in *Tootsie* had me in stiches, men like Wesley Snipes, Patrick Swayze and John Leguizamo in *To Wong Foo, Thanks for Everything! Julie Newmar* left me cold (I failed to sit through the entire film). However, the late, great Robin Williams dressed up as a woman—seriously, what's not to love?

The laughs in a movie like *Mrs. Doubtfire* were obvious enough from the get-go, but to truly consider Williams in a role such as this, in which he played Daniel Hillard, a devoted father who went to extreme lengths to be with his kids during a bitter divorce, was to not only appreciate the man as a comedian, but to also appreciate his tender emotions, particularly with children, that was obvious since *Dead Poets Society* in 1989. Perhaps we didn't know what Williams was like as a father in real life, but to watch his dedication to his children on screen only served to raise the bar of expectations of our own fathers.

As a husband, however, Daniel was considered a nightmare by his wife Miranda (played by Sally Field). He was repeatedly unemployed, never took anything seriously and was irresponsible when it came to caring for the structure and discipline of his household. Miranda was the opposite of the coin—structured, responsible, disciplined and believed in raising their three children according to a set of rules and restrictions (sounds like *my* mother when I was a kid). As a parent, whether you supported her attitude or you thought she needed to lighten up, it was clear that she and Daniel couldn't stay married to each other anymore. This, I suppose, is where not having a steady job would cost you joint custody of your kids. And when you're addicted to your children as much as Daniel was, one Saturday a week wouldn't be enough time.

What to do? Dress up as middle-aged British woman who calls herself Mrs. Euphegenia Doubtfire, of course. This transformation was more than just physical. As Mrs. Doubtfire, Daniel was a completely different person—responsible, disciplined, structured, and one who made sure his kids adhered to a schedule. Clearly, he'd either learned a thing or two from his ex-wife or he was simply treading on very safe waters to keep his job and family intact. However, behind all the new responsibilities was still the classic Robin Williams insanity and wiseass dialogue we'd come to expect from this funny man. In fact, we couldn't help but feel empathy and support when Daniel/Mrs. Doubtfire went out of his way to not only discredit Miranda's new/old love interest Stuart Dunmire (played by a pre-James Bond Pierce Brosnan), but to also make sure Miranda didn't end up sleeping with him. It may have sounded like the wise, old granny giving her the honorable, well-meaning advice of maintaining a level of postdivorce celibacy, but we knew and loved the jealous ex-husband who didn't want to see his ex-wife screw another guy.

To say that *Mrs. Doubtfire* was heavily predictable would be an understatement. Frankly, we wouldn't have it any other way. For as much as we knew that Daniel Hillard would get away with his costumed charade, we also knew the entire scheme would inevitably come crashing down faster than any of us could say "classic episode of *I Love Lucy* or *Three's Company*." And crash down it did. To watch Daniel/Mrs. Doubtfire constantly and desperately run back and forth in a classy restaurant changing outfits between his family and his boss while repeatedly chugging down the alcohol was hilarious and fun to watch. Daniel was found out in the end, and Miranda took her revenge by legally taking his children away from him. In the end, though, anger slowly dissipated when the entire family realized how much Mrs. Doubtfire improved their lives, even if she wasn't real. Upon the surprise of learning that Daniel had brought the character of Mrs. Doubtfire to a new children's TV show, anger was replaced with forgiveness, and a father's love and dedication to his children prevailed. That kind of love may seem excessively sentimental, but Robin Williams shines so brightly that the end result is impossible to ignore or resist.

Now I'll tell you why I needed to see this film with my father. During our postmovie dinner, he and I enthusiastically agreed that he was also the type of man who, while perhaps not dressing up as a woman, would have gone to equally great lengths to be with his kids. He too, went through a bitter divorce with my mother when I was a kid and was determined to make sure he'd remain the devoted father he always was. Those were rough times for the both of us, but it was the love of a film like *Mrs. Doubtfire* that enabled a father and son to realize there were also humorous (if not insane) elements to even the darkest of times.

Schindler's List

Directed by Steven Spielberg
(December 15, 1993, U.S. Release Date)

Some films you want to see. Others you *have* to see. Not just because it's the latest film from Steven Spielberg, but because even before you've gotten on line to buy your ticket, the media and the word-of-mouth have become so strong behind the most important film of the year, you're left with no choice. To have not seen *Schindler's List* when it was released in 1993 would've been borderline irresponsible (and that meant *not* making out in the theater during the film as Jerry Seinfeld so infamously did on an episode of his NBC sitcom). It was the black-and-white epic historical drama of the Holocaust, based on Thomas Keneally's original novel called *Schindler's Ark*, which told the story of German businessman and profiteer Oskar Schindler and the period of his life during World War II Europe in which he saved the lives of more than a thousand Polish-Jewish prisoners by ensuring they were constantly kept under his employment.

This was a film I knew I couldn't see alone. On the other hand, I couldn't just see it with anyone who'd merely consider it just another few hours killed at the movies. I needed to see this with someone who'd appreciate and understand its social and conscience-minded significance in not only translating a piece of important history, but who'd also walk away with me having learned a thing or two. The choice was simple—Daniela. As it turned out, the trip to see *Schindler's List* was an entire Saturday night complete with dinner and another couple joining us (remember my friend *Stuart S.* from the *Cape Fear* chapter of *It's Still Strictly Personal?* The couple was him and his new fiancée). The movie came first, and even before it started, I couldn't help but wonder what sort of appetite we'd have for dinner when it was over.

The film began briefly in color with the traditional Jewish candle lighting and prayers for the weekly practice of Shabbat. The single line of smoke from the burning candle faded out and gave way to a black-and-white shot of smoke. It was World War II in the city of Kraków in Poland, and the local Polish Jews were forced into the overcrowded ghettos by the Germans. Oskar Schindler (played by Liam Neeson) was a German member of the Nazi Party, arrived with the intentions of making his latest fortune. He had to cash to bribe the German armed forces and SS officials to acquire and open a factory of Jewish slave labor to produce enamelware. To help run the business, Schindler enlisted the aid of accountant Itzhak Stern (played by Ben Kingsley) who also had the right connections with the black marketeers of the Jewish business community. As a result, Schindler was able to finance the factory, in which the Jewish labor received no financial compensation. While Schindler enjoyed his wealthy status as *"Herr Direktor"* and maintained ongoing friendly relations with the Nazis, Stern handled financing and administration while ensuring as many Jews as possible were deemed essential work-ers to keep them from being killed by the Nazi guards or transported to concentration camps. This effort proved ineffective when an old man with only one arm was deemed useless and executed. This was also the moment in the film where I noticed that Daniela had begun to cry.

A turning point occurred with the arrival of SS lieutenant Amon Göth, whose job it was to oversee construction of the new concentra-tion camp. This was also when the killing of innocent Jews escalated, as this new lieutenant was psychotic. Upon declaring that *"today is history"* and ordering the liquidation of the ghettos, many Jews were shot and killed in the process of emptying the living quarters. Some survived by hiding in some of the most god-awful places, including a little boy hiding in the community latrine. Schindler himself wit-nessed the massacre and we saw how profoundly it affected him. He particularly took notice of a little girl wearing a red coat. We knew the coat was red because Spielberg deliberately showed the girl's coat color amidst a black-and-white movie (she'd later be among a wagonload of the dead).

Schindler maintained a very careful friendship with Göth, and through bribery and lavish gifts, continued to enjoy his much-needed SS support. Göth was given to periods of drunkenness and routinely shot and killed Jews from the balcony of his villa, and even found reasons to brutally mistreat his Jewish maid Helen Hirsch, whom despite his brutality, had developed a private fondness for her. As time and cruelty progressed (as did Daniela's crying), Schindler redirected his efforts from making money to saving as many Jewish lives as possible. To do this, he bribed Göth into allowing him to build a sub-camp of the one he already had.

The Germans were losing the war, and Göth was ordered to ship the remaining Jews to the concentration camp at Auschwitz. Schindler bribed Göth to allow him to move his workers to a new munitions factory in Czechoslovakia. At this point, Schindler and Stern started their list ("Schindler's List") of over a thousand Jews to be transferred to his new sub-camp, thus saving them from certain death. But something went wrong when the women and girls were mistakenly redirected to Auschwitz and were released only when Schindler bribed the commandant with a bag of diamonds—but not before we all thought they were going to be gassed when ordered into a large community shower room. In fact, at the moment just before the water came on, I thought poor Daniela would lose it.

Life at the new factory was easier, and interference from the SS guards was forbidden by Schindler. He even encouraged the community rabbi to conduct the Friday night Sabbath. By the time the war finally ended in 1945, Germany had surrendered and Schindler was broke. As a member of the Nazi party, he was forced to flee and avoid capture. Although the SS guards in the factory were ordered to dispose of the Jewish workforce, Schindler persuaded them not to, so they'd return to their families as men and not murderers. Before bidding his final farewell to his workers, they gave Schindler a special ring engraved with a quote from that Talmud in which, *"Whoever saves one life saves the world entire.*" Deeply touched, he was also deeply ashamed and broke down crying, feeling he could've done more to save more Jewish lives.

The epilogue was like nothing I could've ever imagined, and yet I would've expected nothing less from a man like Steven Spielberg. In our present day, many of the surviving "Schindler Jews" were shown visiting the grave of Oskar Schindler (while accompanied by the actors portraying them in the film), while placing stones on his grave's marker (this is the traditional Jewish sign of respect when visiting a grave). This was perhaps the most poignant and beautiful moment I'd ever seen on film, and I felt I was on the verge of joining Daniela with my own tears. When the film ended and the credits began, the movie theater resembled a morgue in its total silence. No one spoke. No one wanted to. In fact, it was at least twenty minutes before anyone in my party of four said a word to each other because the emotional impact of *Schindler's List* hit us like a sledgehammer. It wasn't until later in the restaurant, after ordering burgers and beers, that we finally broke down our personal walls and discussed to great length, the motion picture we'd just witnessed and would never forget. I couldn't imagine anyone other than Spielberg who could've done such a thing to our emotions (for that, I thank him).

Nearly thirty years later, my initial feelings for *Schindler's List* are just as strong as they were back in '93. The fact that it's shot almost entirely in black and white is crucial because I cannot imagine this tale told any other way. Color, in my opinion (and in the opinion of many others, I'm sure), is a strong implication of life, joy, and spirit. And while the film may end on a somewhat triumphant note, it's still a bleak and grim telling of the most horrible period of twentieth-century history, so to tell it any other way would've been an injustice. Still, even among its darkness, Spielberg makes an attempt to capture a light moment with a laugh when during a montage, Schindler is interviewing a series of beautiful secretaries who don't possess the required skills for the job. The last interviewed woman is unattractive, old enough to be his mother, and types with great and efficient speed. The look of disbelief and irritation on Liam Neeson's face is enough to put a brief smile on your face during a film in which our emotions are destined to be tried as we face the unspeakable evil and cruelty of the period.

In this film, there are endless Jewish prisoners, some that we've come to know a little more than others, that are given their due screen time (Itzhak Stern and the maid Helen Hirsch, being the best examples). The horrors bestowed upon them by their Nazi captors is as countless as the number of people that are victims of it. Yet amidst the great mass of human beings blended together into a black-and-white tapestry of celluloid, there's the little girl in the red coat. Who is she, and why does the director choose to stand her out among so many in one of the few moments of color in the film? She is perhaps, a symbol and a reminder of the colorful gift of life in a world filled with death. This may be my own opinion, because Spielberg himself confessed a very different approach in that she was meant to symbolize the highest levels of the United States government knowing full-well about the Holocaust's existence and choosing to do nothing about it. As he put it,

> *It was as obvious as a little girl wearing a red coat, walking down the street, and yet nothing was done to bomb the German rail lines. Nothing was being done to slow down the annihilation of European Jewry. So that was my message in letting that scene be in color.*

Keeping an optimistic tone in a tale without optimism, there's a scene where a young Jewish boy and girl choose to marry, even while they live as scared prisoners. They're married by a woman who confesses to not being a rabbi, but will perform the ritual, nonetheless. As a cynic myself, it's extraordinary that I can appreciate and even be touched by such an optimistic and hopeful institution as the vows of marriage take place right smack in the middle of the refugee prison.

Throughout the journey, we come to understand early on that Oskar Schindler is a kind-hearted man deeply affected by the course of action being a member of the Nazi Party takes on his life and his business. There are light moments of mercy and sympathy in a world of darkness that saves the lives of many of his workers, but it's the heat of the train cars and the hoses that draws me in. Trapped like animals inside the boxcars, prisoners are suffering in the scorching heat. In an almost trivial and nonchalant manner, Schindler urges Amon Göth to indulge him and spray the water hoses at the car openings to cool the prisoners off. By his facial expression, he treats the entire matter as if it were comical, but we know his heart is in the right place in showing mercy to those who are suffering. To be obvious about his intentions in front of his SS superiors would surely mean trouble for him, even as he's forced to listen to Göth when he declares, *"This is very cruel, Oskar. You're giving them hope. You shouldn't do that.* That's *cruel!"*

So what shall our final reflection and interpretation of *Schindler's List* be? How shall we, our children, and our children's children come to view what is undoubtedly the most respected motion picture of Steven Spielberg's magical career? Shall we say that the big kid who loved aliens, archaeological adventures, Peter Pan and dinosaurs finally grew up with this one? No, I don't think so. As far as I'm concerned, he did that back in the '80s with *The Color Purple* and *Empire of the Sun*. Shall we say that Spielberg finally came to terms with his Jewish roots and faith, something he may have chosen to dismiss throughout most of his life prior to the making of this film? That's a reasonable enough assessment, as he's clearly sought to make a motion picture that is, by far, the most personal, intense and deeply uplifting piece of cinema he's ever offered us. Or shall we simply say, with immense gratitude, that the film finally tells a tale of the human spirit behind its will to survive during one of the darkest times of our own humanity that should never be forgotten? Yes. That's what I'll tell my son when his time comes to watch *Schindler's List*. Perhaps I'll even go to YouTube and show him the introduction by Spielberg himself that he recorded when NBC premiered the film on February 23, 1997, uncut and uninterrupted by commercials (at his request) in which he stated,

> *I want you and especially parents to know that* Schindler's List *is more explicit and more graphic*

than anything you may have seen before on network television. I made the film for this and future generations so they would know and never forget that six million Jews were murdered in the Holocaust and that history cannot be denied. I cannot be honest to that history or to the memory of its victims without depictions of violence and suffering. So tonight, in your homes, you will experience the story of Oskar Schindler, a German businessman, a member of the Nazi Party, a womanizer and a war profiteer, who saved the lives of more than eleven hundred Jews.

For my own personal closure of this film, it came on March 21, 1994 when Steven Spielberg finally got his just dues when *Schindler's List* won the Oscar for Best Picture of 1993, and *he* won the Oscar for Best Director, two awards he long deserved ever since getting royally screwed against *Out of Africa* in 1986.

Philadelphia
Directed by Jonathan Demme
(December 22, 1993, U.S. Release Date)

By this time, I was getting to know Jonathan Demme a little. After *The Silence of the Lambs* won the Oscar for Best Picture of 1991, I took notice of some earlier work including *Swing Shift*, *Married to the Mob*, and even his Talking Heads concert film *Stop Making Sense*. Still, I suppose after you've just made a very scary and controversial thriller about a deranged cannibal, perhaps the only logical procedure is to continue stirring the shit storm by taking on the subject of AIDS, homosexuality, and homophobia, though adding men like Tom Hanks and Denzel Washington and even a slow opening ballad by Bruce Springsteen may soften things up. It all sounded to me like a great Oscar contender during the 1993 holiday season. Of course, like *Schindler's List* before this, I needed to experience this one with Daniela, as well, though it would likely mean watching her cry during the movie again.

The film was based on a true story (it seemed that *every* worthwhile story was) of a real-life gay lawyer unjustly terminated from his law firm because it was discovered he had AIDS, and subsequently won his lawsuit against his firm before succumbing to the deadly disease. This would stir our emotions and convictions of not only law and justice, but our personal feelings toward AIDS and those who carry the virus. As Andrew Beckett, Tom Hanks was the film's protagonist and hero fighting for his legal and human rights in the face of prejudice and bigotry. His role in *Philadelphia* was, I suppose, the turning point in which Hanks finally grew up after years of cinematic stupidity (though funny and popular as much of it was). Denzel Washington, who'd blown me away as Malcom X only a year ago, seemed the perfectly solid and gifted actor fit to play lawyer Joe Miller, whose first purpose was to defend the law that was broken (despite advertising himself on TV as just another personal injury ambulance chaser with a reputation throughout the city as *the TV guy*") and still battle his own demons of homophobia and bigotry.

I couldn't help but wonder if the character of Joe Miller was intentionally cast as a black man. Perhaps it was meant to further stress the implications of oppression from one man to another, and the aid and support they bring to each other's lives. Predictably, Joe started out as a closed-minded man of ignorance and prejudice, and eventually realized the importance of the human being he got to know in Andrew as he defended him in a court of law. In what I thought was a negative decision about casting, though, Mary Steenburgen was often irritating as the attorney for Andrew's former bosses considered the "bad guys" of the film. I always considered her a reasonably pleasant actress in general, but her character here was wooden and practically "textbook." Daniela and I were infuriated every time she repeated the word *"fact"* during her opening statement at the trial in which she listed, well…the *facts* about Andrews's homosexual life and supposedly incompetent work habits. Were it possible to physically reach out and hit someone on the screen, we would've done it.

When Andrew's case went before the court of Philadelphia, the partners of his former firm took defense in claiming he was incompetent and that he'd deliberately tried to hide his life-threatening condition. The defense repeatedly suggested he'd *"invited"* his illness through his reckless homosexual acts and was therefore not a victim (sounds like what many said during the Ronald Reagan era). But as the law and personal feelings of social anxiety toward AIDS and homosexuality came to pass during the trial, Andrew's triumph over those who wronged him became clear to us and to the jury who'd find for Andrew. Unfortunately, as justice prevailed, Andrew's health deteriorated and he ended up in the hospital where he died by the end of the film (hope I didn't spoil it for you, but how did you expect a story like this to end?). Our hero was dead, but his spirit of the big fight lived on in our minds and hearts forever.

In the final sequence that was a real tear-jerker, director Jonathan Demme really knew how to tear at our hearts. What could choke even the toughest person more than watching a home video of the beloved deceased when he was just a little angelic boy running along the beach with his family? Add to that the soft, sweet voice of Neil Young with that, and even the most cynical son-of-a-bitch (like myself) couldn't help but shed a tear. Certainly, Daniela shed many tears.

It's impossible for me to write about *Philadelphia* without addressing my own personal feelings about homosexuality. How shall I address it? If there's one consistency in my books, it's that I've never held anything back with regard to my true feelings and opinions—until now. As a man and a human being of this great country, I don't believe anyone has the right to tell anyone else how to live their own lives, whatever those choices may be. However, that admittedly admirable conviction compared to my own personal feelings about homosexuality are *not* necessarily one and the same. That's all I'm willing to say. To write any further is to likely offend a few, some or many of my readers, and I won't do that. Just know that like it or not, popular or not, I'm still human, which means I'm loaded to the brink with faults.

As for AIDS, I can only say that I'm old enough to remember its history and the controversial talk that surrounded it when it first emerged to the public in 1981. I remember coming of sexual age during a time in the '80s when extreme caution and protection was all I ever heard about (not too unlike today when the world is living with the Covid-19 pandemic). Today, I can only feign a certain degree of ignorance about AIDS. I know it still exists, and I know there's still no cure yet, but it appears to be under control a lot more than it was decades ago. You just don't hear about it too much anymore. This is what I know and perhaps all I'll ever know, as such matters have never hit home on a personal level for me.

Well, there's one exception, and here it is—at the start of the summer of 1994, about six months after my seeing *Philadelphia* for the first time, my brother Kevin came out of the closet and formally announced to me and my mother at a Chinese restaurant that he was gay. Upon "officially" hearing this, I remained more or less unaffected and untouched by his news because I think I knew that deep down, I wasn't surprised by his announcement. In fact, I think I wondered what took him so long to come out. My mother, on the other hand, was a different story in that she'd chosen to remain deaf, dumb and blind about the possibility of her son being gay throughout his entire upbringing. Despite being in a public restaurant, she broke down and cried in disbelief. It would be years after that night before she'd finally accept things as they were, and probably for no other reason than she had no choice.

For myself, I only remember me and Kevin driving home that night and my not having much to say about the entire matter. What I do remember is warning him to be careful about his activities and to not do anything in which he could contract AIDS. Keeping in mind that I often relate my own life's experience and emotions (and those of others) to the movies, I concluded my friendly warning by asking him, "Did you see *Philadelphia*?"

*****

This is the last film of 1993 I shall discuss in any great detail.

Since the close of the 1980s, I've come to mark the time and periods of my life with each consecutive New Year's Eve, not only with the movies, but with people too. Since Caren came into my life, the way each year opened and closed seemed more vivid and more significant to me. The year 1993 was a milestone because she and I went through various stages of our relationship. In the beginning, we remained platonic as we'd been for years. By the summer, we'd gotten back together, broken up, and gotten back together again. By the year's close, it was the beginning of the end for us. And while most relationships tend to deteriorate over time, it was one particular night in her house that was solely responsible for our parting.

At this time, the economy was still on shaky ground and I had trouble finding a job with an architect. I'd worked at the local Great

Neck book store for a little over a year now, and Caren had concluded that I was a man without a future as long as I was working there, while she was convinced that *she* had a bright future ahead of her as a lawyer, believing her father would get her into law school at Hofstra University, thus using all of this as reasons for us not to be together. On the one hand, part of me wasn't surprised that a girl this fickle was breaking up with me again. What I couldn't accept, however, was a girl I'd come to care for, trust, and love over the years losing her faith in me during a temporary career setback in my life, and placing herself on a higher pedestal than me. In fact, if you take a moment to think back to Season 2 of NBC's *Friends*, and the episode called *The One with the List*, you may recall these words Rachel Green said to Ross Geller, and you'll know exactly how I felt:

> *Imagine the worst things you think about yourself.*
> *Now how would you feel if the one person that you*
> *trusted the most in the world not only thinks them,*
> *too, but actually uses them as the reasons not to be*
> *with you?*

Interestingly, as things turned out many years later, the one who supposedly didn't have any viable future (that would be *me*) became an architect and a published author. The one who concluded that I had no viable future (that would be *her*) never got into law school, and has under her belt, a failed marriage, numerous postmarriage failed relationships, at least one failed business venture, and as of this writing, earns part of her income by serving coffee at Starbucks (it's funny how life can turn out for some people, isn't it). It's just *my* opinion, but I think the average person worth a damn might respect a bookstore as a place of employment over the local coffeehouse chain. What do you think?

As you might guess, that evening at her house didn't end well between us, and I left a broken man, though I didn't exactly end things with her then and there, though I certainly *should have* (seems I was still too weak a man to do that). I saw her a couple more times after that, but I gradually realized what sort of poison this girl was in my life. It was on December 31, 1993, at Caren's New Year's Eve party that I finally experienced a moment of clarity and realized what I had to do once and for all. Shortly after the stroke of midnight, I gave Caren a long hug and said goodbye. At the time, she presumed I was parting for the night, and whatever friendship we still had would continue. It was, however, what I decided would be my last hug and my final goodbye to this girl.

I wish I could tell you I felt free and exonerated from years of personal turmoil, but life isn't that kind. I spent days alone, never leaving my apartment, and barely getting out of bed. I knew this was a period of sorrow I'd have to go through until I didn't feel so bad anymore. Of course, to get myself through it, I watched a *lot* of movies. But even as time passed, there was that part of my brain wishing I'd have done things differently. My mind raced back to New Year's Eve 1989, when I wished I'd done what Billy Crystal did at the end of *When Harry Met Sally*, and told Caren how I really felt before the new decade began. This time, however, my thoughts were occupied on how I could've parted from her differently. I wished I'd not shown up to her party, allowing her to consider the possibility that something bad might've happened to me. I would've ignored her phone calls and permitted her to presume the worst, just to teach her a painful lesson (I know that sounds silly and immature, but I wasn't exactly thinking straight at that time). One thing I knew for sure was that I spent too much time and energy loving her. I woke up loving her, I managed through my day loving her, and I went to sleep loving her. Now it was time to *stop* loving her.

It would be four years before I'd ever speak to or see Caren again. I'll tell you about that later. For now, I will tell you that it was, as you may have guessed, a *movie* that inspired me to reintroduce her into my life.

And that, my friends, was the year 1993 for me.

THE YEAR WAS 1994...

- During the U.S. Figure Skating Championships, American figure skater Nancy Kerrigan is attacked and injured. Her rival Tonya Harding and ex-husband are held responsible for the attack.
- Fifty-seven people are killed and more than 8,700 are injured after a violent earthquake strikes the Greater Los Angeles Area.
- Kurt Kobain, front man of the rock band Nirvana, is found dead at his home at the age of twenty-seven from a self-inflicted shotgun wound to the head.
- Nelson Mandela is sworn in as the first democratically elected president of South Africa.
- O. J. Simpson's ex-wife Nicole Brown Simpson and friend Ronald Coleman are murdered outside the Simpson home in Los Angeles. Days later, O. J. Simpson and friend Al Cowlings flee, driving a white Ford Bronco in a televised low-speed chase that ends with O. J.'s surrender.
- *Woodstock '94* takes place in Saugerties, New York, commemorating the twenty-fifth anniversary of the original *Woodstock* in 1969.

...AND THERE WERE MOVIES!

It's impossible to know what sort of outcome life will throw at you, even during your worst moments. In the summer of 1994, I took part in the Westhampton Beach share house for the second year, only this time I was helping to run things, allowing me a free share with my own room. It turned out to be one of the best summers I ever had. During a time of great personal pain, a summer filled with the fun of friends, barbecues, beer, rock and roll, and great sex with a new girlfriend was just what I needed to help me get over Caren. While not exactly taking the summer off, I worked as little as possible as a freelance architect with the firm I'd interned for in my younger days, getting paid in cash off the books. That combined with the money I collected from unemployment insurance gave me sufficient funds to afford myself a fun summer.

Even during what promised to be a wild and crazy summer, I still longed for good movies to help me escape the immediate pain of today. The year 1994 began with a lot of crap, in my opinion, despite some titles offering mild entertainment and escapism when I needed it like William Friedkin's *Blue Chips*, the British comedy *Four Weddings and a Funeral*, and even Ron Howard's *The Paper*. Like so many years before, I looked forward to the new summer blockbuster season when I hoped movies like *The Crow*, *The Flintstones*, *Beverly Hills Cop III*, *Speed*, *True Lies*, and *Blown Away* would blow *me* away and (temporarily) erase the pain of a broken heart. While the action films of Keanu Reeves, Arnold Schwarzenegger, and Jeff Bridges didn't fail to deliver what it promised, the high expectations I had for the other films I mentioned were grossly disappointing, particularly Eddie Murphy's pointless (and painful) third go-around as Detroit cop Axel Foley. Of course, I stayed away from *When a Man Loves a Woman*, because like *Ghost* four years before, the last thing I needed was a tender love story to remind me of my own broken heart.

Nope—'94 began unexpectedly for me with an in-your-face slap of the reality many of my fellow American Gen Xers were challenged with as we faced new chapters of career, responsibility, and lifestyle choices in the age of '90's grunge music—and it really *bit*!

Reality Bites
Directed by Ben Stiller
(February 18, 1994, U.S. Release Date)

I've always been considered a responsible person—by my wife, family, friends, and myself. Even when I was a kid, I was considered the more responsible one between me and Kevin, and it often put extra pressure on my shoulders to constantly do the right thing. It's practically been a stigmata to have to live with. After only a few months into '94, the local bookstore I'd worked at for a year and a half went out of business, and I was unemployed. Sure, I looked for an architect job so my college degree wouldn't go to waste, but I didn't do it with much drive or enthusiasm. I still experienced personal heartbreak, and all I lived for was returning to the weekend fun and partying of the summer share house.

I didn't see *Reality Bites* until the fall of '94 when it was just another one of my many video rentals from the local Blockbuster store. I had no preconceived ideas about it. For all I knew, it was just another postcollege tale in the spirit of *St. Elmo's Fire* or *Less Than Zero* by a director I'd never heard of, and starring that girl from *Bram Stoker's Dracula* and that nervous kid from *Dead Poets Society*. I couldn't have been more wrong.

It began with four best friends recently graduated from their college in Houston, Texas. Aspiring videographer Lelaina (played by Winona Ryder) and coffeehouse musician Troy (played by Ethan Hawke) were obviously attracted to each other, but kept things strictly platonic between them. Troy was a bum, having lost several minimum wage-paying jobs. Lelaina was valedictorian of her university and had aspirations to become a serious film documentarian, though her current job as a production assistant to an obnoxious TV host wasn't what she had in mind. Lelaina's roommate Vickie worked at the Gap and kept her romantic life limited to a series of one-night stands and short relationships with different guys (this sort of lifestyle led to the fear of her having possibly contracted HIV later in the movie). Her friend Sammy was gay, still a virgin, and trying to figure out how to come out of the closet to his conservative parents.

When the ladies got into a car accident (while singing along to *"Tempted"* by Squeeze), Lelaina met Michael (played by Ben Stiller) after she accidentally threw a cigarette into his convertible. He worked as an executive at a cable channel called "In Your Face," which he described as *"MTV with an edge."* They started dating, and he was interested in airing the documentary she was putting together about herself and her three friends. After an impulsive act of revenge against her boss, Lelaina lost her job and was forced to look for work beneath her technical and educational abilities. Her relationship with Michael dissolved after he helped to sell her documentary to his network and they poorly edited it into a stylized montage compromising and degrading her original artistic vision.

Meanwhile, Lelaina and Troy's friendship inevitably turned sexual and even had an admittance of love. The next morning, though, Troy left her house, avoided her for days, and then got into a messy confrontation with her. He left town and wasn't seen for some time. Even as Vickie learned that her HIV test was negative, it did little to ease the ongoing tensions between these friends. When Troy finally returned after losing his father to cancer, he forced himself to reevaluate his relationship with Lelaina, as well as his life. He and Lelaina made amends and were presumed to live the life of Hollywood "happily ever after."

From time to time throughout my writing, I've cited movies that were more about *timing*, and not necessarily whether or not they were great movies. *Reality Bites* is *not* a great movie. Hell, it's hardly even a *good* movie. As a love story, it fails miserably in my opinion because Wynona Ryder has *zero* chemistry or charisma with either of her male costars, Hawke and Stiller. If fact, her character would've probably improved as a lesbian because she seems to have the best rapport with actress Janeane Garofalo, whose own life in this story is about as interesting as her managerial shirt-folding abilities at the Gap. Even her brief brush with HIV is told with a matter-of-fact attitude, and any chance of some serious thought-provoking drama is lost.

For me, the first time I watched *Reality Bites* was a moment I realized how much I related to a couple of misfits like Troy and Lelaina, who'd come to the point where they didn't feel like doing much with their lives. Their fictional roles seemed to echo my own existence at that time. How much echo? Well, by the time the year was up, I'd had *four* jobs under my belt (two of them with architects), I'd broken up with my summer girlfriend, and my dad and I came to blows over my less-than-responsible attitude toward life.

Yes, if ever there was a time in my life I was on the verge of becoming a *bum*, 1994 was it. I did very little, and I cared even less… and it was because of a movie like *Reality Bites* that I suddenly realized I didn't want to end up like Ethan Hawke's character, which I'd come to define as *loser* with a big 'L'. Clearly, I got bent out of shape because I didn't care for the negative statement the film made about the youth of my Generation X in the '90s. Mind you, I'm not saying I suddenly found my ambition and rolled up my sleeves to change my life when the movie ended, but it *did* give me pause to realize the only way I'd ever get over my past was to fight like hell to have a worthwhile future.

So thank you, Ben Stiller. You didn't make a great movie, in my opinion, but you gave me a reason to give myself a good kick in the ass. You also gave me a reason to fall in love with *"My Sharona"* by The Knack all over again.

Forrest Gump
Directed by Robert Zemeckis
(July 6, 1994, U.S. Release Date)

I couldn't decide what it was about *Forrest Gump* that made me want to see it after seeing the trailer. Was it the dynamic star power of Tom Hanks or was it the simplicity of the film's premise that took me back to when Peter Sellers showed us the world through the eyes of a simpleton in Hal Ashby's *Being There* in 1979? The easy answer is *both*. Or perhaps it was the thought-provoking message behind Gump's simple belief that *"life is like a box of chocolates...you never know what you're going to get."* If that was a true life lesson, then my own life over the years had turned out to be a pretty damn big box of chocolates. Robert Zemeckis's new film depicted several decades in the life of Tom Hanks as Forrest Gump, a naïve and slow-witted southerner who witnessed, and in many cases, influenced some of the defining events of the latter half of the twentieth century. Intriguing as well were the extensive visual effects used to incorporate his character into archival footage of history alongside historical figures to further develop the scenes.

We met Forrest in 1981 sitting on a bus stop bench in Savannah, Georgia as he recounted his life story to strangers sitting next to him. As a child in the early 1950s in Greenbow, Alabama, Forrest was fitted with leg braces to correct his curved spine and improve his walking. Living alone with his mother (played by Sally Field), they met *"all sorts of people"* who passed through their boarding house, including a young, unknown man with a guitar named Elvis Presley.

On his first day of school, Forrest met the girl who'd become the love of his life, Jenny. The two of them became best friends, *just like peas and carrots."* Forrest was bullied because of his physical disability and lack of intelligence. It was while running away from bullies that his leg braces broke off and miraculously revealed him to be a very fast runner. His running abilities enabled him to receive a football scholarship at the University of Alabama, where he witnessed Governor George Wallace's stand at the Foster Auditorium door on June 11, 1963, and eventually joined the All-American team, thus meeting President John F. Kennedy at the White House (though he had to pee real bad).

Upon graduating college, Forrest enlisted in the U.S. Army and met fellow soldier nicknamed "Bubba." They became best friends and even went to Vietnam together. During their tour of duty, they agreed to go into the shrimping business together as soon as they returned home. But during a violent and bloody ambush while on patrol, Bubba was killed in action. During the battle, Forrest saved several wounded members of his platoon, including his lieutenant Dan Taylor (played by Gary Sinise, who I'd seen only once before in his 1992 remake of *Of Mice and Men*), who lost both of his legs and resented Forrest's effort to save him, believing it was his destiny to die with honor on the field of battle. Returning home, Forrest was awarded the Medal of Honor for his heroism by President Lyndon B. Johnson (even showing LBJ the bullet wound on his ass).

Now in Washington, DC, Forrest was unwittingly caught up in the antiwar "March on the Pentagon," though he wasn't smart enough to realize what he was caught up in. It was there he was reunited with Jenny as an adult (played by Robin Wright, who I only barely remembered from Rob Reiner's *The Princess Bride*), who lived the carefree life of a hippie. He'd also developed a real talent for playing ping-pong, escalating him to the status of a sports celebrity, competing against teams in China and even earning him a spot on the Dick Cavett Show in 1971 alongside John Lennon. Shortly before he was discharged from the army, it was Forrest who reported a light burning at the Watergate complex in 1972, thus accidentally exposing the Watergate scandal which eventually forced President Richard Nixon to resign his presidency in August 1974.

Returning home to Greenbow, Forrest kept his promise to Bubba to go into the shrimping business. With his earnings from a ping-pong paddle endorsement, he bought a shrimping boat and was surprised to find Lieutenant Dan Taylor waiting for him one day, fulfilling his own promise to be Forrest's first mate. Shrimping was a failure at first, until their boat got caught up in Hurricane Carmen, which they not only survived, but also enabled them to pull in huge amounts of shrimp, thus creating the Bubba-Gump Shrimp Company. Once bitter about his physical disabilities, Lieutenant Dan thanked Forrest for saving his life and finally made his peace with God during a cleansing swim in the Bayou. To cap off their success, Lieutenant Dan invested their new fortunes in what was then a brand-new computer company called Apple, which Forrest presumed was *"some kind of fruit company,"* making the two of them millionaires.

Time progressed and took its toll on Forrest's life. His mother died of cancer, and in 1976, Jenny returned after a long, troubled life of drugs and physical abuse to live with Forrest in his house in Greenbow. Turning down his proposal of marriage, she loved him, nonetheless, and they made love for the first time, though she left him the next morning. It suddenly occurred to me while watching this movie that Jenny and her fickle, unpredictable behavior reminded me a lot of Caren. Heartbroken and confused, Forrest decided one morning to go for a little run, which inevitably became a three-year marathon across the country, bringing him fame once again.

The film then caught up with itself back at the bus bench in 1981. We learned that Forrest was there waiting for a bus so he could visit Jenny at her request. Reunited with her again, she introduced him to their little son Forrest Gump Jr. But what should have been a moment of joy and closure turned tragic when Jenny revealed she was sick with an incurable disease. She and Forrest married, Lieutenant Dan walked again with artificial titanium alloy legs, and Jenny died. When Forrest placed her grave under their favorite childhood tree, he reminded us that life perhaps was a combination of both destiny and pure chance. His life, however, found peace and meaning with his new role as a loving father.

Leaving the theater, my first thought was that *Forrest Gump* would surely win the Oscar for Best Picture of 1994 (it *did*). I remember wanting to see this film again as soon as possible because I was so taken by the simplicity and the magic of this man's extraordinary life which often played out by mere chance of circumstance and history. Forrest Gump is, indeed, not a smart man. On its surface, his story is an intriguing balancing act of drama, comedy, sadness, and magic. But his story also shows us that even the dumbest of people can express the simplest of philosophies what will sustain them through life. In his case, Forrest always listens to his mamma, he loves only his Jenny, maintains a never-ending loyalty to his best friends Lieutenant Dan and Bubba, and he runs great distances across the country to find his own personal meaning and purpose. I suppose if you're a true optimist of life (which I'm often *not*), that may be all you need to get by in this world.

Regarding Forrest's love and loyalty to Jenny—while incredibly admirable, there are times when I consider him to be an absolute schmuck. After all, Jenny treats him like dirt and abandons him more than once. Who would continue to love a girl like that? Apparently, only Forrest Gump would (and *me* a long time ago). I suppose I can justify that it all pays off in the end when he finally wins her heart and becomes the father of the child she bears him (unbeknownst for years), thus rewarding him with the destiny of fatherhood, which can be argued as the most important thing in this life. As a father myself, there's surely no argument in that.

Decades later, there's one moment at the end I'm still drawn to. After Jenny dies and Forrest walks away from her headstone, he witnesses a flock of birds flying overhead, symbolic of how when he and Jenny were children, she prayed to be turned into a bird so she could *"fly far, far away"* from her abusive father and troubled life. Yes, symbolism can be very corny on film, but it can also touch our hearts and remind us of what love really is. Because as Forrest himself so bluntly put it, *"I'm not a smart man…but I know what love is."* Perhaps after watching life and the world through the sentimental eyes of *Forrest Gump*, I understand the sweet and charming simplicity of life and love a little better too.

The Shawshank Redemption
Directed by Frank Darabont
(September 23, 1994, U.S. Release Date)

Throughout much of the '90s, I did a lot of "movie hopping" at various multiplex theaters. If you're unfamiliar with that term, it's when you pay one ticket price for one movie and then proceed to move around, or "hop" throughout the building catching more than one movie. Back when I did it, security at these buildings was incredibly lax, so moving around was never an issue. It was simply a matter of planning ahead to make sure the movie start times worked conveniently with my schedule. This saved me a lot of money and I really caught up on my movies. Yes, it was dishonest and I wouldn't condone it today, and the theaters likely lost money because of people like me, but I didn't care back then.

One night in the fall of '94, I had *no* intention of seeing *The Shawshank Redemption*. Believe it or not, I went to a local multiplex in Queens to see *Wes Craven's New Nightmare* (aka *A Nightmare on Elm Street 7*). I actually paid good money intent on seeing this sort of crap. Somehow I'd gotten it into my thick head that because Wes Craven was back in the director's chair and actress Heather Langenkamp returned to her role that made the original film of *A Nightmare on Elm Street* such a hit (a film I no longer care for), this new film in the franchise might prove to be worth something. Wrong. When it was over, I decided to compensate my time and money wasted on this slasher dud by watching something else. Without much thought, I walked into the theater showing *The Shawshank Redemption* simply because of the convenient start time. Despite the fact that the movie poster indicated it was based on a novella by Stephen King (whom I loved to read), my thoughts and expectations of the film were minimal, at best. Again, wrong.

It was 1947 in Portland, Maine and banker (and the movie's protagonist) Andy Dufresne (played by Tim Robbins) was convicted of murdering his wife and her lover (a crime he didn't commit), and sentenced to two consecutive life sentences at the Shawshank State Penitentiary even before the movie's opening credits were over (much like the opening of *The Fugitive*). Andy kept much to himself at first and then finally opened up to Ellis "Red" Redding (played by Morgan Freeman), the man known throughout the prison as *"the guy who can get it for you,"* by requesting a small rock hammer and a poster of Rita Hayworth. While adjusting to the hell of prison life, Andy was frequently assaulted and raped by a group of men infamously known as "the Sisters."

In May 1949, things turned around for Andy when he inadvertently helped a brutal prison guard keep his entire inheritance tax free by offering his sound financial advice on how to legally shelter the money by giving it to his wife as a one-time gift. The price for this valuable advice was merely three cold beers apiece for his fellow prison mates while tarring a building roof on a hot day. In that moment of verbal risk, Andy turned things around for himself with not only the prisoners, but the guards too, who now relied on his financial services at tax time every year (his favor with the guards also got "the Sisters" off his back for good).

The years rolled on, and the routines stabilized for Andy at Shawshank, as did his purpose there, including obtaining government funds to improve the decaying prison library. He also remained a man of the hope and spirit other prisoners lost long ago. In a moment of great defiance, Andy played an excerpt from a record of the opera *The Marriage of Figaro* over the public address system. The shot of the inmates gathered together in the prison courtyard as they looked up in awc and wonderment at the beautiful sounds of two Italian ladies singing their hearts out was not only visually breathtaking, but also a reminder of how music, any music, never failed to touch even the most tormented of souls. Nonetheless, Andy was placed in solitary confinement as punishment for his defiance against the warden's authority.

By 1963, the prison warden (named Norton) exploited prison labor for public projects, and profited by underbidding skilled labor contracts and accepting bribes. He used Andy's banking skills to launder the money by creating a phantom alias known as "Randall Stephens." Sometime later, a young kid named Tommy Williams arrived at Shawshank for breaking and entering. Andy took him under his wing to help him pass his high school GED exam. Tommy then revealed to Andy and Red that his former cellmate at another prison had confessed responsibility for the murders of Andy's wife and her lover, for which Andy was wrongly convicted of. When Andy approached Norton with the information, Norton refused to listen and threw Andy back in solitary confinement when Andy mentioned the illegal money laundering between them. To protect his corrupt activities and illegal profiting, Norton had Tommy killed in the prison courtyard under the guise of an escape attempt.

By now it looked like Andy had reached the end of his rope, facing a lifetime at Shawshank. He sat down with Red and shared his dream of spending the rest of his life in a small coastal town in Mexico. He spoke of a specific hayfield, asking Red that if he ever got out of prison, to promise to dig up a package buried under a large isolated tree. But Red was fearful that Andy had finally reaching his breaking point and might do something drastic to himself that night.

In the history of movie plot twists, turns, and revelations, the moment when we discovered that Andy had escaped from Shawshank and had, for the last nineteen years, been systematically planning that escape, was one of the best I'd ever seen. From the moment that Norton furiously threw the rock at the poster of Raquel Welch hanging on Andy's wall and revealed the large tunnel Andy had been digging every night with the small rock hammer he'd gotten from Red at the beginning of the film, it was astounding to finally realize that all the while, we'd been victims of a major deception that ultimately put our hero on top. We knew Andy was innocent of his crime all along, and we took pleasure in his personal triumphs during his prison life.

But nothing put such a smile on my face as when Andy's final act of defiance and revenge was to not only escape to the beaches of Mexico, but to also steal Norton's money and take him down in the process. By the time Red told us, *"I guess I just miss my friend,"* and the picture faded to black, I was sure the movie was over and I got up from my seat to leave the theater.

In what was practically an epilogue to this great story, Red was finally paroled and released from Shawshank after having served forty years. Fearing he'd never adjust to life outside the prison, he broke parole by keeping his promise to Andy and visited the hayfield and tree Andy spoke about. What Red dug up was a box containing money and a letter from Andy asking him to join him in Mexico—a letter Andy had clearly written *after* he escaped, though he'd spoken of it before, as if it was already something that existed. Finally feeling and understanding his own hope, Red crossed the U.S. border in Texas and was reunited with Andy on the beach. And as I left the theater that night, the memory of a failed attempt at Wes Craven's new horror film was easily forgotten, as I'd just experienced an amazing feeling that one can only feel when they've spent time at the right movie at the right time in their lives. It was not only Andy and Red's triumph that made me feel so good, but also the idea of thinking back on Andy's actions, small as some were, and realized how they all came together to make him and Red free men. I (and I'm sure others who loved this film) loved not only that initial good feeling, but also the feeling of finally having been let in on the ultimate plan taking place behind our backs the entire time.

Admittedly, I haven't seen many prison films. While I consider black-and-white dramas like Mervyn LeRoy's *I Am a Fugitive from a Chain Gang* and John Frankenheimer's *Birdman of Alcatraz* classics, crap like Sylvester Stallone in the 1989 film *Lock Up* can really put a crutch on the genre. I'm also probably the only person who's never liked Paul Newman's classic *Cool Hand Luke*. However, despite my personal cinematic tastes, the prison drama has become its own genre over time. To call *The Shawshank Redemption* my favorite prison film of all time (which it is) is too easy since I have little basis of comparison. In almost any prison story, the formula doesn't change much, in which you have the protagonist who's either innocent of their crime, or grossly misunderstood as a human being, despite the crime they're guilty of. The latter description would best fit Red who, despite being convicted for murder, is a gentle man whose prison reputation not only identifies his purpose in life, but also shows his kind heart in making conditions for the convicted felons a little easier.

The integrity and feelings of self-worth among men are, perhaps, the strongest themes of Frank Darabont's film. In prison, where life seems hopeless, it's the simplest things that make them feel like men again, and not animals; whether it's the cold beer on a May morning or even a brief excerpt of opera music. Still, even those moments of freedom are threatened by the hard fact of being institutionalized. As Red so bluntly puts it, *"These walls are funny. First you hate 'em, then you get used to 'em. Enough time passes, you get so you depend on them."* By that reckoning, being free on the outside proves to be a form of imprisonment in of itself. Friendship, while being nonsexual, is also very strong, as it proves the bonding love between men who have come to depend on each other for survival. There are moments that are wonderfully satisfying and uplifting, particularly when we feel our own sense of triumph and validation when at the end Red, now a free man, strolls along the isolated beach to be reunited with not only his best friend Andy, but the promise of hope and freedom.

Author Stephen King himself declared *The Shawshank Redemption* to be one of his favorite film adaptations based on his own work. For myself, I consider it to be one of my top ten favorite films of the '90s (and it's all due to my initial stupidity of wanting to see a *Nightmare on Elm Street* movie). Still, my night at the movies in the fall of '94 proved once and for all that sometimes the things you expect the least from shall deliver the most in return…and return, it did.

Pulp Fiction

Directed by Quentin Tarantino
(October 14, 1994, U.S. Release Date)

Twenty-eight years ago, if you'd asked me what my single favorite film of the 1990s was, I'd have told you it was Quentin Tarantino's *Pulp Fiction*. Ten years ago, if you'd asked me what my single favorite film of the 1990s was, I'd have told you it was Quentin Tarantino's *Pulp Fiction*. And if you came up to me on the street tomorrow and asked me what my single favorite film of the 1990s is, I'd tell you without hesitation that it's Quentin Tarantino's *Pulp Fiction*.

By October '94, I'd moved into Manhattan and lived in a one-bedroom apartment on East Eighty-Sixth Street, and it was the word-of-mouth and media frenzy behind it that drove me to see *Pulp Fiction* on a Saturday afternoon at a twin movie theater just down the street from where I lived. Perhaps the biggest piece of news behind this new independent film was that John Travolta had finally scored a hit after more than a decade of duds. Even before the rolling credits began, I realized I was required to pay strict attention to every word spoken, every pause, and every facial expression in between. The beginning was a simple Los Angeles coffee shop and the childish plotting between two lovers bent on robbing the very coffee shop they sat in. But even this was misleading because as the robbery began, it froze and then the film began—I mean *really* began.

Its story and narrative were told in a nonchronological order and followed two interrelated stories of mob contract killers Vincent Vega (Travolta) and Jules Winnfield (played by Samuel L. Jackson), and prizefighter Butch Coolidge (played by Bruce Willis). It began with Vincent and Jules driving together on their way to do a mob hit while listening to Kool & the Gang on the radio. These were no ordinary mob killers, though. These were thinking men who not only carried on intelligent conversations (including McDonald's food in Europe), but also engaged in theological reasoning and speculation (including foot massages). I recall my immediate reaction from listening to just their first conversation was, "Oh man, I love these guys!" I was surely witnessing the notion of the two-sided coin with these men because I knew they were about to commit a violent job regardless of their intellect, but not before continuing their engaging conversations with the very boys they came to kill. One minute it was a deep biblical passage and whether or not *they speak English in What,"* and the next minute it was violent *bang, bang, kill, kill* gun action. Sick yet brilliant.

Following the violence and mayhem, we saw the lighter side of Vincent Vega as he spent the evening on a platonic "date" with his boss Marsellus Wallace's wife Mia. It began innocently enough at a 1950's-style diner with steak, hamburger and fries, a five-dollar milkshake, and then some dancing to top off the experience (we got to see John Travolta *dance* again). But even as all this seemed innocent and lovely, it ended with a cocaine overdose and the desperate effort to save the big boss's wife so that Vincent wouldn't be killed for allowing it to happen. And if that image of Uma Thurman with the hypodermic needle sticking out of her heart didn't convince me or anyone else never to use drugs, I don't know what would have. How could I or anyone else have kept from jumping out of our seats when we heard the sound of the needle penetrating her breast plate and then watching her freak out. When it was over, the sequence concluded with a rather "happily ever after" moment complete with a corny joke about a family of tomatoes and a kiss blown into the wind from Vincent.

The story of Butch the prizefighter was a darker one. He was a man haunted by his past, both in childhood and professional choices he made with his boxing career. As a child, he learned of his father who died in Vietnam through a family birthright gold watch delivered to him after having been up the asses of two men. Despite all the great work Christopher Walken had done up to that point in his career, his brief and brilliant cameo may be how I'd want to remember him best. As a boxer, Butch accepted a high payoff from Marsellus Wallace to throw his last professional fight. Instead, he screwed everybody by winning the fight (and killing his opponent) and taking off with Marsellus's cash, as well as money due him through his bookie. In a twisted case of irony, Butch and Marsellus were together again and almost killed by a couple of sadomasochistic redneck assholes practically taken from John Boorman's 1972 film *Deliverance*. This incident may have been just bad luck when Butch went back home to retrieve his father's gold watch, but the real irony was Butch saving Marsellus's life and squaring his debt with the gangster. Again, in a sick way, another case of "happily ever after" when Butch and his girlfriend drove off together on one of the redneck's motorcycle (sorry, *chopper*).

Returning to the opening scene of the hit by Vincent and Jules, another boy who was hiding in the bathroom all along, burst into the living room and fired his gun wildly at both hitmen, missing every shot. After Vincent and Jules shot him dead, Jules professed their survival as a miracle of God, which Vincent disputed. In the car, Vincent accidentally shot their associate Marvin in the face, covering themselves and the car's interior with his blood. Desperate to get the car off the road in broad daylight, they hid the car at the home of Jimmie (played by Quentin Tarantino himself), who demanded they deal with the problem immediately before his wife Bonnie got home and raised hell. The clean-up man known as "The Wolf" (played by Harvey Keitel) arrived and directed Vincent and Jules to *"pretty please, with sugar on top, clean the fucking car"* and dispose of their bloody clothes before taking the car to a junkyard. Again, as if nothing bad had happened, there was that "happily ever after" feeling again as the hitmen (also friends) decided to have breakfast together.

Now into the film's epilogue, we returned to the coffee shop, and the robbery between the two lovers was under way. We also learned that Vincent and Jules, two hit men with guns of their own and great balls of steel, were in that same coffee shop eating breakfast. The robbery didn't go as expected, but it concluded with some of Jules's deepest, theological thoughts on not only the Bible quote he repeated during the film, but also the sum total of his life until now, and how he might redeem it before it was too late. We didn't know what would happen to Jules or Butch (we already knew what happened to Vincent when he was shot dead by Butch earlier in the film), but part of the story's originality was its ambiguity.

When it was over, I was so taken and blown away by what I'd just watched, my immediate reaction to myself was, "Eric, this isn't a film you watch just once and then go home. You have to stay and watch it again right now. They'll never let you stay in your seat like they used to when you were a kid, but you can go sit on the men's room toilet for half an hour and then return to the theater to watch it again. You *have* to!" That's just what I did, and by the time two back-to-back showings of *Pulp Fiction* were concluded, day turned into night, and I rewarded myself with a large sausage pizza for having had the privilege of experiencing the art of cinema in a startling new way.

Before seeing this immortal Tarantino classic for the first time, it was obvious that I was ignorant to the possibilities of what film and storytelling *could be*, beyond the conventional bullshit textbook format that every "how to" screenwriting book insisted you had to follow to get a screenplay made into a movie (I say fuck all of you so-called "how to" experts who write your books still insisting on the traditional three-act structure). *Pulp Fiction* took everything I and others knew about the unconventional nonlinear story line, bloody violence, ironic humor, casual and eclectic dialogue, pop-culture reference, and stylized film direction and tuned it upside down on its ass.

Let's discuss the questions of the film and the issues that force us to use our analytical heads and *think* for a change. Let's start with the infamous suitcase, what's in it and why it glows. Everybody's talked about it and speculated what it could be. There's never been a correct answer on the subject, but I'll tell you which theory I personally agree with (perhaps you do too). The glow inside the suitcase is likely the *soul* of Marsellus Wallace, and Vincent and Jules are the two unconventional *angels* charged with delivering it to him. It's a solid biblical theory that makes the most sense to me. Is there any other theory than them being angels that explains how they survive the bullets repeatedly fired directly at them? Is there any other theory that explains Jules's repeated reference to the biblical passage of Ezekiel 25:17, and connections toward which direction God wants him to go in? On the other hand, if they *are* angels, why is Vincent so easily gunned down outside Butch's bathroom? Is it because his angelic powers no longer exist, having completed their mission of delivering the briefcase? Also, take careful notice of the first time we meet Marsellus Wallace, which is from the back of his head with a Band-Aid on it. This bandage very likely covers the skin cut in which his soul either once left his head or the one in which his soul will return to his head. Let's not also forget the character of Lance (played by Eric Stoltz) is meant to look just like Jesus Christ, complete with long hair and dressed in a robe. Is all this coincidence? I'd like to think it's all possible, and it's the great possibilities of the film that are a treasure to experience.

Still, I'm no expert on *Pulp Fiction* because I haven't figured everything out yet, particularly the scene when Butch is riding in the back of the taxi and the background in the rear windshield is black and white. What does it mean? Is it an homage to the Golden Age of black-and-white Hollywood film noir, or is there something more to it that I don't comprehend? The answer must lie somewhere— the truth is out there. Nonetheless, let me conclude by thanking Quentin Tarantino, John Travolta, Samuel Jackson, Bruce Willis, Uma Thurman, Ving Rhames, Harvey Keitel, Tim Roth and Amana Plummer for their tremendous efforts of stylized performance and artistic filmmaking. It's been a miraculous revelation in cinema that, every once in a great while, renews my faith in the possibilities of what motion pictures *can* be.

As much as I love *Forrest Gump*, I think *Pulp Fiction* should've taken home the Oscar for Best Picture of 1994. It is, after all, in my opinion, the single best movie of the 1990s.

Clerks

Directed by Kevin Smith
(October 19, 1994, U.S. Release Date)

By the time I finally saw *Clerks* on video in early 1995, I was in between architect jobs and working instead at the Banana Republic just blocks away from my apartment. I stayed at that job for only five weeks, and it was one of the worst experiences of my life, because much like Kevin Smith's movie poster tagline, just because I served the customers didn't mean I liked them. Truth is, I despised every customer who asked me to help them with anything. Sure, I put on a smile and acted like I gave a damn about what I did to earn my meager paycheck, while inside I was screaming and begging for someone to put me out of my misery. In fact, with the exception of the local Great Neck bookstore and the summer of 1985 I spent working at *LeSportsac* in Westhampton Beach (I had a crush on the girl I worked with), I spent my youth avoiding retail positions whenever possible.

As a debut independent black-and-white film, *Clerks* wasn't exactly Orson Welles's *Citizen Kane*, but it seemed a bold enough effort at low budget comedy, and its subject matter was on par with what I felt at the time—young men who have a job to do, but hate the people involved. Dante Hicks was such a man who worked as a retail clerk at the local Quick Stop convenience store in a small New Jersey town. On this particular day, he was asked to come to work on what should've been his day off. Not long after opening the store for the day, Dante's best friend, wiseass slacker Randal Graves, arrived to open the local video store next door. While these buddies hated their tedious customer service jobs, Dante would grin and bear it every day and treat each customer with respect. Randal, on the other hand, had no problem doing what many probably often fantasized about doing—telling the common difficult customer to fuck off.

Despite their different attitudes, they equally neglected their jobs, with Randal often closing the video store to hang out with Dante at the Quick Stop. Surprisingly, these guys weren't idiots. They passed the time engaging each other in philosophical discussions on a wide variety of topics including relationships, sex, and the deeper meaning behind the destruction of the second Death Star in *Return of the Jedi*. What they repeatedly agreed on was the difficult customers they had to deal with day in and day out—customers who were angry, demanding, irrational, impolite, clueless, and those with inexplicable idiosyncrasies, like the man who sat on the floor and examined each egg to form the perfect dozen, the four-year-old girl who managed to buy cigarettes, and the old Jewish man who politely requested a porn magazine before using the Quick Stop bathroom. In between discussions, they found reasons to leave the store and slack off, from a twelve-minute hockey game on the roof of their building to a wake for one of Dante's ex-lovers, ending with them being chased out of the funeral parlor.

Dante was torn between two women—his current girlfriend Veronica who doted on him, urged him to go back to school, and confessed to having given oral sex to thirty-six men before him, which Dante didn't take too well. Despite her devotion to him, though, he was still hung up on his ex-girlfriend Caitlin, whom he secretly communicated with. When Caitlin returned from school unexpectedly, Dante tried to rekindle his relationship with her, despite her history of repeatedly hurting him (sounds like me and Caren). The rekindling wasn't to be, because Caitlin was traumatized and catatonic after she had sex in the dark Quick Stop bathroom with whom she *thought* was Dante, but instead turned out to be the old Jewish man who died of a heart attack while masturbating and still maintained a rock-hard erection even after death (this incident would later be referenced in Kevin Smith's 1997 film *Chasing Amy*).

Throughout the events of this day, a pair of drug dealers called Jay and Silent Bob (Bob played by Kevin Smith himself) loitered outside the Quick Stop and the video store. Aware of Dante's romantic dilemma, it was Silent Bob who finally broke his silence and helped Dante to see that he truly loved Veronica. But Randal had already opened his big mouth and confessed to Veronica that Dante wanted Caitlin instead of her, which prompted Veronica to dump Dante, which in turn, provoked a fight between Dante and Randal, trashing the Quick Stop.

(Are you following this little soap opera with me?)

Despite their physical brawl, Dante and Randal were still friends and experienced a moment of clarity when after Dante repeated that he's *"not even supposed to be here today,"* Randal chewed him out by telling him that he could've left work any time and prevented the day's chaos if he chose to. After all, they were just *clerks* and not nearly as *"advanced"* as they chose to think they were. If they were that advanced, they wouldn't be stuck in such low paying, low self-esteem jobs. I suppose such a declaration at the end of the work day, even in a movie, might have given me pause to appreciate that even while I despised working at the Banana Republic, at least I wasn't a convenience store clerk (or mopping floors at McDonalds—or serving coffee at Starbucks).

I didn't know it at the time, but *Clerks* was practically autobiographical because Kevin Smith worked in a Quick Stop convenience store before becoming a filmmaker. What little I've seen of him in real life would suggest he's just as subdued and relaxed as his infamous character, Silent Bob, so I imagine that as a store clerk, he was a lot like Dante Hicks. I'd like to think that he had a friend who despised customers as much as Randal. I'd also like to think that there's someone out there who'd deliberately go out of his way to offend a mother and her little girl by ordering a barrage of blatantly vulgar porn video titles (including *Cum on Eileen*) over the phone to validate my own fantasies of wanting to tell the customer where they can go and where they can stick it.

Still, I have to give Smith the proper credit for chasing and making the necessary sacrifices to achieve his cinematic dreams. He sold off a large portion of his extensive comic-book collection, maxed out a series of limited credit cards, used a portion of his college money, and spent his insurance money awarded to him after losing his car in a flood to fund his film project. The story was also filmed at the actual Quick Stop convenience store Smith worked at.

As previously stated, despite its cult film status, *Clerks* is hardly another *Citizen Kane*. It's a film you take at face value, as well as your own personal experiences in the world of retail commerce (if any). The middle-class characters of New Jersey are quirky and interesting, and the dialogue is comical, weird, brilliant and more than quotable. Kevin Smith doesn't apologize for his vulgar approach to life for the twentysomething male who can't figure out what to do with himself. It's ultimately a film that speaks for and to the slackers of the world in a way that goes beyond anything *Reality Bites* achieved in its own right during my brief period of "slacker-ness." One thing that remains unchanged throughout my career, though, is my ongoing desire to avoid dealing with difficult and stupid people. Fuck them all!

Star Trek: Generations
Directed by David Carson
(November 18, 1994, U.S. Release Date)

When I wrote my first *It's Strictly Personal* book, I covered many of the films of my childhood, which comprised of a great deal of science fiction. These were life-changing movies to a child which may not have had the same emotional or spiritual meaning to an adult. As I got older and (hopefully) more mature, I'd pick and choose which films I felt were more significant and life-changing for me (I write about those now), and very often that didn't include science fiction—until now.

In the history of television's syndicated run of *Star Trek: The Next Generation* (1987 to 1994), I watched the show only *twice*. The first was the pilot premiere of *Encounter at Farpoint* on September 28, 1987. The second was the series finale *All Good Things* on May 23, 1994. In between, nothing. But even before the series finale aired, word was out that the first *Next Generation* motion picture would be released in the fall of '94, and it would somehow feature *both* Captain Jean-Luc Picard and Captain James T. Kirk (the movie poster of both Patrick Stewart and William Shatner confirmed that). How would *that* happen? How do you have two *Star Trek* captains in the same movie that's supposed to be separated by an entire generation? I suppose the world of sci-fi time travel would permit the idea, but I hoped the story wouldn't go that route (*Star Trek IV: The Voyage Home* covered that well enough).

The world of the original *Star Trek* and the twenty-third century gave us one last visit with three familiar faces—James Kirk, Scotty and Chekov, as they returned to attend the maiden voyage of the starship USS Enterprise-B, under the command of the guy who played Cameron Frye in *Ferris Bueller's Day Off* (he seemed just as goofy and unsure of himself as captain of a starship). What should've been a routine "shakedown" flight became a dangerous rescue mission to save two ships from a strange energy ribbon in space. The new Enterprise captain, unprepared for this crisis, turned to Kirk for assistance. As always, Kirk saved the ship and the day but was (presumably) killed when the ribbon caused an explosion across Enterprise's hull, where Kirk happened to be located.

Seventy-eight years later, we were reunited with the crew that *Next Generation* fans (except me) followed on TV for seven years. During a computer simulation to celebrate the promotion of Worf, Captain Jean-Luc Picard learned that his brother and nephew were killed in a fire, and it looked like he'd be the last Picard in the long family line. The energy ribbon was also reintroduced, and with it, the eccentric (if not mad) scientist Dr. Tolian Soran (played by Malcom McDowell) who obsessed about getting himself back *inside* the mysterious ribbon called the "Nexus," even if it meant destroying the Amargosa star and killing millions (including the crew of the Enterprise). The Nexus was described as an extra-dimensional realm existing outside of normal space and time, where time had no meaning, or as Whoppi Goldberg simply put it, *"being inside joy. As if joy was something tangible, and you could wrap yourself in it like a blanket, and never in my life have I been as content."* Her words, which I suspected were a simple part of the film's dialogue, hit me on a personal and emotional level when I heard them…but I'll get into more detail on that shortly.

Determined to stop Soran, Picard travelled to the planet Veridian III, while the Enterprise engaged a Klingon Bird of Prey in battle. The Enterprise was victorious, but was also headed for destruction as Picard was unsuccessful in stopping Soran from launching his destructive missile at the Amargosa star. The Enterprise and her entire crew were destroyed along with Veridian III from the shock wave of the exploding star. Picard was now inside the Nexus ribbon and surrounded by a loving family on Christmas Eve in a fictional world straight out of Charles Dickens. For the briefest time, he was no longer the last of the Picard family line, and he discovered what pure joy meant to him as he embraced what he never had before, declaring to himself, *"These are my children."* But it was in a moment of silence within himself as he stared into the ornament of his Christmas tree that he realized everything he felt and experienced was wrong, and simply an illusion of his own mind and desires. His mission to return to Veridian III and stop Soran was still a reality, and he'd need help to do it.

It was now time for the powers-that-be in Hollywood to live up to their promise to come up with *something* to satisfy the dilemma of how Picard and Kirk could achieve a hallmark meeting in the same movie, and that something turned out to be more convincing than I could've imagined. It was simple—Kirk was still alive because he was sucked into the Nexus ribbon where time, and his death from the previous century, had no meaning. Kirk, entranced by the opportunity to make up for past mistakes and regrets, had no intention of leaving the Nexus. Though he soon realized his life constantly required excitement and danger. Realizing they could travel wherever and whenever they wanted, they left the Nexus and returned to Veridian III to stop Soran, save the Enterprise and humanity itself. But the price paid was that after many decades of following his heroic adventures, the great and legendary James Tiberius Kirk would finally meet his end, and it would be the other great captain of the galaxy, Jean-Luc Picard, who'd bury him on Veridian III in a sweeping overhead camera shot that I still enjoy watching today. If there wasn't something so perfectly *poignant* about that, then I don't know the true meaning of the word (though I still feel Picard should've said a few words instead of just placing his Federation pin on the burial rock).

Something I became aware of before seeing *Generations* was that Leonard Nimoy and DeForest Kelly declined to appear in the new film because they both felt there were problems with the story and script. If this is accurate, then they should've explained themselves about accepting the story and script of *Star Trek V: The Final Frontier*, which every Star Trek fan and reasonable moviegoer with half a brain considers to be the worst *Star Trek* film in the history of the franchise. In my opinion, the plot point of the Nexus ribbon and its power of time and illusion is as plausible a story for uniting our two captains as anything else sci-fi may come up with. It's a sufficient blend of just the right amount of fantasy and mystery required to define yet another extraordinary force in our unknown universe.

Speaking from a more personal level, *Generations*, despite its reputation as one of the less popular *Star Trek* films in the franchise, is still an original space fantasy tale that deserves more credit and recognition that it's received (though I *do* find Data's experience with the emotion chip silly, annoying and unnecessary), even from those of us who aren't die hard Trekkies. It also provokes thoughts of thematic reflections that I haven't felt from a sci-fi film since *Star Trek III: The Search for Spock* back in 1984. If the Nexus ribbon *were* a viable fantasy in life, how would I use it? What was my idea of joy and contentment at a time when I was feeling at my lowest? The perfect job? The perfect home? The perfect woman? None of them existed in my life yet, and I was desperate to reach out for them in a deep longing that equally matched Picard's. These were questions I could potentially live my entire life without ever getting answers to, but through the unexpected aid of this *Star Trek* film, it was one of life's mysteries that occupied my thoughts and reflections, and that was something I'd hardly expect from a sci-fi film as an adult.

Perhaps it was a lot like the old poster I'd seen as a kid which said, "All I need to know about life I learned from *Star Trek*."

*****

This is the last film of 1994 I shall discuss in any great detail.

The summer of '94 was one of the best summers of my life. I did very little work, I ate plenty, I drank more, I partied, I had great sex, and I was popular with nearly two hundred young men and woman in the share house I was running. I couldn't have possibly imagined a more perfect way to get over my heartbreak. The problem is that summer lasts only three months, and I set myself up for a severe downfall when it was over. As soon as Labor Day weekend came and went, it all came crashing down around me. The distracting fun was over and I had to return to the harsh pain of reality. All the friends I'd made had almost completely disappeared at a time before the convenience of emails and social media, the summer romance with my girlfriend was over as we both went our separate ways, and I was living a very lonely existence in New York City while I continued to try and find a more stable, and status-minded position of employment.

The movies of the year, while plentiful in action, violence and excitement, had done little in the way of pure fun to ease my troubled mind. *Star Trek: Generations* surely took me back to the sci-fi fun of my childhood's past, but in the end, it left me with depressing questions and uncertainty. Too often, I heard Malcom McDowell's words about time hitting me in the face: *"Aren't you beginning to feel time gaining on you? It's like a predator…stalking you."* Yes, I *was* feeling it (sometimes I still do). In the end, the only true life-changing pleasure I experienced at the movies was the unorthodox method of filmmaking and dialogue structure that was Quentin Tarantino's *Pulp Fiction*. I tried to channel that experience as best I could to repeatedly remind myself that at heart, I was a writer with dreams of making myself known to the world someday (a dream I still hold dear today).

And that, my friends, was the year 1994 for me.

THE YEAR WAS 1995...

- In the Oklahoma City bombing, 168 people are killed and 680 wounded when Timothy McVeigh and Terry Nichols set off a bomb at the Alfred P. Murrah Federal Building.
- Windows 95 is released by Microsoft.
- O. J. Simpson is found not guilty on charges of double murder for the deaths of former wife Nicole Brown Simpson and her friend Ronald Goldman.
- The Million Man March, as conceived by Nation of Islam leader Louis Farrakhan, is held in Washington, DC.
- In Tel Aviv, Israeli prime minister Yitzhak Rabin is assassinated at a peace rally.
- The Bosnian War is officially ended with the signing of the Dayton Agreement in Paris.

...AND THERE WERE MOVIES!

The nineties were half over. The year 1995 began, and it was my first full year without Caren in it. Time heals, of course, but not without its moments of pain and anguish. Many times I wanted to break down and call her for any reason or excuse, just to hear her voice, or perhaps to see it there was any way of patching things up between us. Through the verbal grapevine, though, I found out she was living with her boyfriend (also the man she'd eventually marry *and* divorce) in Manhattan not more than a short cab ride from where I was. Whether that made me feel better or worse, I'm not sure. What if I ran into her? Worse yet, what if I ran into her *and* her boyfriend? How would I react and what would I say? Would I be the gracious type, or would I cave in to my temptations and say something obnoxious and spiteful? Thankfully, I never found out because I never ran into her.

For the first time, I was *not* looking forward to the oncoming summer. I was scheduled to take part in running the same Hamptons share house I'd been involved with since '93, but by now, the whole thing was starting to feel old. I longed to return to my own home in Westhampton Beach where I'd spent the better part of my life, but current environmental conditions were still not permitting residents to return to their homes. I finally found a full-time position with a reputable architect in Queens and was learning to settle myself into the daily routing of the subway commute and the grinds of architectural design and drafting. This was my life by day. By night, I failed to get past my loneliness, despite living in a city with millions of single people in it. Sure, I dated. But just like a bad episode of *Sex and the City*, it was often meaningless dinners that failed to go further, and that included *not* getting laid.

Despite the promise of some potentially great summer blockbusters like *Crimson Tide*, *Die Hard with a Vengeance*, *Batman Forever*, and *Apollo 13*, there was always the winter and spring seasons to get through, and they often provided no more than a good reason to get out and spend the day at the local multiplex with whatever seemed interesting enough. Trouble was, titles like *Billy Madison*, *The Brady Bunch Movie*, *Major Payne*, and *Tank Girl* leave you wanting to save your time and money by staying home and seeing what's on the local cable channels. That year, even the more promising titles of early '95 like *Just Cause*, *Outbreak*, and *Dolores Claiborne*, while far from disappointing, were merely temporary entertainment without much thought-provoking content (though I'd argue now that a movie like *Outbreak* during the Covid-19 pandemic gives one serious pause).

As it turned out, it took a movie by the late John Singleton to not only provoke my thoughts and emotions, but to also take me back to the days of my college youth.

Higher Learning
Directed by John Singleton
(January 11, 1995, U.S. Release Date)

When this film was released, I'd been out of school for nearly three years. Still, I couldn't imagine any depiction of college life could be that much different than what I'd experienced because this was still a time before the internet and social media, when emails were still in their introductory period, and when cell phones weren't affordable to everyone who wanted one. But I don't recall going to the movies with the intention of seeing *Higher Learning*. I think it turned out to be one of those extra bonus movies I caught while doing my multiplex movie hopping.

From the moment the movie began, though, I was immediately taken back to the fall of 1985 and what it felt like to be an incoming freshman at SUNY Buffalo, and later an incoming new student at Pratt Institute. I felt lonely, confused, and almost desperate for the type of attention that would help me gain popularity. In a strange way, I also felt like there was a little bit of me in all three of the story's principal characters attending Columbus University—Malik Williams who struggled with his academics and his former track-star status, Remy who was quiet and struggled with his feelings of isolation amongst other students, and even Kristen Connor who was friendly, but felt shy and naïve around people and situations.

Kristen attended her first fraternity party not long after her arrival. It was held by a militantly Afrocentric senior named Fudge White (played by rapper Ice Cube) who was also Remy's roommate.

Remy hated dealing with the loud rap music while he tried to study, so he called campus police to break up the party. These white police officers, however, saw no need to break up another equally loud party not too far away simply because they appreciated rock music instead of rap. Remy eventually moved out of his dorm and into another one with a new roommate who was Jewish. Leaving that party early, Kristen met an openly lesbian junior named Taryn, who warned Kristen about walking around campus alone late at night and invited her to attend a student group involved in antisexism.

Kristen and Malik were both in the same political science class taught by a conservative black man from the West Indies named Professor Maurice Phipps (played by Lawrence Fishburne), who challenged his students to determine who they were for themselves, and not allow themselves to be categorized by others. In one incident, Malik confronted Phipps about the paper he wrote, arguing for a better grade, despite many spelling and grammatical errors. Irritated, Malik called Phipps a *"sellout"* for the so-called white establishment. Phipps angrily defended himself by arguing the world didn't owe Malik a thing and that he must work hard for himself to make a real difference in the world. Malik also got this same truthful attitude from his new girlfriend Deja, who'd later teach him to write a more structured essay.

Sometime later, Kristen was raped by a drunken frat boy named Billy, who tried later to call her, but was put off by her roommate Monet. Angered, he called her a *"black bitch,"* which angered Fudge, who recruited his own friends to confront Billy at a frat party, forcing him to apologize to Monet. This act of revenge, though, was all about the disrespecting of a black woman, and little (if anything) to do with the fact that a white girl had been raped. Despite her attack, though, Kristen found the strength to try and move forward. She joined Taryn's student group for harmony between different races and cliques, and even opened up herself to a new relationship, with both Taryn (her first lesbian experience) and another boy who treated her right.

Remy slid further into darkness, becoming increasingly angry and isolated, and finally joined up with a group of neo-Nazi skin heads, who repeatedly preached their racist beliefs and convinced Remy that the white man was becoming an endangered person in the wake of blacks and Jews. Remy confronted Malik with racial slurs and accusations, even pulling a handgun on him and his Jewish roommate, then finally packing his stuff and leaving the university. In a gang rumble between the skin heads and Fudge's friends, the skin heads got their asses kicked, which only enraged and intimidated their determination to commit an act of violence. Remy was given a sniper's rifle by one of his new friends and challenged to kill for the white race, a challenge Remy claimed he was ready to take on.

In an attempt to create a campus of peace and harmony, Kristen organized a peace festival. Among the many students, Malik and Deja were there, and it was Deja who was hit with a gunman's bullet when Remy opened fire from a rooftop. She died in Malik's arms, and he was quick to intercept Remy while trying to escape the building. Malik tried to strangle Remy, but was stopped when the campus police immediately grabbed him instead of Remy for no other likely reason than his color. Regretful, Remy apologized before shooting himself in the mouth. Despite this horrible tragedy, Malik persevered and won the respect from Professor Phipps. In what seemed like a poignant ending, Malik and Kristen introduced themselves while standing in front of the spot where Deja was killed. And before I was allowed to leave my theater seat, I was forced to contend with a single word intended to provoke my actions, as well as my intellect, and that word was *UNLEARN*.

So much of *Higher Learning* was familiar to me. The wild fraternity parties, the drunken frat brothers and sisters, the personal conflict with dorm roommates (including different tastes in music), and the challenges faced in various classes with various types of college professors (including the foreigners with thick, incomprehensible accents). What *wasn't* familiar to me, believe it or not, was the racial tensions at the heart of this college tale. Strangely, after having survived life at not one, but *two* colleges, I never experienced even a single incident of racial unrest or prejudice. I'm not saying it didn't exist (I'm not stupid). What I'm saying is that I never saw it. I never witnessed any racism on campus, any anti-Semitism as a

Jewish person, nor did I come into conflict with a member of the African American race. In fact, my first roommate at Pratt Institute was a black guy named Leland and we were very good friends. I was never seduced by a member of the same sex, I never forced myself on a girl, and I knew of no neo-Nazi skin heads on or anywhere near the campus. What does all this mean? Was I ignorant to what was going on outside my private college world, or was I just lucky?

John Singleton's purpose is strong enough in his attempt to paint a thought-provoking picture in the same manner as he did for his 1991 debut film *Boyz n the Hood*. College life may be fun and full of ideologies, but it's far from pretty or perfect, even if you can't personally relate to all of its problems of racism, integration and even separatism (as I couldn't). He manages to interweave a series of events and characters forcing us to ask the hard questions about how we can all relate to each other at such a young age in such a hard world. While I'm personally no longer in the position to ask these questions anymore, it does force me to contend with the racial problems existing in the world today with not only the American police force, but also the ignorant American citizen. There are things and people in this world that are scary, and if I'm forced to consider what it must feel like for the incoming college freshman, then I can only look ahead to the future when my son Sam will likely leave home to begin his new life at a university. What will I tell him about the world outside his parent's home and the town he grew up in? How will he learn to handle the potential for clashes with other members of the human race? How will he understand the need to accept those who are different from himself, be it cultural, sexual or even someone who enjoys music that he hates?

Perhaps the answer will just be to have him watch the movie *Higher Learning*.

Before Sunrise

Directed by Richard Linklater
(January 27, 1995, U.S. Release Date)

As previously mentioned, it was a whole year now without Caren in my life. They say that time is a healer, and that my wounds wouldn't be the same. That *sounded* great but was my faith strong enough for my emotions to handle going to see a love story at the movies? The answer was no, and I waited a few months to watch *Before Sunrise* on video.

The movie poster and what little I'd heard about this movie on TV were clear enough in that it was a simple romantic drama about a young American man and a young French woman who meet on a train and disembark together in Vienna to spend the entire night walking around the city, getting to know each other, and inevitably falling in love. Even before I pressed play on my VCR, I felt cynical about the idea of falling in love that quickly. I've never believed in it. Everybody is different, of course, but it didn't happen that fast for me with either Caren or the woman who eventually became my wife. But it happened to Jesse and Céline, and this is *how* it happened…

Jesse (played by Ethan Hawke) was travelling on a train from Budapest and met Céline (played by Julie Delpy) when they both chose to move away from an arguing married couple. From the moment their conversation started, they learned about each other quickly. Jesse was travelling to Vienna to catch a flight back to the United States. Céline was returning to her university in Paris after visiting her grandmother. When they reached Vienna, Jesse suggested that Céline get off the train with him, and I have to say, I was very impressed with his pitch when he said,

> *Think of it like this—jump ahead, ten, twenty years, okay, and you're married. Only your marriage doesn't have that same energy that it used to have, you know. You start to blame your husband. You start to think about all those guys you've met in your life and what might have happened if you'd picked up with one of them, right? Well, I'm one of those guys. That's me, you know, so think of this as time travel, from then to now, to find out what you're missing out on. See, what this really could be is a gigantic favor to both you and your future husband to find out that you're not missing out on anything. I'm just as big a loser as he is, totally unmotivated, totally boring, and uh, you made the right choice, and you're really happy.*

Wow. If I'd been a girl, I'd likely fallen for all of that and gotten off the train with Jesse myself. Céline fell for it and they decided to spend the night roaming around Vienna. They walked, talked, visited landmarks and came to know each other's secrets, passions, peeves and fears. It was at the top of a Ferris wheel when the moment was perfect for them to share that first kiss. Continuing their journey on foot, their talks opened up about life, love, sex, religion and their personal observations of the city. Céline confessed that her last boyfriend broke up with her because he claimed she *"loved him too much."* Jesse revealed he'd come to Europe to spend time with his girlfriend, but they broke up soon after his arrival.

As the threat of morning approached, Jesse and Céline couldn't avoid admitting their attraction to each other and how their night together made them feel, despite a mutual understanding that they'd likely never see each other again. Making the most of the time they had left, they ended their night with only the implication of a sexual experience between them, realizing that sex would only make parting more painful, though Jesse confessed that if given the choice, he'd marry Céline instead of never seeing her again. Their final goodbye at the train station was painful, despite their promise to each other to return to the same train station in six months, without the traditional exchange of contact information.

When the film was over, and I listened to the video tape rewind, I suddenly realized something about myself—I'd just watched a tender love story and I was still standing. In my own way, I'd taken a big step forward in getting over my own pains of love by watching others in the movies. This may not sound like much, but it felt important to me at the time. As a motion picture, though, *Before Sunrise* leaves me with much to consider. The plot is minimal because not much happens aside from two young people walking around Vienna and talking to each other, although each of their views and perspectives of life and love are highly detailed. Jesse is cynical, but is open to romantic ideas (like me). Céline is a seemingly romantic soul, but not without her doubts. Even as they draw closer to each other, the limitations of a single night are always on their minds, and perhaps it's their limited time together and the thought of never seeing each other again that inspires them to reveal so much about each other. Even as love inevitably develops into a wonderful fantasy, the threat of time prevents it from becoming a reality.

Let's talk about fantasies—I mean *male* fantasies for a moment. Not the obvious sexual kind, but the kind that involves conversation, beauty and intimacy. What if you were traveling alone on a train and you met a beautiful young woman like Julie Delpy who was willing to spend the night walking and talking with you, with the mutual understanding that your time together would end in the morning? What will happen? Will you be unsure of yourself and permit awkwardness to take over, or will you take a chance by sharing and discussing the most intimate details of your life? Will she share all of this with you? What will happen when you inevitably realize you're falling in love with this woman? How will you handle knowing you'll never see her again? How will you say goodbye when you're struggling with the pain of falling in love with her in one night, and knowing she's fallen in love with you too? And finally, if you both promise each other that you'll meet again in six months, will either of you show up?

Life and love offer so many questions, and much of this is pure fantasy. During Jesse and Céline's journey, the weather in Vienna remains perfect and every person they meet is nice and helpful. No one in the streets harasses or robs them, and even the club bartender is nice enough to give them a free bottle of wine on the promise that Jesse will send him the money when he returns to the United States. Like I said, it's a fantasy in a simple tale of unexpected love that depends on dialogue and the cinematography of the beautiful city these two kids occupy. What can I say—the fantasy works for me, and it worked with audiences and critics at the time of its release. Thanks to the performances of Ethan and Julie, the art of modern love is warm, intelligent, thought-provoking and beautifully filmed by Richard Linklater. Their conversation throughout the night is a witty and colorful marathon of ideas and attitudes toward life in the eyes of twentysomething people in the '90s, whom unlike misfits in *Reality Bites*, offers promise that young people are *real* people too. This may be considered fantasy by someone like myself with little faith in people, but when love fails you in real life, you rely on the fantasy and possibilities of love to sustain your faith in human actions and emotions.

In the years that followed, I watched the two sequels, *Before Sunrise* in 2004 and *Before Midnight* in 2013 for no other reason than curiosity. It seemed almost inevitable, but by *Midnight*, our two lovers ended up as just another bickering married couple (not too unlike the bickering couple they were both determined to get away from on the train before meeting in *Sunrise*). Truth be told, I was prepared to be disappointed with both of these films even before watching them because I've always been a strong believer in the art of cinematic ambiguity and relying on one's imagination to determine one's destiny. I liked (hell, I *preferred*) the ambiguous notion of not knowing whether or not Jesse and Céline would ever see each other again because it's what makes the notion of lost love so intriguing to not only myself, but I suppose to anyone else who's experienced the painful loss of love.

That ambiguity, is perhaps also part of the fantasy.

The Bridges of Madison County
Directed by Clint Eastwood
(June 2, 1995, U.S. Release Date)

When I started working at the local Great Neck bookstore in the summer of 1992, it was merely daily routines without much excitement in discussions and sales. Then in August, a small hardcover romance novella of 192 pages was released entitled *The Bridges of Madison County* by first time author Robert James Waller. It told the story of Francesca Johnson, a married Italian American bride of World War II living on a farm in Madison County, Iowa in the 1960s who had an affair with Robert Kincaid, a visiting photographer on assignment for National Geographic to create a photographic essay on the covered bridges in the area, while her husband and two children were away for the week. It debuted on the New York Times bestseller list and stayed there for over three years. It was *the* book everyone was talking about. We couldn't keep enough copies in the store, and the woman I worked with (also went to high school with) repeatedly sang its praises to the customers.

Printed love stories didn't interest me, but it was impossible for me to avoid reading this thing amidst all the hype. It took up only two evenings of my life and it remains the only love story I've ever read. When I finished it, two thoughts occupied my mind. The first was that reading this sentimental love story while I was in the process of carrying a torch for Caren wasn't exactly an uplifting experience to my spirits. The second was that I immediately pictured this story as a Robert Redford-directed film, with Redford as Kincaid and Meryl Streep as Francesca, in a project reuniting the two stars of *Out of Africa*. Turns out, my prediction was *half* right, and the idea of Redford was instead directed and starred by tough guy Clint Eastwood.

When it comes to love on screen, I prefer watching a straight-forward love story rather than a silly romantic comedy. The basic formula for rom-coms almost never changes. Guy meets girl. Guy or girl may or may not be immediately interested in each other. Guy and girl inevitably get together in the end. Guy's best friend is a goof-ball. Girl's best friend is also a goofball girl or a flamboyant gay man. Still, in a summer filled with the likes of John McClane and Batman (both for the third time) and Tom Hanks declaring, *"Houston, we have a problem,"* the prospect of Eastwood showing his tender side with this love story was intriguing. I wish I could tell you I went to see this movie on a romantic date with a happy ending, but alas, I went to see it with a woman who was only a platonic friend.

It was the present day, and adult siblings Michael and Carolyn Johnson arrived at the Iowa farmhouse of their recently deceased mother Francesca to settle her estate. They were shocked to learn that she wanted to be cremated and to have her ashes scattered from the local Roseman Covered Bridge instead of being buried at the family plot next to their father. While sorting through her posses-sions, they discovered unknown photos of their mother taken at a covered bridge, letters to her from a strange man, and three note-books describing in detail, the story of Francesca's secret four-day affair with this unknown National Geographic photographer named Robert Kincaid while her family was away at the Illinois State Fair.

The film flashbacked to the year 1965, when Francesca met Robert while he was passing through on assignment for his magazine to photograph the county's historic covered bridges. He stopped to ask Francesca for directions, and she rode in his truck to show him where Roseman Bridge was. This meeting grew into a connecting of two lonely people sharing food, drink, sentimental stories, and private confessions. For four days, Francesca and Robert grew closer to each other's souls and spirits, until they could no longer control each other's feelings of physical passion—and they acted on it, both in bed and in the bathtub.

Moving past the shock of their mother's infidelity, as Michael and Carolyn continued to read the notebooks, they came to understand the affair's deep and lasting influence on both their mother and Robert. They'd fallen deeply in love with each other and came very close to running away together. But despite Francesca's feelings of confinement to family, routine and a passionless marriage, she ultimately decided against abandoning her loyal husband and impressionable teenage children. I became enthralled by not only the forbidden love between these two people, but also in Francesca's final explanation of why she couldn't go with Robert:

> *When a woman makes the choice to marry, to have children; in one way her life begins, but in another way it stops. You build a life of details. You become a mother, a wife and you stop and stay steady so that your children can move. And when they leave, they take your life of details with them. And then you're expected to move again, only you don't remember what moves you because no-one has asked in so long. Not even yourself. You never in your life think that love like this can happen to you.*

I felt a sense of dread from her words. Was *this* what my future wife (whomever she might be) had to look forward to later in life if she married me? Was I going to someday become merely a woman's *routine* until the day came when she met another man who rocked her world more than I ever could? These were questions that I would or wouldn't get answers to someday. For right now, the answers on the screen were that Francesca and Robert would *not* be together after their brief encounter, that he'd leave town never to see her again, and she'd spend many painful years wondering what might have or could have been.

After her husband's death, Francesca tried to contact Robert again, but he'd left the magazine and no one knew how to find him. Later, she learned he'd died a few years after her husband, and had left all of his belongings to her. His ashes were scattered from Roseman Bridge (which is what *she* later wanted). As Michael and Carolyn finally closed this chapter of their mother's life, they each had newfound knowledge and direction on dealing with their own troubled marriages and lives. The film ended with them honoring their mother's final wish, scattering her ashes at the covered-bridge of Madison County.

The Bridges of Madison County may be considered slow and excessively sentimental, but it's irresistible, nonetheless. And just when you think Clint Eastwood's film characters aren't capable of much more than shooting a .44 Magnum or punching somebody's lights out, it turns out he's a very gentle and tender lover (what a guy). As director and star, he turns Waller's famed book into something very moving. Not just in the forbidden love that can never be, but also in Meryl Streep's portrayal of a plain housewife who yearns for deep passion in a world that doesn't go too far beyond ordinary and conservative Iowa farm life in 1965.

Life in her world is at an unhurried pace and indulges itself in moments of silence and reflection, even when she simply spends her evening reading a book on her front porch and allowing the gentle night's breeze to wash over her naked body beneath her clothes. In her world, passion carries with it not only anticipation, but consequences, as well. When does anticipation allow for the right move to be made that won't end in rejection? What happens next when erotic heat between two people matures into something more? What are the consequences of the affair for a woman like Francesca, who's been faithful to her husband, if she's found out by not only her family, but by a conservative town that will talk about it for years? Perhaps while we're finding the answers, we'll consider the possibility that this film is tough guy Eastwood's message (or even gift) to not only the women of his audience, but all the women he's loved in his life.

The personal impact of *The Bridges of Madison County* had little to do with me, but rather the story of my mother. She came to the United States from Egypt in the early '60s, met my father, married him, and the rest is…well, never mind that. In the summer of 1996, my mother flew to Los Angeles to visit Kevin while he attended law school at the University of Southern California, and made a phone call that would change the rest of her life. She contacted the man she had *previously* been engaged to in Egypt before the engagement was called off and she came to this country with her family. By chance, her old flame was divorced and available. Two years later and they were married and they remain married today. When they first reunited, though, I couldn't help but draw similar parallels to how my mother and her long-lost sweetheart were living out their own version of *The Bridges of Madison County*. I bought my mother a copy of the book and insisted she read it. When she did, she said her soul was hardly moved at all, citing that her own story between herself and her lost love was enough to sustain her without comparisons to fiction (this was the same woman whose only reaction to *E.T.* was that *"it was cute"*).

As for myself, I remain haunted even today by these words spoken by Francesca Johnson, not only for the love of my past, but even for my marriage today—*"Love won't obey our expectation."*

Il Postino (The Postman)
Directed by Michael Radford
(June 16, 1995, U.S. Release Date)

I hadn't been to Italy for three years. What I mean is, I hadn't been to Italy on the big screen for three years (I've not yet been to Italy) since I'd seen *Mediterraneo* back in the summer of '92. Since then, I'd made it my business to get to know the classic black-and-white films of Fellini and De Sica, practically ignoring the colorful splendor that such a beautiful country had to offer. I often reminded myself that amidst a world of Hollywood blockbuster bullshit, it was imperative that I continue to educate myself in the world of foreign subtitled cinema, especially since living in Manhattan offered a good selection of screen options. When the opportunity came to see a new foreign film that wowed audiences, critics, and Oscar voters, it was also an opportunity for my mother and I to further connect on a cinematic level, which remained one of the few ways we *were* able to connect in my adult life. Besides the media Oscar buzz for *Il Postino*, there was also the tragic news that its star Massimo Troisi had died suddenly of a severe heart attack the day after filming was completed. It wasn't until the spring of '96 that we both went to see this film at Lincoln Center's Lincoln Plaza Cinemas, the perfect venue for art-house cinema.

This was a simple story of a simple man—a fictional tale in which real-life famed Chilean poet (and Communist) Pablo Neruda (played by Philippe Noiret, whom I'd never forget from *Cinema Paradiso*) and his wife were exiled to a small and beautiful Italian island in 1950 for political reasons. One of the island's locals, Mario Ruoppolo (Troisi) led a disappointing life with his fisherman father. Armed with nothing but a bicycle and the ability to read and write, Mario secured a temporary job hand delivering mail to (only) Pablo Neruda. Shy at first, Mario slowly developed a dialogue and eventual friendship with Pablo, in which he was influenced by the man's poetry, political views, and unique ability to craft clever metaphors.

Meanwhile, Mario fell in love with the village beauty, Beatrice Russo, who worked in her aunt's café. It suddenly occurred to me that no matter how many times I witnessed love at first sight in the movies, I refused to believe it existed in real life. It didn't happen to my parents, it never happened to *me*, and it never happened to anyone else I knew. Love took time and effort, in my opinion. But I suppose that's what the movies, particularly love stories, were for—to make us believe the unbelievable in the world of love. In *this* world of love, Mario was very shy with Beatrice, but soon found ways to communicate his love to her thanks to Pablo's help with poetic words and metaphors. Despite her aunt's diabolical disapproval of Mario and his highly sensual poetry (including references to Beatrice's naked body), she eventually responded favorably to his love for her niece. Mario and Beatrice were married, though the village priest refused to allow Pablo to serve as Mario's best man because of his political and communist views. However, when the local politician stepped in for Mario, the matter was resolved. It was at the wedding that Pablo and his wife received welcome news that they were permitted to return to their own home country of Chile.

Time passed, and Mario wrote letters to Pablo that saw no reply. When he finally *did* receive a letter, it was from Pablo's secretary asking that Mario forward Pablo's old belongings to Chile. Although he made very light of it, Mario was clearly hurt that his old poet friend had apparently forgotten all about him. To ease his pain, he used an old phonograph to record the beautiful sounds of the island onto a cassette, including the heartbeat of his soon-to-be-born child, which he insisted be named Pablito (in honor of Pablo). Five years later, Pablo returned to the Italian village and found Beatrice and her son Pablito at the same café. He learned that Mario was killed before their son was born when he was scheduled to recite his own poetry at a large communist gathering in Naples, and the demonstration was violently broken up by the police, resulting in his death. Beatrice gave Pablo the recordings Mario had made of the island sounds. The story ended with Pablo walking on the beach where he'd talked with Mario in the past, showing us at the same time the communist gathering that led to Mario's tragic death.

I previously used the word *simple* to describe this film. Simple is a key word because like Peter Sellers in *Being There* and Tom Hanks in *Forrest Gump*, someone like me learned about the world through a simple man like Mario Ruoppolo, whose existence on a forgotten island in Italy seemed nearly worthless to most, but unique and extraordinary to those who'd open their eyes, minds and hearts to see what was possible in life. Mario isn't a man of wisdom, experience or courage to face life's challenges, or to make his existence known to the most beautiful and tempting woman on the island. Like simple men before him, he needs the help of someone wiser and well-versed to get what he wants. But at the same time, the film realistically reminds someone like me that even that happiest of stories don't necessarily result in "happily ever-after." Complications and political circumstances end in tragedy, with only memories of the past and the hopes for the future to sustain us.

That's what *Il Postino* teaches us, in my opinion. That's what it taught *me*, anyway. It also taught me to cautiously approach the common Hollywood multiplex feature that offers little other than a quick Friday night fix of entertainment. Admittedly, we *need* that fix every once in a while to sustain our anxieties and frustrations in life. But a film like this one, and many others of its foreign genre, also teaches me to smile because sometimes in the life of cinema, it's the simplest stories, the simplest pleasures, and the most simple of beautiful world locales (gorgeous Italy) that puts that smile on my face (and perhaps yours, too).

I couldn't have known this at the time, but as it turned out, *Il Postino* was the last film my mother and I would see together, just the two of us. Less than a year later, she'd relocated her life to Los Angeles to be with the man who'd become her second husband. I'm thankful, though, that our private cinematic "swan song" ended with a film of intelligence, wit, and beauty—something I think we both desperately needed when continuing to broaden our mother-son relationship through the art of the movies.

The Usual Suspects
Directed by Bryan Singer
(August 16, 1995, U.S. Release Date)

Summer was coming to an end, and so was the season at the Westhampton Beach share house. Nearly every movie I'd seen that summer was by myself either because I was alone in Manhattan, or I hadn't made any friends at the house worth spending any time at the movies with. Not that I minded going by myself, especially when it was a film requiring an element of thought. This certainly wasn't what I expected when I went to see *The Usual Suspects* at the Hampton Arts Twin over Labor Day weekend. The director was unknown to me, as was the entire cast in the police lineup on the movie poster. The only familiar thing was the film's title itself, taken from one of Claude Rains' most memorable lines from the classic black-and-white film *Casablanca*. As it turned out, Singer's second feature film hit me in a way I hadn't felt since Tarantino's *Pulp Fiction*.

The film opened with a scene unfolding at a ship docked at a California bay. Hardened criminal Dean Keaton sat badly wounded against the side of a ship, looking as if he'd just been through some sort of hell. He was approached by a mysterious figure whom he referred to as "Keyser" before he was shot dead and the entire ship was set ablaze. The next day, the police discovered many bodies and only two survivors. One was a badly burned Hungarian mobster already hospitalized, and the other a low-life con artist with cerebral palsy named 'Verbal" Kint (played by Kevin Spacey, whom up until now, I only recognized from the 1992 film *Glengarry Glen Ross*). Customs agent David Kujan arrived to interrogate Kint, who proceeded (via flashback) to describe the events that led himself, Keaton and other criminals to be aboard that doomed ship.

Six weeks earlier in New York City, Verbal and four other criminals (including Keaton) were arrested as "usual" suspects in a recent truck-hijacking, only to be released thanks to Keaton's girlfriend lawyer. Banding together, the group pulled a carefully planned jewel heist to take revenge against the New York Police Department and their corrupt taxi service (driving smugglers and drug dealers around the city), or as Verbal put it, *"A little* fuck you *from the five of us to the NYPD."* Their heist netted millions and also got many cops arrested. To fence their stolen goods, they travelled to California to meet their contact, who connected them with another offer for a jewel heist. This heist, however, went badly and the men learned the job was arranged by a lawyer named Kobayashi. Meeting with Kobayashi, he informed them that they were chosen to not only be arrested together back in New York, but to come together to perform yet another job; because as it turned out, each of them had unwittingly stolen from a mysterious Turkish crime lord named Keyser Söze, and now they each owed a debt to compensate. Mr. Söze rarely worked with the same people for long, and those people never knew who they were working for. As Kobayashi so perfectly put it, *"One cannot be betrayed if one has no people."* This new job was an order for them to raid a ship manned by Argentinian drug dealers and to destroy a shipment of cocaine worth $91 million, an amount those who survived would split in cash, thus exonerating them from their debt to Keyser Söze.

This flashback so far, had its grip on me and I made sure not to miss a single word spoken. Kevin Spacey's voice was of a gentle storyteller telling a story that was hardly gentle. I knew this story would lead to a startling conclusion, but I had no concept of what that conclusion was yet. Storytime was definitely not over yet, boys and girls.

During Kujan's continued interrogation of Verbal, we learned of the legend behind Keyser Söze in that he began his criminal career as a small-time drug runner who blatantly murdered his own wife and children as they were held hostage by rival Hungarian mobsters to display his true power. He then massacred the mobsters, their families, friends and even people they owed money to before disappearing into an urban myth. Did Keyser Söze really exist? Did others believe in him? I think Verbal said it best with these words, *"I don't believe in God, but I'm afraid of him. Well, I believe in God, and the only thing that scares me is Keyser Söze."* He also said what I consider to be the best piece of dialogue from the film, *"The greatest trick the Devil ever pulled was convincing the world he didn't exist."* Even though I don't believe in God or the devil, I couldn't help but think those words were intriguing enough to spark debate even among the most serious of nonbelievers and atheists.

As Verbal's story drew to a close, the men raided the ship during the night, killing several Hungarian and Argentinian gangsters before ultimately discovering there was no cocaine on board. Then men everywhere started dying, killed by an unseen assailant, until it was down to a wounded Keaton sitting where he was when the film started. The ship was set ablaze as Verbal looked on from a hiding place on the dock. When it was over, Kujan deduced that Keaton must be the infamous Keyser Söze. Keaton was apparently a man with enough of a powerful history to pull off such a deception to the police, the underworld, and the movie's audience, including *me.* Desperate and defeated, Verbal finally confessed that Keaton was the man behind everything, though Verbal refused to testify in court. His granted immunity permitted him to post bail and he was released.

What happened next was something I couldn't possibly prepare myself for. Moments after Verbal left the police station, Kujan realized that Verbal had fabricated his entire story of what happened by carefully piecing together detailed items posted on a bulletin board in Kujan's office. He also discovered the name "Kobayashi" came from the bottom of the coffee mug he'd been drinking from the entire time. Meanwhile, Verbal was free and walking outside, and his cerebral palsy gradually disappeared. He walked normally and flexed his supposedly disabled hand. In a panic, Kujan ran after Verbal, and a fax arrived from California showing a facial composite of Keyser Söze, bearing a near-perfect resemblance to Verbal Kint, confirming that we'd all been the victim of a perfect con. *Verbal Kint* was *Keyser Söze!* Kujan missed Söze only by moments, and Söze disappeared into a car driven by his loyal associate "Koayashi"—and just like that, he was gone.

As I previously mentioned, not since *Pulp Fiction* was I so taken aback by a film and the possibilities of original storytelling. And like *Pulp Fiction*, I was determined not to leave the movie theater yet, choosing to hide out in the men's room until the next show began so I could reexperience this film with a fresh perspective behind the story and the big reveal. I knew who Keyser Söze was now, but it seemed a far more rewarding experience to watch things unfold again and carefully reconstruct all the dots to make them fit together in my head. This was the power film had over me and my thoughts, and I welcomed it with an open mind and willing heart. Before that day at the movies, I'd never heard of director Bryan Singer or screenwriter Christopher McQuarrie. After that day, I'd never forget their names.

Singer's shooting and editing manages to take a simple plot of a crime gone wrong and turn it into a layer cake filled with twists, turns, deceit and violence before finally allowing us the privilege and pleasure of being let in on the big, unexpected secret—a secret that in its most simple state, is still nothing more than a reveal of one's true identity, and yet we cannot help but be taken in by it because it forces us to realize just how easily we can be fooled, and how much we don't *mind* being fooled. Kevin Spacey and the rest of the cast give fine performances that effortlessly come together despite great differences in the characters. The film is one you want to watch repeatedly and even try to reinterpret, because each time it may turn out to be a different film than the one you watched for the first time back in '95, maybe even a *better* one.

On the night of March 25, 1996, I watched the *Academy Awards* on TV and took personal pleasure in watching Christopher McQuarrie walk away with the Oscar for Best Original Screenplay for *The Usual Suspects*. I was so excited about the possibilities that one's work (the second screenplay of his career) could earn such a distinguished honor in Hollywood, that I immediately called my friend (also watching the Oscars) and told her that someday that would be *me* standing up there accepting the *same* Oscar statue. I was inspired and pumped to continue moving forward with my dream to get my screenwriting not only noticed, but recognized for the awards they'd someday deserve, and it was all due to the magic and possibilities of *The Usual Suspects* and Keyser Söze.

Dreams change. Old dreams die and become new ones, maybe even better ones. I don't regret my old dreams. I'm glad I had them.

Get Shorty

Directed by Barry Sonnenfeld
(October 20, 1995, U.S. Release Date)

I spent the entire decade of the '90s (and well into the 2000s) obsessed with making a name for myself as an unknown screenwriter. I entered writing contests, attended writing seminars, wrote endless query letters to literary agents, and even attended a weekend Hollywood pitch festival in August 2000. None of it amounted to anything (if it had, perhaps I wouldn't have written my books). In between my writing, I looked to the movies for inspiration and information on how and why certain writers made it in Hollywood and some didn't. Robert Altman's *The Player* suggested luck and circumstance. The 1994 film *Swimming with Sharks* suggested Hollywood was nothing but a world of backstabbing, ruthlessness and two-faced revenge. It left me wondering what Elmore Leonard's tale of Hollywood moviemaking had to offer me.

Something else for me to consider—despite John Travolta's revived popularity in the '90s, I couldn't help but wonder if anyone remembered what he did with his career in between his 1980 romantic Western *Urban Cowboy* and his turnaround film *Pulp Fiction* that put him back on top? Sure, he worked, but what of it was truly memorable? *Perfect* with Jamie Lee Curtis? *Look Who's Talking* sequels? I don't think so. *Get Shorty* seemed the perfect vehicle for Travolta's streetwise attitude giving him the opportunity to bring a blend of comic timing and dialogue alongside the traditional cliché of the Mafia tough guy.

As Miami loan shark Chili Palmer, Travolta unwittingly found himself working for Ray "Bones" Barboni after the big boss Momo dropped dead of a heart attack at his own surprise birthday party. Chili and Bones despised each other, and he ordered Chili to fly to Las Vegas to collect a debt from Leo, who faked his own death to claim $300,000 in an insurance fraud scam. While he was there, he took on a second job of collecting another debt from a small-time Hollywood film producer named Harry Zimm (played by Gene Hackman). Arriving in Los Angeles, he warned Harry to pay what he owed, and even managed to pitch his own idea for a movie based on his own life, including Leo's insurance scam. Harry also owed a large sum of money to drug dealer Bo Catlett, who'd already invested in one of Harry uncompleted films. Coming to Harry's aid, Chili threatened Bo not to interfere with Harry's latest script called *Mr. Lovejoy*.

Instead of repaying the debt, Bo offered to finance Harry's *Mr. Lovejoy* with a large sum of money stored inside an airport locker. Suspecting it was a trap, Chili agreed to retrieve the money himself, and immediately suspected there were DEA agents at the airport watching the locker. Outsmarting them, he opened an adjacent locker instead, and despite being questioned by the agents, was released. It seemed as if Chili was constantly surrounded by stupidity and inflated egos in Hollywood, particularly by big shot movie star Martin Weir (played by Danny DeVito) whose poster-boy face was plastered all over every magazine cover in Hollywood. Martin's ex-wife, horror movie actress Karen Flores (played by Rene Russo) pointed out that movie stars had no idea what things cost and never picked up a check at a restaurant.

Meanwhile, Chili and Karen pitched Chili's movie idea to Martin to get him to portray Chili's character in the film, which Harry intended to produce. Harry alerted Bones that Chili had recovered the scammed money from Leo, and Bones immediately flew to L.A. to collect that money himself. During their final confrontation, Chili informed Bones of the stashed money inside the airport locker, which Bones intended to collect. Just at the moment when it looked like Bones would open the locker, the scene changed to a film production's version of the same shot, with actor Harvey Keitel playing Bones, and the late Penny Marshall directing. It appeared Chili Palmer had made it as a Hollywood big shot in a very short time (lucky bastard).

As a Mafia gangster, it hardly surprised me that Travolta could pull it off so easily. Instead, what I immediately connected with was Chili's passion for the movies. As the film begins, he expresses how upset he is that they're closing his favorite local movie house, and that he wishes he could run the place himself and show old James Cagney movies. As I studied the awe-inspired look on his face while he watched the end of Orson Welles's classic *Touch of Evil*, I recalled my own sense of gratification whenever I sat inside the Film Forum on West Houston Street in Manhattan watching some of my favorite black-and-white revival films. That's the passion that burns deep for cinema that speaks to us. I knew it, and I loved that Chili knew it too.

More than passion, *Get Shorty* afforded me a glimpse of the pompous demeanors and outrageous self-promotion that clearly infected the bullshit world of "La-La Land." Although at the time, I hadn't visited L.A. yet, I suspected that despite Hollywood's tendency to exaggerate with its own artistic liberties, author Elmore Leonard and director Barry Sonnenfeld weren't distorting the facts about the movie business, either. It's cold and cruel, and will eat you up to the bone if you're not prepared for it, even if someone like Chili Palmer suggests that strength and attitude help to make it work in your favor. After all, if he wants Martin Weir for his movie, *"I'm gonna take a gun, I'm gonna put it to his head, and say sign the fucking papers, Martin, or you're dead."* In his mind, that'll work, and there's no reason not to believe him.

Despite the sharp, satirical entertaining comedy and traditional Hollywood gangster formula of *Get Shorty*, watching it for the first time in '95 gave me a sense of both enthusiasm and discouragement in moving forward and attacking the dream I had back then of becoming a screenwriter. I didn't see the city of Los Angeles for the first time until the summer of 1996, when my mother and Kevin were living there. I often flew there to visit them, and it didn't take more than a few trips to realize just how predictably-off-the-wall phony that entire town was. I'd actually go out of my way to tell people that L.A. residents wouldn't survive one week on the streets of New York City—at least whenever I thought I could get away with saying it.

The American President

Directed by Rob Reiner
(November 17, 1995, U.S. Release Date)

Bill Clinton was President of the United States throughout the bulk of the 1990s. During that bulk, there were notable films featuring the president as a (fictional) key character and even hero whenever challenged. In 1996, Bill Pullman and Jack Nicholson matched their skills and wits against attacking aliens from space in *Independence Day* and *Mars Attacks!*, respectively. In 1997, Harrison Ford personally fought Russian terrorists in *Air Force One*. In 1998, Morgan Freeman gently and honestly prepared us for a comet to strike our planet in *Deep Impact*. Love him or hate him, Clinton was a popular president, and Hollywood was eager to cash in on that popularity. Those are days my generation can look back on with fondness, especially after living through the dramatic and turbulent years of George W. Bush and Donald Trump (looking back on Clinton's years, it seems our country's biggest concern in the White House was blowjobs from Monica Lewinsky).

Even during the trailer, I was intrigued at the prospect of seeing *The American President*. Not just because Michael Douglas looked as if the part of our Commander-in-chief was perfect for him, but also because there was something strangely perfect about the simple concept of the president of the United States going on a date. On the surface, it was harmless, and yet, I saw its potential for disaster and how it would be perceived by the voters and their twisted views on American family values and any other bullshit they could use against the president. As popular (and widowed) Democratic president Andrew Shepherd, Douglas was everything we'd wish the President to be in real life—caring, honest, and dedicated to serving the best interest of the American people. He was also running for re-election, and that meant anything was possible. Shepherd's approval rating was at sixty-three percent, and he was prepared to get a crime control bill passed through Congress. But the conservatives didn't want it, and the liberals thought it was too weak. If it passed, though, Shepherd would secure his re-election.

Meanwhile, we met environmental lobbyist Sydney Ellen Wade (played by Annette Bening), hired to persuade Shepherd to pass legislation committing his Administration to reduce carbon dioxide emissions by twenty percent, something he believed would never pass at more than ten percent. During their first meeting, Sydney insulted Shepherd behind his back, but he was intrigued with and attracted to her, nonetheless. In private, they struck a deal in which if she secured twenty-four votes for the environmental bill by the State of the Union address, he'd deliver the last ten votes. However, Shepherd didn't believe Sydney would get enough votes to meet her end of the deal, thus releasing him from his responsibility if the bill failed to pass.

In the meantime, Shepherd was conflicted about whether or not he'd be in his right place by asking Sydney to accompany him as his date to a state dinner honoring the president of France. His White House Chief of Staff (and best friend) A.J. (played by Martin Sheen who'd later play the president himself in NBC's *The West Wing*) bluntly told him, *"The president can't just go out on a date."* Even as I heard that statement, it seemed dead-on correct, and yet I couldn't help but ask myself why not? According to Shepherd, Thomas Jefferson did, and so did Woodrow Wilson (if that was true, I had no idea until this movie). The brief conversation between them grabbed my attention, in which Shepherd said,

> *I'm talking about something that in no way is a conflict with my oath of office. I'm a single adult, and*

*I met a woman that I'd like to see again socially.
How's that different from what Wilson did?*

*The difference is he didn't have to be the president on television. You've said it a million times—if
there had been a television set in every living room
sixty years ago, this country does not elect a man in
a wheelchair.*

A.J. was referring to Franklin D. Roosevelt. The arguments sounded logical and convincing from both ends, and I felt caught up with both sides. The whole thing didn't seem like such a big deal, but if that was true, why was I so intrigued to see what would happen next?

After a series of awkward phone calls (including his failed attempts to buy Sydney some flowers without the use of the White House staff), Shepherd asked Sydney to the state dinner. At that dinner, he and Sydney embraced the crowd's attention by dancing together. It seemed obvious the two would fall in love, but not without hurdles. Not just with the public's perception of their new relationship, but also with Republican presidential hopeful Senator Bob Rumson (played by Richard Dreyfuss, who was also in Rob Reiner's *Stand by Me*), who was ready and willing to use Shepherd's new girlfriend for his own attacks, while focusing on Shepherd's ethics and family values, as well as Sydney's past as an activist who once attended a flag burning rally. Shepherd refused to respond to these attacks because he felt his personal life was none of the American public's business. Still, his approval rating went down, and it cost him political support, without which his proposed crime bill seemed doomed to fail.

In time, Sydney secured the votes to meet her end of the deal. However, Shepherd's staff (including Michael J. Fox) discovered he was only three votes short, with no choice but to shelve the environmental bill to secure them, thus solidifying the support he needed from Congress, and also making things bad for him and Sydney. She was subsequently fired from her lobbyist job for failing to fulfill her professional objectives, as well as damaging her political reputation.

When she broke up with Shepherd, he tried to politically justify his actions by defending the crime bill as his top priority, but it failed to repair the damage done to their relationship. He lost the woman he loved, but worse than that, he also lost her vote.

As someone who was invested in this love drama, I had little concern about the two of them getting back together (the couple *always* gets back together in movies like this). What I really waited to see was how Shepherd would triumph *politically* before the story was over. On the morning of his State of the Union Address, Shepherd made a surprise appearance in the White House press room to rebuke Senator Rumson's attacks on his character, his values, and on the accusations against Sydney for supposedly trading sex for political favors. He announced he was withdrawing his support for a crime bill he considered weak, and instead promised to write a crime bill that made sense in which he'd make every effort to get the guns off the streets. In what was probably the best triumph a movie like this could achieve, the president of the United States passionately defended the values he believed in, in the name of himself, the woman he loved, and the American people. The only reaction such a victory left me with was, "Awwww."

There are some things that come to mind when perceiving *The American President*, both when I first saw it back in '95 and now. The first is that, in my opinion, this is the last great film from Rob Reiner which began in 1984 with *This is Spinal Tap* and continued with a string of hits including *The Princess Bride, Misery* and *A Few Good Men*. After the solid story and performances of *President*, they seemed to lose their spark for me. The second is when Sydney arrives at the White House for the first time and declares she wants to *"savor the Capra-esque quality"* of the experience. My mind immediately jumps up and says, "Yes! Frank Capra would've loved this movie. Hell, Frank Capra would've *made* this movie if he'd lived long enough." The man who gave us *Mr. Smith Goes to Washington* knew what he wanted to say about politics and corruption in the 1930s, and Reiner is comfortable in not only paying homage to the famed director of yesterday, but also in making political observations and statements of his own in a decade before the likes of Bush and Trump—a time when our perception of the president of the United States was still a somewhat kinder and gentler notion—when a man like Michael Douglas could make us feel comfortable about the institution of government.

But Reiner isn't being *that* serious or dramatic with us. Andrew Shepherd isn't going before Congress to defend illegal actions against our country. He merely wants to go out on a date with a woman he finds attractive and interesting. Still, the unavoidable reaction from many is like, "Oh my god, how dare he!" Though we still can't help but ask ourselves, why the hell not? After all, when the widowed president of the United States isn't busy with his oath of office, he's still a man capable of dating, sleeping with, and falling in love with a woman, regardless of the media's and the American public's perception of his character and values. Such opinions over his dating debacle have a way of shifting back and forth in American politics like bad mood swings. In the end, we as viewers of these events may want nothing more than the guy to get the girl and live happily ever after. That's what a charming romantic comedy-drama like this wants, and that's what the director wants.

Frank Capra would've wanted that too.

GoldenEye
Directed by Martin Campbell
(November 17, 1995, U.S. Release Date)

Have you ever gone to the movies in a really bad mood? You're probably thinking that the movies are just the thing to cure one of such a bad mood. With me, it's the opposite effect. If I go to a movie in a bad mood, I'm likely to sit there and find endless faults with the movie simply because my present mood dictates that I act like an overly critical, nitpicking son of a bitch. As a result of my tearing the movie to pieces, I leave the theater in an even worse mood than when I arrived. This is what happened to me when I went to see *GoldenEye* during its opening weekend in November '95. But let's first backtrack things a bit.

Ever since I was ten years old and first saw *The Spy Who Loved Me* in 1977, I'd been conditioned to expect a new James Bond film every two years during the summer blockbuster season. That expectation held its course throughout the 1980s right up until we said goodbye to Timothy Dalton at the end of *License to Kill* in 1989. Then something unthinkable happened. Two years came and went and there was no new James Bond film in 1991. Time continued to pass, and still there was nothing. It seemed the James Bond film franchise had come to a screeching halt for the first time since its inception with *Dr. No* in 1962. This was, perhaps, my first lesson in film franchise rebooting. By '95, when I finally saw the trailer for *GoldenEye* starring Pierce Brosnan (the *original* choice to play Bond after Roger Moore), I was overcome with excitement and anticipation.

The film began with the traditional opening white circle and gun barrel sequence, though the opening music was far from traditional. Clearly, this was *not* the iconic scoring of composer John Barry anymore. Although the opening action sequence (in which Bond's partner Alec, aka 006, was killed) was at the tail end of the '80s, the time was now the present in the age after the Cold War and the dissolve of the Soviet Union. The Russians were *still* the enemy, nonetheless. By the time I'd learned the new character of M was a *woman*, I decided I was going to hate *GoldenEye* and that I'd have a stack of what I considered viable reasons—at the time.

Let's remember that overall, I love James Bond films and do my best to stay positive about them. So let's jump ahead six-to-eight months to when I gave *GoldenEye* a second chance and watched it on video, and we'll start over. The Cold War was over and there was change in the air. Yes, M was a woman, but when played by a woman like Judi Dench, she was an extraordinary woman who knew exactly how to handle a sexist relic of the Cold War like James Bond. Over or not, the Russians were still a threat, and Bond knew this when he attempted to prevent the theft of a Eurocopter Tiger attack helicopter during a military demonstration by the beautiful, sadistic and lustful assassin Xenia Onatopp. That stolen helicopter turned up later at a Russian radar facility, and was followed by an electromagnetic pulse that blasted the site, destroying it and the investigating Russian fighter jets. The only apparent survivor was a computer programmer named Natalya Simonova, and also the future Bond girl teaming up with 007.

M assigned Bond to investigate the matter after it was determined the blast came from a Soviet-era satellite armed with a nuclear space-based weapon codenamed Goldeneye. Like many Bond films before this, our hero's adventures were complimented by intense action, beautiful women, fast car chases, a great train wreck, and the occasional verbal puns and innuendos. During all this, we learned that Alec, the former 006 of MI6, was not only alive and well, but also the criminal mastermind behind the Goldeneye threat that would grant him revenge against Great Britain for the betrayal of his parents following World War II. This threat would also devastate London to conceal the theft of financial records from the Bank of England, thus sending the United Kingdom back into the "Stone Age."

In Cuba, Bond and Natalya uncovered a hidden base beneath a large lake, concealing a satellite dish, and attempted to infiltrate it. They were captured after rigging explosives to destroy the base. Natalya managed to hack into the satellite and reprogrammed it to initiate its own self-destruction. They escaped when the explosives went off, destroying the entire site. But there was still the final showdown between Bond and his former trusted colleague—a fight that left Alec dangling below the satellite antenna. When Alec asked Bond if his (Alec's) death was for England, Bond simply replied, "No…for me," before letting Alec plummet to his death. Bond and the girl were safe, the world was safe, and it seemed the film franchise was safe too.

Let's take a step back and remember that I'm watching *GoldenEye* for the second time, and no longer in the bad mood I was in the first time I watched it. My reaction—stop the presses—this new Bond film after a six-year hiatus wasn't bad at all. In fact, it was great. Pierce Brosnan was a tough, no-nonsense Bond who made the film's hardcore action the best I'd seen since the late Sean Connery, and also minimized the silly puns Roger Moore used too many of in his films (the puns, unfortunately, got worse with each passing Brosnan Bond film). And what's this? Judi Dench was damn good in her role as the new M. Suddenly, it all made sense to me. With a franchise reboot such as this, change was not only in the air, it was also necessary to evolve with the times. Because if there's no change, then we're just watching the same ol', same ol' over and over again, and that's not good.

Now let's talk about Bond girls. Isabella Scorupco as Natalya, despite the fact that she's still *another* Russian Bond girl, is as good or bad as anyone else you may appreciate (she's certainly better than Denise Richards in *The World Is Not Enough*). Future *X-Men* Famke Janssen as Xenia Onatopp is another matter entirely. This is a serious, evil bitch who gets tremendous sexual pleasure by killing people, particularly with her long, sexy bare legs (no wonder her first victim had a huge smile on his face when he died). Bond, being *Bond* of course, can't resist her sexual aggressiveness to get his job done and save the world (this is one of those rare times when Bond *doesn't* sleep with the bad girl to get what he wants). And to briefly mention actor Sean Bean as the classic Bond villain, I think it's an original concept of his being a former MI6 agent turned bad that gives his character a more disgruntled point of view as one who's chosen the dark side of life, as well as a man who can anticipate James Bond's every move better than the next guy.

As a member of a long-running franchise, *GoldenEye* brings things into a modern context while not failing to provide the action-packed, high-tech formula we've come to love over the decades. James Bond himself seems more vulnerable and sensitive, especially when it comes to betrayal by his former trusted friend that results in the loss of his own innocence, even though he never fails to give us his natural British charm and wit. All in all, it's pure James Bond action, adventure, thrills and a formula that still works when it remembers not to get too stupid or far-fetched (or to let Madonna sing the opening theme song as she did in *Die Another Day*).

So you see, sometimes a little time, a more open frame of mind, and a better mood can turn a movie that previously sucked into one of the better films of the famed spy film franchise. It's just one of the reasons this British spy will forever matter to a Gen X'er like me.

Nixon

Directed by Oliver Stone
(December 22, 1995, U.S. Release Date)

I was born in 1967. The first United States president I was aware of in my lifetime was Richard Milhous Nixon. The first major political event I was aware of (at the age of seven) was Nixon's shameful resignation from office in August 1974, though I had no idea why. At that tender age, I verbally simplified the event by saying something like, "Did you hear that the President quit?" among my elementary school peers. In May 1977, when I was ten years old, I caught bits and pieces of the Nixon interviews with David Frost on PBS, though I had no clue what they were talking about. On November 9, 1980, when I was thirteen, I watched the 1976 film *All the President's Men* for the first time on the NBC Big Event, and its cinematic implications on real-life political events that took place only a few years prior, became a little clearer to me. Finally, many years after *that*, I wrote a twenty-one-page college term paper on the Watergate scandal (for which I got an A on). So while I hardly consider myself an authority on the subject of Richard Nixon, it's the latter years of his scandalous time in office that inevitably led to his disgrace that I've always been fascinated with. It's no surprise that director Oliver Stone had something to say about him, as well, and I couldn't wait to hear it.

I didn't approach *Nixon* without some skepticism. To begin with, Anthony Hopkins looked and sounded *nothing* like Richard Nixon. I also had to prepare myself for the fact that this film might play out much like Stone's 1991 film *JKF*, not only in its cuts and edits, but also in its content that was likely subject to severe scrutiny and controversy, not only by those who knew Nixon personally, but by historians, as well. If this was supposed to be one's history and biography, how much of it was accurate and how much was pure Hollywood entertainment?

The film began in 1972 with the Watergate break-in and the arrest of the burglars. What followed was what I expected from Stone, and that was a series of flashbacks highlighting Nixon's troubled life, both as a boy growing up with two brothers who died of tuberculosis, as well as the rise and fall of his entire political career. The story highlighted that Nixon and his wife Pat abused alcohol and drugs, as well as his health problems, including his experience with pneumonia and phlebitis during the Watergate crisis. When things inevitably turned to the assassination of John F. Kennedy, Nixon felt responsibility towards it, the implication being that the events played out by the Bay of Pigs Invasion during Nixon's term as vice president to Dwight D. Eisenhower spiraled out of control to inevitably lead to not only the assassination, but eventually Watergate.

There was also an ongoing battle between Nixon and his staff over who Secretary of State Henry Kissinger really was. Was he a security leak in the administration who only cared about his reputation with the press, or was he a loyal member of the team who followed the president's orders? Nixon never knew for sure, but he also never turned his back on him. When his presidency neared its end, however, the film depicted him and Kissinger getting on their knees to pray together. It ended as I expected, with Nixon's resignation in August 1974 and his departure from the White House lawn by the helicopter. What I didn't expect, and was pleasantly surprised by, was Nixon's real-life funeral played over the end credits, with all the living ex-presidents of the time shown in attendance, and president Bill Clinton giving a eulogy.

One thing I learned from watching *Nixon* is that despite obvious flaws in physical and vocal differences between the real man and Anthony Hopkins, the actor has mastered the art of playing Richard Nixon, both the man and the very lonely and isolated president of the United States who always had his back against the wall and the weight of the world that hated him on his shoulders. Just like *JFK*, Stone takes us on a journey through many pivotal political events in history in a nonlinear structure with the same style of film cuts and edits. But whether you were a fan of Nixon or not, one cannot help but feel empathy for a man who experienced so much pain and despair, both personally and professionally. For myself, who was only slightly aware of Nixon's downfall when I was a child, the film offers depth of who he was throughout the highlights of his life; as a boy, a man, a husband, a father, and a president. Of course, while one shouldn't take a cinematic biopic too seriously in its facts and accuracy, I also have to remember my faith and confidence in Oliver Stone as a filmmaker who does his homework and is often compelled to teach us something about history through his films.

One final interesting piece of information—upon the film's release, the Nixon family allegedly issued a statement claiming the film was designed to "defame and degrade President and Mrs. Nixon's memories in the mind of the American public." Excuse me? Really? You don't think perhaps Richard Nixon's illegal and shameful actions within the walls of the White House during the years 1972 through 1974 didn't actually accomplish *that* on its own? Well, you have to figure that with every biopic, there are those who will rise up and shout, "Wrong!" and "Unfair!" Regardless, *Nixon* still manages to give me and anyone who still remembers the latter part of the Nixon era a fuller understanding of the life and career of a United States president that history may forever negatively brand. Whether you choose to view this as true history is up to you. Regardless, the film remains for me, an outstanding achievement in psycho drama in both performance and language. As a "presidential" film, it may also serve as the second act in a trilogy of such films (*JFK* preceding it and *W.* following it).

Now if only Stone would do a film of Bill Clinton (make sure to include some good ol'-fashioned cocksucking by Monica Lewinsky) and Donald Trump (make sure to include *every* single despicable thing that piece of garbage did right up until that fateful day at the State Capitol on January 6, 2021).

Dead Man Walking

Directed by Tim Robbins
(December 29, 1995, U.S. Release Date)

In September 1992, I went to see Tim Robbins's directorial debut film *Bob Roberts*. Although I wrote it off as an entertaining satirical mockumentary film (much like Rob Reiner's debut film *This is Spinal Tap*), Robbins clearly had something valid to say about politics, corruption and the mind of the American voters. Three years later, the death penalty was also something he had a passion for in his new film *Dead Man Walking*, and I was curious to see his position. I went to see the film with the same "crew" (including Daniela) I'd gone to see *Schindler's List* with. You may be thinking the four of us deliberately got together to partake in films that were deeper, more serious, and sparked controversial conversation between us over dinner afterwards. I assure you it was merely a coincidence.

When we met death row inmate Matthew Poncelet (played dramatically well by Sean Penn), we met a monster who participated in the brutal rape and murder of two teenagers. But at the same time, we were asked to look beyond the monster and try to discover the human being inside through the eyes and personal experiences of kind-hearted nun Sister Helen Prejean (played by Tim Robbins real-life wife, Susan Sarandon). Poncelet had been in prison six years, awaiting execution by lethal injection after his conviction for the crime. Held in the Louisiana State Penitentiary awaiting the day of his execution, he corresponded with Sister Helen and asked her to help him with his final appeal. Poncelet was sexist, racist, arrogant and showed no remorse for what he'd done, even claiming he hadn't killed anybody. While she and Poncelet established their relationship, she not only got to know Poncelet's mother, but the families of the victims, as well. These families couldn't understand how she could try to save a monster like Poncelet by *"taking his side"* while they sought justice for their murdered children (I couldn't blame them).

The appeal for Poncelet's pardon was declined. Acting now as his spiritual advisor, Sister Helen stressed that his redemption was only possible if he finally took responsibility for what he did the night of the crime. In the end, he tearfully confessed to raping and killing those two kids. For his execution, he was laid across the table with his arms spread out in the same manner as a crucifixion. It was at this moment I looked over at Daniela to see she was in tears, though I wondered whether it was because the man was about to die or because his death was dramatically and tragically displayed in a Christ-like manner (I'd later learn it was *both*). For his final words, Poncelet appealed to the boy's father for forgiveness and told the girl's parents that he hoped his death would bring them some peace. Then the switches were flipped and Matthew Poncelet was injected with various lethal substances. The monster (or the man?) was dead, and my friends and I were left with the daunting task of intelligently discussing the matter of the death penalty later amongst ourselves… which we would.

In any social situation, there are sensitive subjects that are bound to raise their ugly heads and become a heated topic of discussion: religion, politics, global warming, the use of nuclear weapons, what is and isn't fake news, whether or not someone like me thinks a freak (sorry…*person*) like Lady GaGa should exist in this world (LOL), and I suppose, issues surrounding the death penalty. I've never been shy about expressing my opinions and beliefs, but for the purpose of this book, these sensitive subjects and more are best left alone. I'll leave my personal views on the death penalty out of this and simply stick to the film *Dead Man Walking* itself.

From its beginning, when we meet Sean Penn's character, the film cleverly doesn't give us the opportunity to stay focused on merely one side of the argument. Through momentary flashbacks, we're constantly reminded of the horrific crime he and his accomplice committed. Even at the final moment when he's escorted to his death and strapped down in a manner resembling Jesus Christ on the crucifix, we may find ourselves experiencing a momentary feeling of compassion for the man. We might even think to ourselves, "He doesn't deserve this." But wait—before we get too caught up in our bleeding-heart, liberal attitude, we're shown the crime in its entirely, as if the film were saying to us, "Wait just a damn minute! Take a good, long, hard look at what this man did to these kids, and don't ever forget it!" Back and forth, Tim Robbins and his film refuses to take sides, and that's probably the most reasonable position he *can* take on the matter (I said as much that night to my friends at dinner).

Strictly speaking as an Oscar-nominated motion picture, *Dead Man Walking* is nothing short of a powerful and thought-provoking journey that makes its points on both sides without getting too preachy about the subject. Whatever your viewpoint might be, you can't help but reflect on the film's intelligence, its devastation and even its beauty surrounding what is ultimately a conflict between good and evil. Sean Penn and Susan Sarandon are both strong and absorbing performers who are in touch with not only who they portray, but also the hard topic they represent, which I'm sure they both know will be talked about for a long time after the film has ended.

Oh, by the way, I *support* the death penalty.

*****

This is the last film of 1995 I shall discuss in any great detail.

When you measure the distance of any single year of your life, you may or may not be surprised with the events that unfold. Sometimes things change for the better, like my *finally* getting a respectable job with an architectural firm after searching in vain for over a year while I maintained a series of meaningless non-career-related jobs to pay my rent, including a five week stint at the *Banana Republic* pretending to give a damn about helping intolerable customers pick out their clothes (I had *no* hesitations in quitting that thankless job). Sometimes things stay the same, like my lonely life in a big city where my self-esteem and self-respect was only as good as my last date. There were even desperate moments when I wanted to call Caren to try and work things out between us (hey, people *do* experience momentary weakness). Thankfully, I quickly came to my senses and put the phone down.

Even as I continued to try and fulfill my empty life by writing whatever screenplay I was working on at the time, I knew the movies were challenging in how they inspired and motivated me, because I never knew what would or wouldn't turn me on, and for whatever reason. In the world of the Caped Crusader, Val Kilmer was a gross disappointment in a *Batman* franchise I decided had exhausted itself. And for whatever reason the Academy of Motion Picture Arts and Sciences concluded that *Braveheart* should take home the Oscar for Best Picture of the Year, Mel Gibson and the rest of his mindless savages in that gross epic made me want to get my time and ticket money back. Instead, I searched for whatever classic revivals were at the Film Forum in Greenwich Village because watching a screening of Billy Wilder's *Double Indemnity* or Alfred Hitchcock's *Rear Window* left me with much better and brighter feelings of joy than most anything Hollywood offered. This option at the movies was what I preferred most about living in Manhattan.

While I can't deny that Martin Scorsese's Las Vegas epic *Casino*, which reteamed alumni cast Robert DeNiro with Joe Pesci, wasn't a thoroughly entertaining and spectacular cinematic gangster experience, I've often regarded it as simply another version of *Goodfellas* in that it (again) depicts larger-than-life men (based on real-life people) who create their own downfall by their overambitious and greedy actions, with only slight variations in characters and their general attitudes toward violence and destruction. Perhaps the most significant thing that stands out for me personally is that it remains the one and only time I ever went to the movies following Thanksgiving dinner.

However, in December '95 there *was* a particular day that stands out in my mind when I went to see Michael Mann's *Heat*, which reunited DeNiro with Al Pacino for the first time since *The Godfather-Part II* (though they never actually shared a scene together).

My best friend since college, *Greg C.*, was in from Colorado visiting his parents in his home state of New Jersey for the holidays, and we met in Manhattan for what turned out to be one of the best crime thrillers we'd both seen in a long time. During the sequence when Vincent Hanna and the LAPD intercepted Neil McCauley and his crew making their getaway from the bank, resulting in a massive street shootout, the sound of the gunfire reverberated throughout the entire multiplex theater thanks to their high-tech surround-sound system. Greg and I looked at each other with the same thought that we might go deaf from the noise, while at the same time thinking just how awesome this entire shootout sequence was.

Later, as we enjoyed pitchers of beer and plates of Buffalo chicken wings, we both understood what even a single day like this meant to each other and our continuing and longstanding friendship. Even today, when we both (architecturally) acknowledge Al Pacino's cynical description of what he calls his wife's ex-husband's *"dead-tech, postmodernistic bullshit house,"* it reminds us of that special movie day, and to never take our valuable friendship for granted.

And that, my friends, was the year 1995 for me.

THE YEAR WAS 1996...

- Eastern North America experiences one of its worst bliz-zards in history, closing New York City schools and the federal government for days.
- Hamas explodes two suicide bombs in Israel, killing thir-ty-two people. Israel warns of retaliation, despite Yasser Arafat condemning the killings on television.
- The suspected Unabomber Theodore Kaczynski is arrested in Lincoln, Montana, by the FBI.
- At the Summer Olympics in Atlanta, Georgia, a domestic terrorist pipe bomb explodes at the Centennial Olympic Park, killing one person and injuring 111. Security guard Richard Jewell is wrongfully suspected of planting the bomb.
- The New York Yankees win their first World Series cham-pionship since 1978 against the Atlanta Braves.
- In the United States presidential election, Bill Clinton wins his second term by defeating Republican challenger Bob Dole.

...AND THERE WERE MOVIES!

I almost never make New Year's resolutions. In my opinion, they're a waste of time and one's self-respect because most people never follow through with them. If we don't make them in the first place, we won't feel guilty for having inevitably broken them. However, when 1996 began, I made one resolution which I was determined to follow through with, and that was to end my personal era of summer share house participations and finally make a real effort to reopen the family beach house in Westhampton Beach after four long years of closure because of disastrous beach erosion and coastal storms. It would take time, effort and money, but I was determined to do my best to make it happen. In short, it was time for me to go home again.

During the winter and spring season of each New Year, I came to expect the same lukewarm response from its films, and '96 was no exception. General releases like *The Birdcage* (a remake of the popular 1978 French comedy *La Cage aux Folles*) and *Primal Fear* were entertaining enough in that they occupied my leisure time with some temporary escapism, though they hardly left me with any permanent emotional thoughts or feelings I'd deem worthy of writing about now. These films were just time killed as I waited for the promise of the new summer blockbuster season to arrive.

My new architect's job was going well. In fact, one of the senior partners was a film buff in his own right, with a strong passion for the classics. It was because of him that I first discovered black-and-white foreign art house classics by Federico Fellini, Ingmar Bergman and Akira Kurosawa, because it was these sort of films the cable channel Bravo *used* to air back in '90s before they converted to crap television about real housewives. But in March '96, my classic film-loving boss went on and on about this new film by the Cohen Brothers that took place in Fargo, North Dakota which I simply *had* to see, and he wouldn't get off my back until I finally went to see what he was raving about.

Fargo

Directed by Joel Cohen
(March 8, 1996, U.S. Release Date)

Ever since I saw *Blood Simple* in the '80s, I'd become a somewhat dedicated fan of the Cohen Brothers' movies, and with the exception of *Barton Fink* in 1991, I enjoyed everything they'd done so far. Their new dark comedy-crime film, however, proved to be something I'd never experienced before. I'd seen the trailer more than once and it looked interesting, but I went to see it solely based on my boss's recommendation because I trusted his taste in quality cinema.

Fargo was a film experience where I laughed at quirky characters like sleazy car salesman Jerry Lundegaard (played by William H. Macy), pregnant police chief Marge Gunderson (played by Frances McDormand) and small time criminal Carl Showalter (played by Steve Buscemi)—three actors I knew little about. When we met Jerry, we knew there was something about him we didn't like or trust. Turns out he was in deep financial trouble. Desperate to get the money he needed to bail himself out, he travelled to Fargo, North Dakota and hired a couple of sleazy criminals to kidnap his wife Jean to get the ransom money of $80,000 from her wealthy father, which he'd split with the kidnappers.

Carl and his creepy partner Gaear kidnapped Jean and drove her to an isolated cabin. While driving, a state trooper stopped them near the town of Brainerd, Minnesota for driving their new Oldsmobile without displaying temporary registration tags. When the trooper rejected Carl's attempt at bribery, and subsequently heard

Jean whimpering in the back seat, Gaear shot him dead, and then proceeded to chase down and execute two passers-by who witnessed the scene.

The next morning, Brainers police Chief Marge discovered the dead state trooper was in the process of ticketing a car with dealer plates, and that two men driving a dealership vehicle checked into the nearby Blue Ox Motel with two hookers. These two girls were less-than-intelligent in verbally describing one of the criminals as *"kinda funny lookin,"* and in the way they sounded every time they uttered the word *"y-e-e-a-a-h."* Did people in the upper mid-west really talk like that? After questioning these two dimwitted hookers, Marge visited Jerry at his dealership, where he feigned ignorance of any cars missing from his lot, particularly the Oldsmobile the two criminals were driving.

Meanwhile, Jerry falsely informed his wealthy father-in-law Wade that the kidnappers demanded one million dollars and would only deal though him (Jerry). In light of the blood spilled with the three earlier murders, Carl demanded the entire $80,000 which he still believed was the ransom total. Carl ordered that Jerry deliver the ransom money immediately, but Wade insisted on bringing it himself, as it was his money and his daughter's life on the line. Wade met Carl at an empty parking garage and insisted on seeing his daughter before handing over the money. Enraged, Carl shot Wade, but Wade shot back and hit Carl in his jaw. Carl killed Wade and took the briefcase with the ransom money. Discovering the $1 million inside, he removed $80,000 and then buried the remaining money in the snow alongside the highway. At their hideaway cabin at Moose Lake, Carl returned to find Jean dead and insisted they split their money and go their separate ways immediately. Then they argued about who' keep the new Oldsmobile, Carl justifying his bloody injuries as reason for him to keep the car. But before he could leave with the car, Gaear suddenly appeared and killed him with an axe.

Marge returned to the dealership, where Jerry angrily insisted there were no cars missing and hurriedly exited the office, claiming he'd double-check his inventory, if that's what Marge insisted on. Instead, he fled the interview and Marge called the state police.

Proceeding then to Moose Lake based on a reliable tip about a *"funny looking guy"* bragging about killing someone, she arrived at the cabin to find Gaear feeding Carl's dismembered body into a wood chipper (gross!). She shot Gaear in the leg, arrested him and even took the time to lecture him about the immoral acts of murder he committed for nothing more than a little money. What surprised me about this scene was that it looked as if this mindless psychotic was actually listening to her and taking her words to heart. North Dakota police arrested a broken and fallen Jerry Lundegaard at a quiet motel. Marge and her husband happily embraced the anticipation of their new baby's arrival, and all was happily-ever-after with the world.

Cliché in the movies is a funny thing, because even before anything happens after Jerry's meeting with the scum of the earth, we know that things will go horribly wrong with the best laid plans. Even though the opening credits tell us that the events happened in 1987, we feel the dread that comes with knowing blood will inevitably be spilled. The crimes occurring in the name of financial greed, not just the murders themselves, but Jerry's diabolical plotting against the wife who loves him, are intriguing because we can't help but be impressed by the hero pregnant cop and her capable deductions and conclusions when investigating these crimes. Violence is also a uniquely intriguing element in *Fargo* because even though we may be used to all forms of movie violence, we still can't believe the wood chipper scene, despite the nature of the criminals involved, especially as played by actor Peter Stormare, who's one of the most chilling and disturbing people I've ever seen on screen, not only in this film, but in in other films like Lasse Hallström's *Chocolat* and Steven Spielberg's *Minority Report*.

But what surprises most is that final moment with Marge in bed with her loving husband as they sweetly tell each other "I love you" after all the mystery and carnage we've witnessed. That's *so* cliché, old-fashioned, and perhaps even stupid in the "Hollywood happy ending" sense, and yet it makes perfect sense at the end of the insane day poor Marge has experienced. Cliché or not, it's impossible to deny that the Cohen Brothers' quirky and darkly violent tale of homespun murder delivers wonderful performances from all those involved (Frances McDormand won the Oscar for Best Actress of 1996) in what is an original and stylish crime story (even if it is based on true events). The geographical locales are beautifully photographed, giving one a bleak sense of a part of America that, despite its snowy beauty, has the potential for the nasty and the macabre.

Let me say to my former employer—thanks, Boss. You turned me on to some strange shit in the world of independent filmmaking from a pair of artists who'd already grabbed my attention in the '80s with *Blood Simple* and *Raising Arizona* and would later go on to make the Oscar winner for Best Picture of 2007, *No Country for Old Men*, and for that, I'm grateful. It makes the springtime movie season more hopeful.

Mission: Impossible
Directed by Brian DePalma
(May 22, 1996, U.S. Release Date)

There are two stories that immediately come to mind with the 1996 summer blockbuster *Mission: Impossible*. Let's start with the somewhat *less* important one (the more important one, I'll tell you about later).

When my mother's second husband went to see this movie in Los Angeles upon its release, his reaction was nothing short of furious. Apparently, he's a huge fan of the original CBS television show, and he simply couldn't accept the new film's story changes, particularly the fate of Jon Voight as Jim Phelps. For myself, all I ever knew of the TV show was the iconic opening and its musical theme by composer Lalo Schifrin. I never watched a single episode of the TV show, so I had no basis of comparison to the film. That accompanied by the fact that I have a shameful weakness for many (not all) of Tom Cruise's films. But Tom Cruise as an action star? This was a new idea that would take some getting used to. Brian DePalma as director was easier to embrace because he'd already scored a big hit with another film version of a popular TV show, *The Untouchables*, in 1987. And then there was the trailer with its climactic helicopter blade barely touching Tom's throat and the promise of Memorial Day that had me pumped and ready for summer to begin.

Tom Cruise as IMF (Impossible Missions Force) agent Ethan Hunt and his team had just completed their mission in Kiev, Russia (before the opening film credits) and regrouped with their director

Jim Phelps. Their new mission was to stop the theft of the NOC (CIA nonofficial cover) list from the American embassy in Prague by a rogue agent. As we followed along, we waited for something to go wrong, and it did when Emilio Estevez's character was killed in the elevator shaft. After that, the list was successfully stolen, Phelps was shot, his wife Claire (a young and stunningly beautiful French girl) and another agent were killed in a car bombing, and the rest of the team were eliminated by unknown assassins. Ethan Hunt survived.

At his meeting with IMF director Kittridge, Hunt realized there was a second IMF team at the embassy that night to monitor him and his team. The stolen list was merely a decoy (the real list was safe in Langley, Virginia) to expose a mole within IMF believed to be working with an unknown arms dealer known as "Max," as part of an operation called "Job 314." Since Hunt was the sole survivor, Kittridge concluded he must be the mole. Hunt used his secret "James Bond" type device of explosive chewing gum to mount his escape into the night. Returning to the safe house in Prague, Hunt discovered that "Job 314" referred to the Bible verse Job 3:14, "Job" being the unknown mole's code name. Turns out Claire survived, too, explaining that she escaped the car bombing after Phelps aborted the mission.

Hunt met Max, a middle-aged woman (played by Vanessa Redgrave) and warned her that she'd been handed a fake NOC list disc equipped with a tracking device. She, Hunt and her agents escaped CIA capture, and Hunt promised her delivery of the real NOC list in return for $10 million and the true identity of Job. Claire joined him, believing that because she was alive too, IMF considered her a suspect and coconspirator with Hunt. They recruited two disavowed IMF agents: computer hacker Luther Stickell and French pilot Franz Krieger. Their impossible mission was to infiltrate CIA headquarters in Langley and steal the real NOC list. The security measures as described by Hunt were high-tech and state-of-the-art in detecting anyone who wasn't authorized to be in the secret vault where the computer containing the list was kept. This heist was brilliant and nerve-wracking in the way DePalma filmed it, not only in its use of camera angles, but also in its nonuse of any musical score. As Tom

Cruise silently descended into the vault from the ceiling, I couldn't help but think if we heard nothing but the sound of human breathing, it would've been a wonderful homage to Stanley Kubrick's *2001: A Space Odyssey*.

Their theft successful, the team fled to London. In that time, Kittridge had Hunt's mother and uncle falsely accused and arrested for drug trafficking to bring Hunt out of hiding. Hunt called Kittridge and allowed the CIA to trace his call to London before hanging up abruptly. That's when we learned Jim Phelps was alive. He recounted to Hunt his surviving the shooting, and naming Kittridge as the mole. But even as we listened to this explanation, Hunt realized it was a lie and that Phelps was the mole, having earlier discovered a Bible with a Gideons stamp that Phelps stole from the Drake Hotel in Chicago. In his mind, Hunt pieced together how Phelps betrayed the team, programming the elevator, faking his own shooting, and rigging the car bombs to explode. Hunt also realized Kreiger was an assassin responsible for the deaths of the other agents of his team, having remembered his distinctive hunting knife. We knew the truth now, but Hunt revealed nothing to Phelps. I suddenly realized why my mother's husband got so pissed at this movie—I mean, if you spent years watching and loving the original TV show, Jim Phelps turning out to be a traitor might piss *you* off too.

Hunt arranged the exchange of the NOC list with Max aboard the TGV train to Paris the next day, and even secretly sent train tickets to Kittridge for him to be there. Aboard the train, Hunt remotely revealed the genuine list to Max, and she directed Hunt to the train's baggage car where his money and Job would be waiting for him. Claire went to the baggage car, where Phelps was waiting for her, and tried to discourage him from killing Hunt. Having exposed herself as her husband's accomplice, Phelps pulled off his rubber face mask and revealed himself as Hunt. At that moment, the real Phelps arrived and took the money at gunpoint, believing that only Hunt and Claire knew he was alive. Not so. Hunt put on a pair of video glasses relaying Phelps's image to Kittridge's wristwatch, blowing Phelps's cover as the mole. Phelps then shot his own wife.

The action climaxed on the roof of the speeding train, where Krieger waited on board a helicopter equipped with a tether. Hunt chased Phelps to the roof as he attempted to escape by helicopter. Hunt got ahold of the tether and connected it to the train, forcing the helicopter into the long tunnel ahead behind the train. Finally, Hunt revealed another piece of that infamous chewing gum and blew the helicopter apart, thus concluding with the helicopter blade at his throat (as I'd seen in the film's trailer). Mission accomplished, list recovered, the future (and missions) of IMF agent Ethan Hunt unknown, and my mother's husband likely to *never* go to another Tom Cruise movie for the rest of his life.

Those of us who saw *Mission: Impossible* back in the summer of '96 probably couldn't get the plotline straight in our heads, and I was no exception. It took a second viewing to put all the pieces of the puzzle together, and like any other complicated puzzle, the more you take it apart and put it back together again, the more you understand and appreciate it. Once you've done that, you can step back and admire what Brian DePalma offers us. Like *The Untouchables*, he doesn't overload our eyes and brains with endless in-your-face action, but rather gives us assorted thrilling moments with the chance to *think* about a plot that isn't simple. If you recall, I'm a man who enjoys a good reason to think about what I'm watching on screen, and unlike too many moviegoers (and my mom's husband), I don't throw a fit when the story turns challenging. Yet despite describing all of this, there's still the irresistible and awesome climactic speeding train and helicopter sequence that's very much in our faces, and I love it. It's almost impossible (pun totally intended) not to absorb a sweeping spectacle as this with its stylish special effects and suspenseful thrills, even if the plot and dialogue throw you off some. Who cares—it's all good fun, nonetheless. If nothing else, the CIA break-in deserves enough praise to keep you interested (it's been parodied in other movies, from *Spy Hard* to *Shrek 2*).

Regarding the final scene aboard the plane, though…somebody has to explain *that* one to me. Ethan Hunt has already told Luthor that he's out of the game, yet he's introduced to a new mission on board the plane. His final facial reaction is of shock and surprise. Is he accepting a new mission or does he, like too much of his *Mission: Impossible* audience, not know what the fuck is going on? Whatever the answer is, I suppose it has nothing to do with the inevitable franchise of sequels that followed the original film, some better than others (*Mission: Impossible 2* is my personal favorite).

Now here's the second and somewhat more important story I promised you. As I previously mentioned, my only New Year's resolution was to reopen the family beach house in Westhampton Beach that summer, and I did. It took a lot of time, patience and cleaning to get things up and running again, but I experienced an undeniable feeling of being reborn the moment I switched on the lights of my beloved home that Friday night of Memorial Day weekend after four years of darkness. The house was alive again and ready to breathe and, with it, a new sense of my own identity and meaning. By the time I took a moment to give myself a break from all my hard work that weekend, I decided it was also time to once again go to the movies in town as part of the spirit of my personal life in the Hamptons. *Mission: Impossible* was playing at the Hampton Arts Twin movie theater, and I went to an early Saturday evening show. For all the reasons I loved the film in the first place, there was something extra special about my trip that night because it reminded me that regardless of whatever glitches life threw at me in the past, be they coastal storms, beach erosion, bad jobs, or bad romances, it *was* possible to go home again.

Thank you, Tom Cruise and Brian DePalma, for having a little something to do with that.

Independence Day
Directed by Roland Emmerich
(July 3, 1996, U.S. Release Date)

It was the summer of 1996. My architect's job was going well, the family beach house was open again, and I loved going to the movies in Westhampton Beach. I found enthusiastic reasons to enjoy just about everything I went to see—from Arnold Schwarzenegger in *Eraser* to Sean Connery and Nicholas Cage in *The Rock*. The release of *Independence Day* was the big one to solidify my newfound spirit of returning home to a life I'd cherished in that it rebooted the genre of childhood science fiction action movies with glorious space battles (was it any wonder the trailers for the special editions of George Lucas's original *Star Wars* trilogy were shown before *Independence Day*)? Since *ID4*, it seems aliens and monster have been endlessly invading and crushing our planet (often in New York City). Even the original teaser trailer didn't need to say much to get people excited to see it come July:

> *July 2—the day they arrive.*
> *July 3—the day they attack.*
> *July 4—the day we fight back.*

Simple, to the point, and quite gripping for the sci-fi lover. However, unlike the many alien invasion films from the 1950s I'd watched on Turner Classic Movies, I'd soon discover that director Roland Emmerich focused less on the science of the aliens and why they did what they did, and instead gave us more of the action, blood and guts we likely craved from this genre…and we'd get Will Smith, fresh off of last summer's *Bad Boys*, to boot.

Beginning on July 2, the enormous mothership orbited around our planet and positioned multiple fifteen-mile-long flying saucers over Earth's major cities. In Los Angeles, Captain Steven Hiller (Smith), a Marine pilot and aspiring astronaut, was on military leave with his stripper girlfriend Jasmine and her son Dylan. That leave was abruptly cancelled as soon the ships arrived and Steven was ordered back to his base. In New York City, MIT-trained satellite technician David Levinson (played by Jeff Goldblum) decoded a signal embedded within Earth's transmissions and concluded it was the aliens' countdown to a coordinated attack. Desperate, he travelled with his father Julius to Washington, DC, to warn the White House Communications Director, who was also his ex-wife. They gained access to the Oval Office to alert the President of the United States Thomas Whitmore (played by Bill Pullman) of the pending threat. The president ordered evacuations of all the major U.S. cities, but it would be too late. The aliens' countdown ended and it was, as David put it, *"checkmate."*

The attack by the alien ships on our major cities was the most visually destructive spectacle I'd seen on screen (big or small) since *The Day After* on TV and Sarah Connor's dream sequence in *Terminator 2: Judgement Day*. The explosions were gargantuan, killing millions of people and incinerating the targeted cities. But even as I watched the destruction of Manhattan, I noticed the filmmakers had (shamelessly) placed the Empire State Building in the geographically *wrong* location for no better reason than to enhance the effects of the shot. To anyone who didn't live in New York City or close to it, they didn't realize how bogus that was. One thing was undeniable, though, and that was everyone in the theater cheered when the White House was destroyed by the destructive beam above. It didn't matter if you were a Democrat or Republican—watching our government destroyed brought us undeniable joy. Amidst all the destruction, though, the president, the Levinsons and others escaped aboard Air Force One as the capital was destroyed.

Continuing on July 3, the first wave of counterattacks against the aliens had begun, and we laughed when Steven expressed his anxiousness to *"get up there and whoop E.T.'s ass."* That enthusiasm came crashing down when we learned the alien ships were protected by force fields and could each launch a swarm of their own fighter ships equipped with individual shields. Our own jet-fighter squadrons were no match for the aliens' technology. Still, Steven was too much of a badass pilot to give up easily. After angrily declaring to the spaceship that shot at him, *"Oh no, you did* not *shoot that green shit at me!"* (that line still cracks me up), he lured his attacker to the enclosed spaces of the Grand Canyon before ejecting from his own plane, causing his enemy ship to crash-land. We finally saw one of the aliens up close, and he was an ugly, slimy son-of-a-bitch. One punch in the face later, and the alien was knocked out. *"Welcome to Earth!"* (looks like the alien got bitch-slapped by Will Smith twenty-six years before Chris Rock did at the 2022 Oscars).

Steven delivered the unconscious alien to the infamous Area 51, where President Whitmore's party had already landed, and learned unbeknownst to him, that a faction of the government was involved in a UFO conspiracy ever since one of the alien attack ships crashed in Roswell, New Mexico in 1947. That refurbished ship was still there, as well as three alien corpses recovered from the crash. While one of the scientists (whom I recognized as Brent Spiner from *Star Trek: The Next Generation*) examined the newly delivered alien, it awoke and attacked, telepathically invading the scientist's mind and using his vocal cords to demand its release. The alien declared there would never be peace between his race and the people of Earth, and was then shot dead by Secret Service agents.

With no choice left, the president reluctantly ordered the use of nuclear weapons against our attackers. The first strike against one of their warships hovering above Houston, Texas remained intact after the detonation, and further use of nuclear weapons was aborted. Elsewhere, Jasmine and her son survived the attack on Los Angeles and were en route to reunite with Steven, picking up other survivors along the way, including the critically injured First Lady, who died later after she was brought to Area 51 and reunited with her family.

Concluding on July 4, David brainstormed a computer virus to disrupt the alien ships' shields and allow our own jet fighters to strike and destroy. The virus needed to be uploaded into the mothership in space, and it would take David and Steven piloting the refurbished alien fighter to complete the mission successfully. Thus began a global campaign in which through Morse code, our own military advised other nations of the world how to launch their own counter-offensive against the aliens. For our own attack, military pilots were in short supply, and anyone with flying experience was needed, including Randy Quaid as a hopeless drunk, and President Whitmore himself, a fighter pilot veteran of the first Gulf War.

This was finally where the *Star Wars* element of battle action kicked in with the massive attack on the warship above Los Angeles with laser fire and exploding ships. Out in space, Steven and David entered the mothership, uploaded the virus and deployed a nuclear missile, thus destroying the ship and weakening its subsequent reinforcements all over the world. With their shields now deactivated, our squadron led by our own president could fight back and cause some destruction, though it was slow-going and ineffective. As the warship prepared to fire its ultimate weapon, the hopeless Randy Quaid sacrificed himself by flying his jet with an armed missile into the ship's weapon and destroyed it. The world was saved. Yay for us!

As a kid, I knew alien invasions were fun, and often still are. But where *Independence Day* takes things further is its reminder that such a world event is terrifying, as well. A gifted actor like Will Smith may be a perfect addition to provide humor to make things lighter and funnier, but it's only a diversion to our own inevitable destruction. From the moment the aliens arrive and surround our planet, we know they're likely *not* friendly, even if we choose to pretend they are and dance around like idiots on the roof of an L.A. skyscraper. When our major cities are obliterated by laser weapons, the balls of inferno and the panic in the streets send chills up your spine if you allow yourself the imagination to take it all in. They're destructive pleasures reminding me how much fun sci-fi was when I was a kid, and how much fun it still can be when it's done right.

What is *right*, though? Sci-fi plots can be thin, and so can character development. Will Smith, Jeff Goldblum, and Bill Pullman are fine actors, but they hardly offer dramatic compensation to what is effectively (even stereotypically) a thrilling, spectacle-filled awesome summer blockbuster, and for those of us who grew up with the original *Star Wars* trilogy, this grand comeback of sci-fi action is all we need to feel like kids again. And in the 1990s, which seemed to be the era of presidential heroes in the movies, *Independence Day* can easily be called the Bill Clinton-era sci-fi film (Clinton himself loved this movie). Pullman as President Whitmore even bears a slight resemblance to our former president. The fact that he's a former fighter pilot willing to go up in the air and take part in the battle with the rest of our brave boys is either, as political commentator John McLaughlin put it, *"A, ultra-brave or B, fool-hardy?"* You decide for yourself. I tend to go back-and-forth with it.

My thoughts and memories for this sci-fi summer blockbuster are not all fun and fancy-free, however. Some of them of are somber, and I'll share them with you now. I went to see the movie the weekend after it opened at the Westhampton Beach Theater, a place I'd frequented since I was ten years old. I didn't know it that night, but *Independence Day* would be the last movie I'd ever see there. One month later, the theater closed after more than six decades. Two years later, it reopened as a performing arts theater, though it still includes independent art film screenings as part of its program (I went to the movies there one last time to attend a screening of Fellini's 1961 black-and-white classic *La Dolce Vita*). So while the theater itself was saved from demolition, a big part of my childhood died when mainstream movies ended there. I also went to see *Independence Day* with my childhood friend *Jim R.* and his girlfriend (eventually becoming his wife and then ex-wife). Jim has passed on now, and with him the memory of every movie we ever saw together since first meeting as kids in 1980. I'll miss him and our close friendship for the rest of my life.

Finally, there's the unavoidable story of myself on the morning of September 11, 2001. I was walking to work along the sidewalk of Christopher Street in Manhattan when I looked up and saw the smoldering plume of smoke coming from the first tower of the World Trade Center. As I watched in disbelief, I witnessed the explosion at the second tower, though still not realizing that our nation was under attack. When I saw that fireball in the sky, the first thoughts that popped into my head were the attack scenes from *Independence Day*. I couldn't help it. It just happened. After the attack, I was caught up in the controversies of whether or not our Hollywood system of destructive moviemaking inadvertently contributed to the inspiration of Al-Qaeda's attack on our country that day. Did movies of the late '90s that systematically struck the island of Manhattan like *Independence Day*, *Godzilla*, *Deep Impact*, and *Armageddon* indirectly contribute to our own destruction? This debate can repeatedly go both ways, not too unlike deciding whether or not Stanley Kubrick's *A Clockwork Orange* was responsible for copycat crimes in England in 1972, or whether or not the lyrics of *"Suicide Solution"* by Ozzy Osbourne was responsible for the death of John McCollum, who took his own life after listening to the song.

I hope rational minds prevail when ultimately deciding these matters. In the meantime, let's continue to try and have fun at the movies.

To Gillian on Her 37th Birthday
Directed by Michael Pressman
(October 18, 1996, U.S. Release Date)

At the close of 1993, I mentioned that after finally cutting Caren out of my life, it was four years before I'd speak to her again. I also mentioned that it was a *movie* that inspired me to reintroduce her into my life. Welcome to that movie (I'll get into the details of how and why later).

I've always been a sucker for poignant stories that take place at the beach (*Summer of '42*, as an example), so my interest in *To Gillian on Her 37th Birthday* was immediate. But it didn't play at many theaters or stay in release for too long, so I missed its theatrical run, and it wasn't until August 1997 that I watched it on video at the beach house. My expectations were a ghost-related love story in the tradition of *Ghost*, but without the thrills and the Whoppi Goldberg wisecracks. I was drawn to the character of David Lewis (played by Peter Gallagher) and his Nantucket beach house's isolation from neighbors and the town. The beach and the ocean right outside his doorstep was an easy way to lose himself in his own private world after the loss of his beautiful wife Gillian (played by Michelle Pfeiffer) two years earlier when she foolishly climbed the mast of their sailboat and fell to her death (on her birthday).

David was so traumatized by her death that he willingly and knowingly communicated with her spirit as if she were standing right in from of him, while unwittingly neglecting their daughter Rachel (played by Claire Danes). During a family weekend gathering on what was to be the second anniversary of Gillian's death, David's sister-in-law Esther and her husband brought with them a woman they hoped would spark a romantic interest in David's heart. No such luck, because *"live people can't compete with dead ones."* David ignored her and proceeded with a series of rituals to celebrate his deceased wife's birthday. The events of the weekend prompted the grown-ups to reexamine their own lives and relationships, while Rachel's best friend Cindy had no problem acting provocative, even while showing off her developing body on the beach.

It wasn't until Rachel's vivid nightmare of her mother that David finally realized his isolation and self-indulgent fantasies were hurting his daughter, and thus agreed to her moving in permanently with her aunt and uncle. He also realized that to move on with his own life, he'd have to close the beach house, move back to Boston, and give up the ghost of Gillian, while not betraying her beloved memory. As someone who'd spent the better part of his life on the beach, I felt a strong, personal feeling of sadness in the permanent nature of boarding up the house, and the likelihood that it would be sold and passed on to another resident. I'd spent years closing up my own home, and even though it was only for the winter season, there was an undeniable sadness I had to reckon with every year.

It would be easy enough to dismiss *Gillian* as just another tearjerker that could've easily been a Lifetime cable TV movie instead of a theatrical release. Its story and performances of those in pain and anguish (particularly Claire Danes as the troubled daughter) are solid enough, though hardly Oscar-worthy. Its strength, in my opinion, are the exterior shots of the beach and the ocean offering the traditional, enchanting moonlight and magic one expects from such a setting. If we allow ourselves to examine each one's true persona, though, we may deduce that sister-in-law Esther is a meddling bitch who should mind her own business and allow David the time and energy he needs to grieve in his own way, and that Rachel is happy living a life of peace and tranquility on the beach with her father. David may be grieving in a very nonconventional manner, but he's hardly crazy (acknowledging that Gillian *is* just an illusion) enough to have his daughter taken away from him. Like real life, these are ordinary people with their own personal issues we may choose to compare to our own.

This film *needs* to feel personal to whomever watches it. As I said, I'm a sucker for beach stories (though not the 1988 film *Beaches*), particularly in its power to heal painful emotions and experiences (works for me). It's because of this, and the timing of when I first watched *Gillian* in my own beach house, that I was inspired to take a daring step in dealing with my painful memories of Caren. I knew if I ever wanted to finally move on with my life, I'd need to contact her to settle my demons and establish closure with the estranged woman I was once in love with.

How would I do it? I'd discarded her phone number years ago, and even if I hadn't, the thought of a phone conversation made me cringe. I'd need to do what I did best, and write down all my feelings and intentions. But even after I did that, I had no mailing address to send a letter to. I did, however, know the location of her Manhattan building where she lived. So after writing her a lengthy letter pouring out everything I felt needed to be said about how she'd hurt me at the end of our relationship, and how I needed to forgive her for all of it to move forward, I hand-delivered the letter to her building's doorman. Now I'd have to wait to see if Caren would respond with an apology, respond by telling me to go to hell, or if she'd respond at all.

Less than two weeks later, I received a letter from her. My heart raced because I had no idea what to expect from her after so many years. To my surprise, her letter had a very apologetic tone, even as she tried to explain her side of things at that time, attributing her hurtful actions towards me to the painful loss of her own mother in 1991 (a loss I was reminded of when watching Danes' performance in dealing with her own mother's death). Sometimes when grieving, people choose someone to lash out at in dealing with their anger at the world, and Caren chose me (*me*—the one who'd always stood by her when her mother died). I didn't understand that sort of twisted human logic, but she was very sorry in her letter to me, and that seemed like enough. In fact, I was so touched by her thoughtfulness, I read the letter several times to absorb her every word.

So in a nutshell, my inspiration and actions based on watching *Gillian* paid off. I'd settled my past with Caren and we were friends again. It was a close friendship with a former girlfriend and lover who was now married to another man (a marriage that didn't bother me, as well as a marriage that inevitably failed), and a friendship that lasted many months until the summer of 1998 when she left New York to move to Las Vegas, Nevada to join her husband already there setting up their new lives. The day we parted, she told me she didn't believe in goodbyes, and I reluctantly agreed with her. But as I walked away from her on that busy Manhattan sidewalk, I knew the truth and uttered to myself, "Goodbye, Caren."

This is the point I've always made with my *It's Strictly Personal* books—that movies have the power to inspire our personal lives. They may not be great movies or popular movies, but if they manage to touch a nerve within us, then they work. Thank you, *Gillian*, for touching that nerve within *me*.

The English Patient
Directed by Anthony Minghella
(November 15, 1996, U.S. Release Date)

Did you ever watch *Seinfeld*? If you did, then you know the show sometimes poked fun at a particular movie. In a season 8 episode called *The English Patient*, Elaine and her date go to see the 1996 movie, which she truly dislikes, thus alienating her from everyone she knows. I bring this up because it's uncanny how silly the human brain is, because despite everything that's intelligent and intellectual about *The English Patient*, the first place my mind goes to is that *Seinfeld* episode (just goes to show you how screwed up even the best of us are sometimes).

By this time in '96, Daniela and I had reached an interesting status in our relationship. We weren't a couple anymore, and we weren't sleeping with each other anymore. What we were, in fact, were *friends* who said at the breakup that we'd remain friends, and actually meant it—friends who were very comfortable with each other, and enjoyed time spent together. I was also one of the few people Daniela knew who lived alone in Manhattan, so it was easy for her to visit me and take advantage of all the city had to offer, including the chance to see quality films on large screens, especially during the fall movie season, when the Oscar buzz for certain films were everywhere. *The English Patient* was one of those films we knew we *had* to see together.

From the moment the film opened over the sprawling sands of the desert, I knew I'd love it because it took me back to the glory days of David Lean and *Lawrence of Arabia*. Set in the latter days of

World War II Italy, a French-Canadian nurse named Hana (played by Juliette Binoche) had recently suffered the loss of two people she loved killed in the war. Exhausted, she got permission from her medical unit to move into a bombed-out monastery to care for her dying, critically burned patient who'd been shot down in his plane—a man who spoke English, but couldn't remember his own name (played by Ralph Fiennes), though he was revealed to be real-life Hungarian aristocrat László Almásy. Almásy had nothing connected to his past except a book filled with notes, pictures and mementos, and his own story to tell his nurse—a story that took us back to the late 1930s when he was exploring and mapping the Sahara Desert near the Egyptian-Libyan border with a group of friends, including British couple Geoffrey and Katherine Clifton, who owned their own plane for aerial surveys. Katherine was a beautiful woman with the spirit to enjoy life and those she shared it with, and it wasn't long before Almásy inevitably fell in love with her. Ironic, because when they first met, he was repelled by her presence and seemingly wanted nothing to with her. Was it because she was married, or because he was incapable of love? We weren't sure yet, though we suspected that ultimately love, erotic passion and personal sacrifice couldn't be denied.

Meanwhile, back in the present time at the monastery, Almásy and Hana were joined by a Sikh in the British Army named Kip whose job it was to clear the mines and unexploded bombs periodically discovered buried in the sands (and one buried inside the old piano Hana played), as well as Canadian Intelligence operator David Caravaggio (played by Willem Dafoe) who had no thumbs as a result of his torture during a German interrogation. He questioned the patient, seeking revenge because he believed him to be one of those responsible for his torture and missing thumbs. The stories continued, and the secrets of the patient's past were revealed through flashbacks in which Almásy and Katherine's extra-marital affair heated up with burning passion. Months later, she ended the affair from fear her husband would discover their secret. Their ongoing archaeological projects were also halted because of the pending threat of war.

Returning to the past for its conclusion, Almásy was packing up his base camp when Geoffrey crashed his plane in an attempted murder-suicide. Katherine was with him. He was killed instantly, while she was seriously injured. Almásy carried her to the Cave of Swimmers, realizing she'd likely die, though he promised that he'd go for help and return to her. After a three-day walk across the desert, he arrived at a British base camp and attempted to explain his desperate situation, but upon revealing his name, was detained on suspicion of being a German spy, and put aboard a transport train. He escaped, secured a plane, and returned to Katherine's cave, where she was already dead. He carried her body from the cave to his plane and took off, but was eventually shot down by the Germans, the flames of his plane causing his serious burns, and thus bringing the story full circle to the desert of the beginning.

As the credits rolled, I recalled my opening comparisons to *Lawrence of Arabia* and asked Daniela is she'd ever seen the film. I cannot recall if she had, but I immediately went into my feelings of homage I thought the director had paid to David Lean's classic. The late Anthony Minghella partially shot his film on location in the deserts of Tunisia, and the exterior cinematography couldn't be ignored in its comparison to *Lawrence*. That was a bold opinion, and I don't suppose there will ever be another film in the same league as that one, but it was still impossible that under Minghella's direction, a very worthy homage was (and still is) certainly credible.

Although we both loved *The English Patient*'s moving and powerful complexity of two perfectly matched English actors as Ralph Fiennes and Kristin Scott Thomas, Daniela didn't talk about it much afterwards. What little was discussed took place as we walked back to my apartment from the theater. I'd gone quiet myself because my mind and memory fixated on one particular line said by Katherine when Almásy carried her injured body to the cave, in which she told him, *"I've always loved you."* I'd gone quiet because those four words were depressing for me to hear. Even though Caren was out of my life for nearly three years, they were words I'd longed to hear her say to me, but she never did. This was a thought I didn't share with Daniela because I suspected she still had some buried resentments toward me for carrying a torch for another girl when we were dating back in college.

Once again, I was confronted about what the movies told me about love. Traditional screen love stories may dictate that its two star-crossed lovers end up together and live happily ever after. But *The English Patient*, like so many other love stories, doesn't obey that tradition, which is one of the things I love about it. I mean, how many times can you keep watching the same old Hollywood outcomes of love before it gets old? After all, Clark Gable didn't get Vivian Leigh at the end of *Gone with the Wind*, Humphrey Bogart didn't get Ingrid Bergman at the end of *Casablanca*, Omar Sharif didn't get Julie Christie at the end of *Doctor Zhivago*, Leonardo DiCaprio didn't get Kate Winslet at the end of *Titanic*…and Eric didn't get Caren at the end of their movie.

Jerry Maguire

Directed by Cameron Crowe
(December 13, 1996, U.S. Release Date)

Do you know what Jewish people do on Christmas Day? Let me put it this way—according to the Old Testament (and Charlton Heston), there are Ten Commandments for those of the Jewish faith to follow as law. There *should* be eleven, and the Eleventh Commandment shall decree, *"Thou shalt go to the movies and then to a Chinese restaurant on every twenty-fifth day of December."* You think I'm kidding? This is what Jews *do* every Christmas Day, and it's practically law. So leave it to me to be the one to break that law, because in my youth, I'd spend that day on the ski slopes. But when you go to the movies on Christmas Day, you can count on extra aggravation because of the increased volume of high-demanding, bitchy people. These conditions are guaranteed to bring out the intolerance in anyone who has a low threshold for such matters…namely *me*. What's my point? My point is that *Jerry Maguire* was and still is one of the few times I've gone to the movies on Christmas Day. Today, my family traditionally goes *bowling* instead, followed of course, by dinner at a Chines restaurant.

I've previously mentioned that with some exceptions like *Cocktail*, *Far and Away*, and *Rock of Ages*, I've always had a weakness for Tom Cruise's movies, many of them being guilty pleasures. By the end of 1996, Cruise was still riding high and hot from *Mission: Impossible* the previous summer. His new film directed by Cameron Crowe already promised to be a contender for the Oscars that year.

Perhaps this was true, but would it be worth my time, effort and patience to go see it with my dad on Christmas Day at a crowded multiplex in Queens? I'd soon find out.

I sat down to watch *Jerry Maguire* with a sense of ignorance, because with the exception of a New York Yankees baseball game once in a while, I don't follow sports, which means I know nothing about the profession of the sports agent. I suppose they're like any other agents who handle artists and performers of a celebrity stature, but this film would show me just how cutthroat the business was. Jerry Maguire (Cruise) was a glossy, sharp, snappy, fast-talking, wise-cracking bullshit artist, and seemingly perfect for his job as a sports agent. As a sample of his character's dialogue, the moment I heard him say, *"I will not rest until I have you holding a Coke, wearing your own shoe, playing a Sega game FEATURING YOU, while singing your own song in a new commercial, STARRING YOU, broadcast during the Super Bowl, in a game that you are winning, and I will not SLEEP until that happens!"* I knew it was surely *Tom Cruise* I was listening to, and that the role was meant just for him.

Jerry was great at his job. He was loved by all who knew him and was engaged to a beautiful woman named Avery (played by the late Kelly Preston), who was tough, insensitive, and even demanded of Jerry, *"Never stop fucking me!"* (who wouldn't want to spend the rest of their life with a woman like *that*?). His life seemed good and in its proper place until he experienced an attack of life-altering consciousness and spent the entire night drafting and printing a "mission statement" directed to the entire staff of his firm, in which he acknowledged the dishonesty of the sports management business and his desire that he and his colleagues work with fewer clients and for less money to produce a better and more personal relationships with them. It sounded perfect on paper, but even as it circulated amongst his peers, Jerry senses he'd just made the biggest mistake of his life. He was right. His mission statement cost him his job, nearly all his clients, his self-respect and his upward mobility. In the end, he was left with *one* client—Arizona Cardinals wide receiver Rod Tidwell (played by Cuba Gooding Jr.) who was disgruntled with his contract, his endorsements, the money he wasn't seeing, and was probably the most obnoxious character to ever grace the screen. Through a very long conversation that cost Jerry his other clients on hold, Rod tested Jerry's resolve convincing him that life was built around four simple words, *"Show me the money."* Leaving his office in disgrace, Jerry announced that he'd start his own agency, inviting anyone to join him. Twenty-six-year-old single mother Dorothy Boyd (played by Renée Zellweger) agreed, having been inspired by his mission statement.

Meanwhile, superstar quarterback Frank "Cush" Cushman was expected to be the number one pick at the next NFL draft and initially wanted to stay with Jerry. However, Jerry's former protégé, the one who fired him, persuaded Cush and his father to sign with him instead of Jerry the night before the draft, the father implying the racist reason that Jerry was *"in the lobby with the black fella."* This new and devastating loss prompted Jerry to break off his engagement to a very disgruntled Avery. Despite the break up meant to be a loss, I was happy to see Jerry break it off with a woman who was so full of herself and the fact that no one had ever dumped her before (someone dumped you *now*, bitch!).

Following his break up, Jerry got closer to and developed a relationship with Dorothy and her little boy Ray. Contemplating a secure new job opportunity in San Diego since Jerry could no longer afford her, Jerry proposed they get married instead. Bad decision on Jerry's part, as seen in their wedding video in which he looked like he dreaded what would happen next. He concentrated all his efforts on Rod, though Rod often accused Jerry of not trying hard enough to get him a worthy contract for big money, and in return, Jerry accusing Rod of being unlikeable, and aloof to his fans and his teammates.

During a big game on Monday Night Football, Rod played well but was injured when he caught a winning touchdown, securing his team for a spot in the playoffs. Rod didn't move, the stadium was halted to a silence, and Rod's family was back home watching the horror play out on TV. Then in what seemed like an impossible miracle, Rod recovered, stood up and cheerfully danced for the wild and cheering crowd, thus winning the fame and respect he'd constantly bitched about. During their televised embrace, it seemed that Jerry and Rod proved their once strictly business relationship was now a close, personal friendship, thus justifying not only Jerry's original mission statement, but also the fine art of cliché in the movies in which a guy like Rod Tidwell gets the $11.2 million contract he wanted (maybe he'd finally shut up now), and a guy like Jerry Maguire realizes the value of true love in a cynical world. Cliché or not, I suppose it's still perfect, nonetheless, and what we all want and expect when we watch a movie like this. Why else would we all fall in love with a line like, *"You had me at hello"*?

In the end, *Jerry Maguire* was a great movie that effectively mixed sports with drama and romance, and probably Tom Cruise's best performance since *Born on the Fourth of July*. And how can I not give actor Jerry O'Connell proper credit for transforming himself from a pudgy, little twerp in *Stand by Me* to a well-built, handsome man who'd eventually have sex with Rebecca Romijn (how *do* these things happen?). Was it worth my spending Christmas Day in an overly crowded movie theater? Probably not. Did Cuba Gooding Jr. really deserve the Oscar for Best Supporting Actor for playing an obnoxious parasite? Probably not. But even as the film gave all these heartwarming feelings to its audience, I couldn't help but feel a sense of anger (even disgust) after I first saw it.

Let me explain—Jerry Maguire is an *ass*. When he loses everything, his immediate mission is to get it all back, or as much of it as possible, and in the process learn something new about himself and his career. But even during that process of passion and determination, Jerry still doesn't cease to be an ass, especially when he contemplates his relationship and marriage to Dorothy Boyd as a simple solution to avoid being alone, despite his inner desire to continue to run scared shitless because of his intimacy issues. When I watched all this for the first time, I was a much younger man still at the start of his own career, and watching a man like Jerry and the entire bloodthirsty nature of his business filled me with anger toward the world and how it operates in not just business, but in life and friendship. How does one realistically make friends in the business world when they may one day be the very ones who fire you from your job? Was this shit going to happen to *me* as my age and career progressed in life? Perhaps these old fears are the reason why even today I make it a rule to never become close friends with anyone I work with. I've found out the hard way that such friendships can end abruptly if the job itself ends. Better to try and be friends *after* you're not working together anymore.

Here's something else I need to get off my chest—am I the only one watching Rod Tidwell's miraculous recovery on the football field who thinks the entire event is all bullshit? Rod is a man who's made it his mission to brazenly shoot off his mouth in ongoing attempts to get what he wants. Does it seem unrealistic that he'd go so far as to fake an injury in front of thousands of screaming fans to triumph on TV and finally score what he feels he has coming to him? I mean, he just doesn't recover…he jumps, dances, spins, climbs the stands, and basically goes completely over-the-top. How convenient it all is, and yet, I've never once heard anyone else who's seen this film share the same opinion I have. Either everyone else is blind, or maybe I'm just a little smarter than everyone else?

Finally, fictional or not, I don't approve of any man who'd switch the car radio station during the Rolling Stones song "*Bitch*" in lieu of Tom Petty's "*Free Fallin*" just because he doesn't know how to sing along with the lyrics. What were you thinking, Tom? You don't *ever* turn off the Stones!

Hamlet

Directed by Kenneth Branagh
(December 25, 1996, U.S. Release Date)

Do you know what a roadshow theatrical release is…or should I say *was*? In the motion picture industry, it was the practice of releasing a film, usually a two hour-plus epic, in a limited number of theaters in major cities for a period of time before its wide release. Beginning as early as 1915 with D. W. Griffith's *The Birth of a Nation* and continuing through the decades with milestone releases like *Gone with the Wind*, *Ben-Hur*, *Spartacus*, *Lawrence of Arabia*, *The Longest Day*, *The Sound of Music*, *Doctor Zhivago*, and *2001: A Space Odyssey*, roadshow engagements were marketed as major events similar to live theater productions with higher-priced tickets sold on a reserved seating basis, and often featured an intermission between the two "acts" of the film, as well as sales of souvenir programs. In my entire moviegoing life, I experienced such an event only twice. The first time was Richard Attenborough's *Gandhi* in 1982 at the single screen Zeigfeld Theatre in Manhattan (it closed in 2016). The second was Kenneth Branagh's four-hour version of *Hamlet* in 1996 at the single screen Paris Theater, also in Manhattan (leased and operated by Netflix today).

Daniela and I already had a history together with the big screen's version of *Hamlet* beginning with Mel Gibson's portrayal back in 1990, so it seemed logical for the two of us to continue the tradition with Brannagh's new version. We also counted on each other as necessary movie companions for the Oscar-worthy contenders of the fall season that also included *The English Patient* and *Shine*. This would require some effort, though—not only for Daniela to trek from the state of Connecticut to Manhattan, but also for me to plan accordingly for tickets, as there weren't a lot of showings per day because of the film's four-hour running time. As it turned out, this was the only time I ever used Moviefone to purchase tickets, and back in '96 before the internet, it was limited to interactive telephone services. Still, our tickets would be waiting for us at the box office, and we'd be guaranteed a seat inside one of the few remaining genuine movie houses left in Manhattan.

As I wrote in *It's Still Strictly Personal*, of all the required Shakespeare readings I had in high school, *Hamlet* was the only book of ol' Billy's titles I had any real interest in. At the heart of this tragedy was a tense-filled tale of a young man plotting his revenge against the uncle who murdered his beloved father, and the kind of content many modern thrillers and action stories were made of (I even referenced actress Joan Plowright's summary of *Hamlet* in the 1993 Schwarzenegger film *Last Action Hero*). By this time, the '90s saw much of Shakespeare on film with previous releases like *Richard III*, *Othello*, and *Romeo and Juliet*, bringing its tales to a more modern age than the original text. Such updated screen versions were not only a bold and original move, in my opinion, but they also brought the world of Shakespeare to a more comprehensible level of understanding to its audience.

At four hours, Branagh's film version surprised me by following the complete text of the play's original plot. My recollection of the book was that of a simple pocket-size paperback, and hardly something I imagined took up four hours of screen time. It seemed my previous *Hamlet* experiences with both Mel Gibson and Laurence Olivier left me short-changed (who knew?). From the moment Branagh's film began with a recognizable actor like Jack Lemmon as Marcellus, it was obvious this new version was not only the most ambitious Shakespearean undertaking I'd seen on film, but it also continued the modern trend of the previously released films of the '90s, with this version taking place at the close of the nineteenth century. The stars were aplenty with outstanding performances—Branagh himself as Hamlet, Julie Christie, Derek Jacobi, Kate Winslet, Charlton Heston, Robin Williams, Billy Crystal, and more. This had to be the largest notable cast I'd seen in a movie since *The Longest Day* in 1962 and *The Towering Inferno* in 1974.

Besides employing the full text, Branagh's *Hamlet* was also a sprawling and breathtaking visual experience, using very long single takes for numerous scenes. It also used flashbacks to depict moments that were either only described in the play's print, such as Hamlet's childhood friendship with poor Yorick, or scenes implied by the play's dialogue, such as Hamlet's sexual relationship with Ophelia (I couldn't argue with a film version giving me a glimpse of Kate Winslet's naked body in bed). There were also colorful special effects, particularly during the visit by the ghost of Hamlet's deceased father. The famous "to be or not to be" soliloquy was a bold and interesting staging in that it placed Branagh in front of a wall of mirrors, King Claudius and Polonius unbeknownst watching him through a two-way mirror to observe his apparent lunacy. Like Gibson before him, Branagh was an experienced actor who knew just how to portray Hamlet as a man driven by very ugly emotions and actions, including fear, rage, jealousy and his profound desire to commit murder in the name of revenge set against a world of royal politics.

I recall feeling entranced and sucked into every word spoken throughout this lengthy tale. Every once in a while, I'd take Daniela's hand and give it a gently squeeze. Not out of romantic affection, but because in my own way, I was telling her how much I enjoyed the film's experience, and at the end of the evening, Branagh's version of *Hamlet* was a complete one. There's was little I could feel about the Prince of Denmark that I hadn't felt already. What I walked away with, though, was the decision that this was definitely my favorite screen version, despite its very long running time. In fact, perhaps it was *because* of its very long running time that I could make that claim because the drama of it was so intense and gripping, thus its running time seemingly irrelevant. This also was (and still remains) as close as I'd come to experiencing the feeling of those theatrical roadshow engagements that made up so much of cinematic history in decade's past. Oh, what it must have felt like back then to enter such a grand movie palace in preparation for what would be a long night of stars and spectacle—not too unlike a special evening at the theater, I imagine.

For myself and Daniela, our so-called evening at the theater felt as complete as Kenneth Branagh's complete version of *Hamlet*, and one I'm happy to have as part of my precious movie memories. However, our complete version also included snacks and a bottle of wine we managed to smuggle into the Paris Theater that night. In short, it was the best platonic date I ever had.

And so, good night, sweet Prince.

*****

This is the last film of 1996 I shall discuss in any great detail.

You'll recall I said that I almost never make New Year's resolutions. In '96, I made only one, and that was to reopen the family beach house, and finally go home again. When I finally made that happen, it was like being born again the night I stepped into my home for the first time in years and turned on the light. Life finally returned to this symbol of my strength, my soul, and my very existence. I grilled again, I walked across the street to the beach again, and I returned to my own home again after going to the movies in town. I was back, and I hadn't felt so good about myself and my life in many years.

That feeling was short-lived because it was about a month and a half after I'd reopened that I arrived to the house late one Friday night to find something inconceivable waiting for me taped to my front door. It was a notice of a legal seizure against the house and those who resided in it. Something was definitely wrong. This *had* to be a mistake. I knew nothing of any irregularities or illegalities against the house or its property. When I immediately called my mother to inform her of this, she claimed as much ignorance as I felt. The best thing I could think of doing at that time was to simply ignore it and get on with my life there.

That hasty decision was also short-lived, because within a week, I learned what had happened. Turns out that during the years the house was closed and inhabitable because of storms and beach erosion, my mother failed to pay her required property taxes. Although she continued to claim ignorance to her actions (or lack thereof), I suspected she'd made the conscious decision to not pay the taxes because of her inability to occupy her own house. Whatever the cause and reason was, the end result was unthinkable. I was ordered not to occupy my home as long as it was seized by the town government. To do so would risk arrest and jail time. The anger and helplessness I felt was beyond imagine. Not only because my family could lose our home, but because its seizure was the result of my mother's negligence, and there wasn't a damn thing I could do about it. My mother hired a lawyer, and I spent the next year of my life making endless phone calls to get on the good side of every legal and elected official in the Hamptons to ensure the return of my family's home to the Friedmann name.

This was a bad time, and it's how I spent the latter half of '96. But because even dark clouds as these potentially had a silver lining, there was a new relationship I had in my life that began during the Thanksgiving holiday, and made the darkness a little lighter. Not a new girlfriend, but rather a new member of an extended family—the eldest daughter of my mom's soon-to-be new husband. Her name is *Michelle M.*, and she's my stepsister. We met briefly back in the summer and got to know each other only a little. In the months since that first meeting, we spoke on the phone often and became very close. The upcoming November holiday weekend would be the first time I'd see her since, as I planned to fly to Los Angeles to have turkey with my mom and Kevin, who both now resided there full-time.

Michelle and I spent a great deal of time together, which included the traditional California tourist attractions like Disneyland and SeaWorld. We also went to the movies, and it was the first and only time I visited the famed El Capitan Theatre movie palace on Hollywood Boulevard in Hollywood. This theater was (and still is) owned by the Walt Disney Company and serves as a venue for the majority of many Disney Studios' film premieres. It was because of this grand theatrical experience that made the 1996 live action film of *101 Dalmatians* with Glenn Close a joyous experience, and one that reminded me of how glorious these classic movie houses once were and still could be. This wasn't a particularly great movie, but it was one of the high moments of that year not only because of the venue I attended, but also the company I kept with someone I was happy to call a very special friend, as well as a stepsister.

And that, my friends, was the year 1996 for me.

THE YEAR WAS 1997...

- In San Diego, thirty-nine members of the UFO religious cult known as *Heaven's Gate*, led by Marshall Applewhite, commit mass suicide.
- In the United Kingdom's general election, Tony Blair becomes prime minister in a landslide majority.
- Timothy McVeigh is sentenced to death for his part in the 1995 Oklahoma City bombing.
- J. K. Rowling's first *Harry Potter* novel is published in London.
- Princess Diana of Wales is killed after a car crash in the Pont de l'Alma tunnel in Paris after being chased by the paparazzi. Her funeral is watched by two billion people worldwide.
- Sixty-two people are killed by Islamic terrorists outside the Temple of Hatshepsut in Luxor, Egypt.

...AND THERE WERE MOVIES!

I'll say this once again—time has a strange way of repeating itself in landmark periods. The year 1980 was the worst year of my childhood because of events surrounding my parent's marriage and my own personal issues. Ten years later, 1990 was the worst year of my youth because of events surrounding my education, my employment prospects and the fact that I was in love with a girl who didn't return that love. This theory of time, fortunately, works the other way too. The year 1977 was a great year of my childhood because of new experiences of home not only at North Shore Towers, but in our first summer in the Hamptons. Ten years later, 1987 was the best year of my youth because of events surrounding school, summer internships and the fact that I finally lost my virginity. Ten years after *that*, 1997 proved to be one of the best years of my adulthood because of events of uncertainty that finally worked themselves out.

Nothing last forever—nothing good and nothing bad. The year 1996 was very trying because of legal issues surrounding the beach house. That finally ended when all debts were paid, all legal issues were settled, and the police padlock was finally removed in July 1997, and I returned to the one and only home I knew and loved. I remember feeling a tremendous sense of pride as I took my place once again inside the walls of where I grew up. It wasn't just the victory of claiming what rightfully belonged to my family, but also the satisfaction I felt in showing my neighbors that the Friedmann family had *not* been the victims of a shameful property seizure, which I'm sure was the subject of much gossip. I still remember standing on my front deck looking out over Dune Road in front of me and thinking to myself, "Fuck all of you if you thought we were beaten!"

This was just the beginning of new and wonderful things to come. During that summer, I was let go from my architect's job of more than two years, but that was good because I found a better job in Manhattan almost immediately, where I spent many years and even met the woman who'd someday become my wife. During my spare time, I'd developed a new and passionate hobby for black-and-white photography, and my subject was what remained of the single-screen movie houses in Manhattan (many of these theaters are long since gone), not only as architecture, but of a moviegoing experience that was sadly replaced by the impersonal environment of multiplex theaters. As I already briefly mentioned, I settled the bad blood between me and Caren, and rekindled our close friendship again for a brief period before she moved to Las Vegas to join her husband. I also had a close relationship with my stepsister Michelle, which I looked forward to continuing every time I visited my family in California. But like I said, nothing lasts forever, particularly not the good. But I'll get to that later. For right now, there was much for me to rejoice about, and surrounding it all was the continued pleasure of going to the movies.

During the first three months of '97, new movies meant nothing. The only thing on my mind was the big rerelease of the original *Star Wars* trilogy in its new special edition format. While it was great to see these giant sci-fi epics on the big screen again, little did we all know what a butcher job of editing and newly added computer-generated effects and dialogue it would all turn out to be. To this day, George Lucas may never be forgiven for altering the confrontation between Han Solo and Greedo, in which Greedo infamously shoots first. Personally though, I give Lucas a few extra stock points for slightly improving an inferior film like *Return of the Jedi* be getting rid of the entire *"Yub-yub"* musical number during the final Ewok celebration.

Still, when this twenty-year celebration was over, the upcoming summer blockbuster season promised much, including a return to the world of *Jurassic Park*, men dressed in black fighting aliens on Earth, and Harrison Ford playing the president of the United States. Though right now, there were only two big screen issues on my mind. The first was the anticipation of seeing famous radio shock jock Howard Stern star in a movie of his own life. The second was an answer to a question that had personally nagged at me for the past five years, and that was what the hell ever happened to director David Lynch?

Lost Highway

Directed by David Lynch
(February 21, 1997, U.S. Release Date)

I'd been patient for five long years since *Twin Peaks: Fire Walk with Me*, which bombed with critics, but scored with me and other fans of David Lynch's work. Creepy, freaky, spooky, surreal, hypnotic, psychological, incoherent, lurid, sick…choose any of these adjectives, and you'd understand the mind of a filmmaker and artist like Lynch. True fans as myself consider just about anything the man does a work of genius, even the stuff that doesn't sit well with the modern audience and critics (what the hell do *they* know anyway?).

You recall when I mentioned my black-and-white photography of Manhattan movie theaters? This new hobby managed to perfectly coincide with my desire to see Lynch's new film *Lost Highway*. There was no doubt I'd see it as soon as it opened, but during one of my outings of picture taking, I stumbled across the 34th Street East Theater, one I'd never been to before, nor did I even know existed (Manhattan is a big island, and one can't know of *everything*). This was once an arthouse theater owned by the Cineplex Odeon Corporation in an isolated part of the east side of the city. I shot the building and theater marquee from every angle, and when I was finished, I put my camera away and purchased my ticket to *Lost Highway*. I didn't know what to expect, except that I probably wouldn't understand it the first time, and that I'd also love the fact that Lynch would continue to challenge my intellect and my imagination.

Bill Pullman (still fresh in my mind as the President of the United States in *Independence Day*) played Fred Madison, a saxophonist married to Renee (played by Patricia Arquette) and living in Los Angeles. The mystery began one morning when he responded to the outdoor intercom and heard a strange voice say, *"Dick Laurent is dead."* What that meant, and who Dick was, we didn't know yet. Then the couple found a VHS tape on their front porch containing footage of the outside of their house. After they had sex, Fred described a strange dream to her, and then for a moment, saw her face as a pale, old mystery man. Days passed and another VHS tape arrived with overhead footage of the two of them asleep in their bed. Panicked, they called the police, but the two detectives offered little assistance or comfort.

At a party thrown by Renee's friend Andy, Fred encountered the "mystery man" from his dream who told him, *"We've met before, haven't we."* Fred knew nothing of this man, but the man claimed he was at Fred's house at that very moment they were talking, and even answered the phone when Fred called him. According to Andy, the man was a friend of Dick Laurent's. But who was Dick Laurent, and was he really dead? Terrified, he and Renee fled the party and arrived home to suspect there was, in fact, someone inside, or at least the illusion of someone.

The next morning, another VHS tape arrived which Fred watched alone. To his horror, the footage contained him hovering over Renee's dismembered body, covered in her blood. Immediately, the scene switched to the police station, where he was interrogated and beaten by the very same detectives who'd previously visited him and Renee. They accused him of killing his wife, though he had no knowledge or memory of doing so. Nonetheless, he was sentenced to death for her murder. While on death row, Fred was tormented by painful headaches, visions of the mystery man and a burning desert cabin. While experiencing excruciating head pain, he experienced some sort of metamorphosis. Then the picture blurred. What the hell had just happened?

The next morning during a cell check, the prison guard discovered to his horror the man sitting inside the cell was *not* Fred

Madison, but rather a young auto mechanic named Pete Dayton. Although the story didn't directly reveal it, it seemed that Fred had transformed into Pete during a moment of very painful stress and torment, and that this was a "Lynchian" tale of two lives behind the same being, each identity having no idea of the other's existence. Pete, now released into the care of his biker parents, was followed by two detectives trying to learn more about him. Returning to work at the garage, Pete met with his gangster friend Mr. Eddy (played by Robert Loggia) to repair a problem with his car. During their drive together, Pete watched an enraged Mr. Eddy beat a tailgater nearly to death. At their next meeting, Mr. Eddy arrived with his beautiful mistress, Alice Wakefield, who looked exactly like Renee Madison, except for her blonde hair.

She and Pete began a lustful affair, but she feared that Mr. Eddy suspected them. To try and escape him, she devised a plan where she and Pete would rob her friend Andy (the *same* Andy) and leave town. She also revealed that Mr. Eddy was actually an amateur pornography producer named Dick Laurent whom she met while seeking out a job. That night, Pete got a phone call from Mr. Eddy and the mystery man, which scared him so much that he chose to go along with Alice's plan. He attacked Andy and accidentally caused his death when Andy's head went flying into the corner of a glass coffee table. I realized then that despite having seen my fair share of slasher movies, this was perhaps the most gruesome way I'd ever seen anyone die. The pool of blood on the floor was beyond description. There was also a framed picture on Andy's table of Alice and Renee together. When the police found the same picture later at the scene of Andy's death, Alice was inexplicably missing from the picture.

Pete and Alice arrived later to an empty cabin in the desert. While waiting for their contact to arrive, they had sex on the sand outside, which ended with Alice telling Pete, *"You'll never have me."* and then standing up naked (Patricia Arquette had an amazing body), leaving Pete outside confused and distraught, while she disappeared into the cabin. When Pete stood up naked, he'd transformed back to Fred Madison. The mystery man reappeared and videotaped a panicked Fred leaving the desert cabin in his car. Driving down the dark highway, Fred arrived at the Lost Highway hotel and discovered his wife Renee having sex with Mr. Eddy. After Renee left, Fred grabbed Mr. Eddy, shoved him into the trunk of his car, and then later slit his throat when a knife was mysteriously placed into his hand by the mystery man, who then shot Mr. Eddy to death. When Fred drove back to his own house, he pushed the button on the outdoor inter-com and said, *"Dick Laurent is dead,"* before jumping back into his car to outrun the police chasing him. The chase went into the night, with Fred helplessly screaming as his car sped down the dark, lost highway.

When I left the theater, the streets of Manhattan were dark, and there were only two things on my mind. The first was that I was glad I'd stumbled upon this isolated single screen movie theater to see David Lynch's latest cinematic vision. Something about watching *Lost Highway* in this theater made it more like an art film experience instead of just another day at the movies. The second was that I knew I had to see this again as soon as possible to further understand any holes in the story I didn't quite get the first time. I did, but it was at a multiplex theater after watching the rerelease of Wolfgang Peterson's extended director's cut of his 1981 World War II film *Das Boot*. Like *Fire Walk with Me*, *Lost Highway* didn't score well with audiences and critics upon its release, and for the life of me, I can't figure out why. Was it too hard to follow? To that I say, screw you, man up and see it two or three times if you need extra time to understand the artist's screen vision and to enrich the experience of it.

Despite being a fan of David Lynch ever since *Blue Velvet* in 1986, I realize even today that to truly understand the man's art form, it's important to know that there are always questions, and the answers aren't always clear. *Lost Highway* is a psychological thriller with elements of neo-noir, but it's important to keep an open mind on how it translates on screen. Lynch never officially made a horror film before, but there are too many creepy and spooky moments in the film to not recognize it as one of the most haunting and fright-ening piece of work I've ever seen. Like so much of Lynch's work, there's never a completely cohesive structure, and we're taken through a world that seems dream-like and contains the possibility of two alternate realities, and two worlds that come together in incomprehensible conflict. Who is Fred Madison really, and does he actually transform into a completely different man as Pete Dayton when he's under extreme and painful duress? Who is Renee really, and does she actually exist as the hot, young piece-of-ass-blonde-lover of Pete and the hot-tempered Mr. Eddy? Is Mr. Eddy really the man known as Dick Laurent? And finally, who is the very freaky "mystery man" in black portrayed by actor Robert Blake? Many questions, but never any clear answers.

The film's biparty structure also exploits the opposition of two different horrors in two worlds. There's the phantasm horror of the nightmare noir universe of perverse sex, betrayal, obsession, trauma, and murder, as well as despair of our ordinary, drab, and alienated daily life of sexual impotence and distrust of one's partner in life and marriage. It's difficult to comprehend when you watch it for the first time, but knowing full well you're about to experience the mind of David Lynch, would you expect anything different? It happens this way in *Lost Highway*, and it happened again in his films that followed, *Mulholland Dr.* and *Inland Empire*. Critics and impatient moviegoers should probably be *forced* to sit through it and watch it again so they don't walk away with the wrong and premature reaction of unfortunate negativity.

Upon the release of *Lost Highway*, the late Gene Siskel and Roger Ebert both gave the film "two thumbs down," and Lynch used this to his advantage by claiming it was "two good reasons to go and see Lost Highway," thus printing the thumbs down in newspaper ads. I don't know if it worked, but who cares. We choose to love certain films for our own reasons, and if others can't agree with or understand them, then to hell with them. Their misunderstanding perhaps gives our own reasons a stronger meaning and purpose.

Private Parts

Directed by Betty Thomas
(March 7, 1997, U.S. Release Date)

I grew up on Long Island. I went to school in Brooklyn. I lived in Manhattan. I love classic rock. All of this put together has in common the fact that for nearly twenty years (beginning in the mid-'80s), my radio time was directed at one New York City radio station called 92.3 FM K-Rock, with classic rock all day and American radio personality *Howard Stern* all morning. This station's format is long-since gone, and Howard himself has since moved to Sirius XM Satellite Radio, but there was a time when this station ruled the New York FM airwaves. Ironically, I only first discovered *The Howard Stern Show* by accident during his afternoon drive show when he first joined K-Rock in 1985. I mistook his on-air shenanigans at first as merely a quick radio plug or commercial. The longer I waited for the talking to end and the classic rock music to begin, the more I realized this man was no fluke, but rather a strong and daily presence on the radio. That was when I had to decide how I felt about him and his comic routines—love him or hate him. I chose love, and I loved him every day I listened to the radio up until the day he left FM and switched to satellite radio in 2006. The love affair ended, because I refuse to *pay* for any form of radio broadcast.

During my long "honeymoon" with Howard, there was the movie *Private Parts* based on his first book. I remember when it was published in 1993. I was working at the local Great Neck bookstore and we couldn't keep enough copies of it in stock. I never read the book, because somewhere in the back of my mind, it seemed illogical to place an actual "life" with the man I listened to on the radio. For me, Howard was an act and an illusion that served as entertainment, and try to humanize him in any way seemed a futile purpose. This didn't mean I wasn't interested in *Private Parts* when it was released in 1997. Howard was funny on the radio, and there was no doubt he'd be funny on film. I was also curious to see what sort of actor he'd be, this being his first (and only) time in the movies.

Despite my love for Howard's outrageous radio routines, I had much to learn about the man himself and his life. But listen to how I sound—I'm speaking as if I'm referring to some significant cultural figure worthy of a substantial biographical epic motion picture. Geez, it's Howard-fucking-Stern! I love the guy, but let's face it—*Private Parts* wasn't exactly telling the story of the triumph of the human spirit, facing life's insurmountable odds and obstacles. No, this was a movie about shock, disgust, filth, a hot chick sucking on very long kielbasa, and even more important, the first live naked girl in the history of radio. Well, all I could say to *that* was turn out the lights and let the fun begin.

The film began with Howard Stern's appearance at the 1992 MTV Music Video Awards as his fictional superhero character *Fartman*. Backstage, Stern was gazed upon as an immature idiot by musical celebrities as Ted Nugent, Dee Snyder. MC Hammer, Slash, and Ozzy Osbourne. On his flight home, Stern sat next to a beautiful woman who was visibly repelled by him. He told her the story of his life, beginning with the verbal abuse he received from his father Ben Stern when he was a child. Ben worked as a radio recording engineer and was influential in Howard's own dreams of being on the radio, despite the fact that he was a quiet, socially-awkward teenager with (according to him) a very small penis. Nonetheless, Howard went on to study communications at Boston University, where he also became a DJ on the college radio station, and subsequently met Alison, the girl who'd become his future wife.

After graduating college, he got his first professional radio DJ job at WRNW in Westchester County. His boss was a jerk who told Howard that he sucked as a DJ, but because he worked hard and was always on time, he was promoted to a management position which included firing one of his fellow DJs, which Howard couldn't stomach. He left that job and he and Alison moved to Hardford, Connecticut where he took a job as a DJ with WCCC. There he befriended radio personality Fred Norris and adopted a more casual and personal attitude on the air, becoming open and upfront without fear of consequence. After he and Fred attended the premiere film of a 'B' movie actress, the three of them ended up in her bathtub. Her sexual behavior toward Howard was his first loyalty test toward Alison. He was loyal, but was stupid enough to hide his wet underwear under the car seat, which Alison eventually found. Believing him to have been unfaithful, Alison left him, and Howard left Hardford for his new DJ job at WWWW in Detroit, Michigan. Alison soon forgave him, and he left *that* job as well when they suddenly decided to switch their musical format from rock to depressing hillbilly country music (I can't blame him).

Howard then joined WWDC in Washington, DC. and met the woman he'd work with for the rest of his career, Robin Quivers. She quickly adapted to his spontaneous riffs on the air and joined his refusals to accept the boss's orders to drop their offensive on-air antics, which included getting a female caller to reach orgasm by straddling her huge stereo speaker. At the point of nearly firing him, the station discovered a huge boost in their ratings because of Howard's show. This enabled Howard to convince them to bring Fred Norris on board. Meanwhile, Alison was pregnant, but lost the pregnancy because of complications. Although the two of them made light of it in private, Howard stepped over Alison's line when he joked about it on the air with his listeners.

Howard then landed his dream job with WNBC-AM 66 New York (and Alison was pregnant again), though higher management was ignorant to Howard's radio show and style when they hired him. Program director Kenny Rushton (dubbed "Pig Vomit" by Howard) vowed to keep him and his radio team in line to the point where Howard would either conform or quit. No such luck. Howard's show continued the way he wanted it, with dirty match games, an actress swallowing a whole kielbasa and a totally naked girl (thank you Jenna

Jameson) giving Howard a massage on the air. By the time his show reached number one in the ratings, the film jumped ahead to 1985 (the year *I* discovered his show) and the man was a national star before a massive crowed of adoring fans. During a rock performance by heavy metal band AC/DC (love them), Alison went into labor and gave birth to the first of their three daughters, who were all there to meet Howard at the airport when the flight, and subsequently Howard's story, ended.

As *Private Parts* is starred by and narrated by Howard Stern himself, one of the first things he tells us is that he's constantly misunderstood. Whether we choose to believe that is up to us and how devoted we are to his stardom. The average listener only knows what they hear on the radio which is (presumably) just an act. The film, however, attempts to actually humanize a man like Stern who made his rise to fame by being offensive, obnoxious and disgusting. Those who still listen to him know this all too well, and frankly, don't give a shit. They…*we* like him that way. This is why we listen to him, or as the film suggests, we want to see what he'll say next. However, director Betty Thomas wants us to see the *real* Howard Stern—the off-the-air loving and loyal husband, the excited-father-to-be, and the loyal friend to those he works with. From his beginnings as a small radio disc jockey, Howard is committed to staying with those he depends on, including Robin, Fred and Gary Dell'Abate, who all play very convincing versions of themselves. We may only laugh at a man who just wants to have fun while doing his job on the radio, but the film's purpose is again, humanization. Should we choose to take the human angle seriously, then it's safe to say that Howard's claim of being misunderstood is right on.

Despite the so-called happy Hollywood ending of a man and his devoted wife and family, Howard Stern in real life was divorced from Alison in 2001 and married Beth Ostrosky in 2008. Does that make the film's happy ending any less valid? Maybe, but who cares. We don't watch a movie like *Private Parts* to satisfy our emotional need for human drama that one might experience when watching a Merchant-Ivory film. We watch it for the more important and entertaining things in life—filth, shock, disgust, naked women, and because diehard fans love Howard Stern.

Chasing Amy
Directed by Kevin Smith
(April 4, 1997, U.S. Release Date)

May 1997 saw another one of my family visits to Los Angeles to see my mother for Mother's Day. I stayed with Kevin at his apartment in West Hollywood just up the street from the former (and famous) Tower Records on the northwest corner of Sunset Boulevard and Horn Avenue. Across the street from that was an independent movie theater amongst a string of cafes and stores. One of the films was Kevin Smith's *Chasing Amy*, which I had enough interest in because I loved his debut film *Clerks*. More than that was the desire to experience the movies in the theaters of Hollywood whenever possible, which (at that time) I'd come to symbolize as the definitive moviegoing experience because of the town's history. First I grabbed a bite at a cafe and struck up a brief conversation with African American actor Glenn Plummer, whom you may recall from films like *Speed*, *Strange Days* and *The Day After Tomorrow* (he's one of less than ten celebrities I've ever met in my life).

I was about to discover a new twist in what might be considered the simplest of love stories. Simple? That may have been impossible in the hands of Kevin Smith, especially if it also involved characters Jay and Silent Bob (how can you *not* love those guys?) This film explored the concept of a romantic relationship between a young heterosexual man and a pretty young lesbian (something different, for sure). Best friends and comic book artists Holden McNeil (played by Ben Affleck, and still a new face to me back then) and Banky

Edwards (played by Jason Lee) met fellow comic book artist Alyssa Jones (played by Joey Lauren Adams) at a comic book convention to promote their book *Bluntman and Chronic*. Holden was immediately smitten with Alyssa, and wasn't prepared for the shock of watching her make out with another girl at a club, thus revealing her sexual orientation.

Regardless, they spent a lot of time together and developed a close friendship. That friendship eventually turned to desperation when Holden finally confessed his love to Alyssa. She was pissed off at first that he'd drop that kind of bomb on her, but nonetheless, they had scx and began a romantic relationship (much to Banky's disapproval) and causing a new tension between himself and Holden. Banky soon uncovered dirt on Alyssa's past in which she participated in a sexual threesome in high school. This upset Holden, who labored under the delusion that he was the only man Alyssa had ever been with, and he shamelessly baited her into confessing her past while they were at a hockey game. She didn't deny the threesome, but refused to apologize for her past sexual experiences. Despite that fact that she still loved Holden, he couldn't live with this new revelation and broke it off with her.

Surprisingly, it was a chance lunch with Jay and Silent Bob that turned things around, when Bob revealed he'd once been in a relationship with a girl named Amy that was similar to Holden's. Despite the fact that he was in love with Amy, he allowed his anger about her sexual past get in the way of their relationship, and it eventually ended. Since his mistake, he'd *"spent every day since then chasing Amy, so to speak."* Touched by his story, Holden decided the best way to fix his relationship with both Alyssa and Banky was for the three of them to have sex together, concluding that Banky was actually in love with him. Banky agreed to participate, but was relieved when Alyssa got offended and refused. She and Banky left Holden alone with his mistakes and regrets.

One year later, the friendship between Holden and Bank was over, as they promoted their solo comic books at the next convention. Banky smiled when he saw Holden, but it was easy to see the sad regret in his face. Holden had an emotional reunion with Alyssa and gave her a copy of his new comic book based on their relationship called Chasing Amy. Teary-eyed and smiling at seeing him again, she referred to him only as *"just some guy I knew"* to her new girlfriend.

You've heard me say before that I'm a sucker for great dialogue in a movie. I'm even more of a sucker when that dialogue is Kevin Smith-style. Sitting there in my Los Angeles movie theater seat, I was struck by some of the funniest and smartly paced dialogue I'd heard since Stanley Kubrick's *Full Metal Jacket* back in 1987. But unlike the dark comedy of life in the Marines, the dialogue of *Chasing Amy* was not only funny, but idiotic and even slapstick. This was some of the most outrageous and sexually charged dialogue I'd heard outside of a porn film, though not at the level of just being mindless or without relation to the story. It's sharp dialogue that not only drives the film's different relationships, but also the raunchy frankness of understanding one's sexuality, gay or straight. Even as Banky contemptuously slams Alyssa's sexual orientation and its impact on his friendship with Holden, he can't help but take advantage of it when it serves his own experiences, particularly when the two of them compare their injuries from going down orally on girls in a hilarious homage to the scar-comparing scene between Robert Shaw and Richard Dreyfuss in *Jaws*.

Still, wisecracking insults and sexual frankness can be wonderful in comedy, especially when it's as politically incorrect as this. Holden may be a conservative stiff to some, but it's Banky's free-floating mouth of raw honesty that's fun to listen to. He's perhaps the most offensive character you're likely to listen to outside of TV's Archie Bunker or radio disc jockey Howard Stern. Regardless, you laugh when you hear him talk, especially when he sketches out the four-way road and the hundred-dollar bill to prove that a male-friendly lesbian is just a figment of Holden's *"fucking imagination,"* alongside Santa Claus and the Easter Bunny, because *laughing* is the whole point behind comedy. And Joey Lauren Adams, while playing her role wonderfully…well, what shall I compare her high-pitched voice to? A sex kitten on helium? Yeah, that's it. Love it or hate it, her voice has the potential to hypnotize our ears, and it does.

Allow me to get a little more serious about this film, and turn back the clock in my mind (and this book) to the film *To Gillian on Her 37th Birthday*. I told you it was that film that inspired me to patch things up with Caren and bring things with her to a necessary closure. That was late '97 into the summer of '98. But when I watched *Chasing Amy* for the first time, it was spring '97, and even though Caren was out of my life for more than three years, it was impossible not to think of her during the film, because Kevin Smith addressed something about love that went far beyond the traditional romantic comedy. The average movie of that genre uses silly, bullshit obstacles to get in the way of what will eventually turn out to be true love. I think Smith was trying to tell me and everyone else that being in love isn't always funny. It's a serious event in our lives that can make us sick and put our entire existence in jeopardy.

The thoughts running through my head were an endless string of confusing questions of what I *might* have, *could* have, and *should* have done. I was over Caren, but it was impossible not to wonder if there was some of *my* own dialogue that would've made a difference in our past relationship. As I listened to Holden McNeil pour his heart out to Alyssa in an endless soliloquy of love and emotion, it occurred to me that such speeches exist only in real life when they become necessary for one to win over the other. Let's face it—if two people fall in love without obstacles, there's no need for heartfelt speeches because the prize of each other's love is already won. But when you have to fight for love and pull out every gun you can think of to make it happen, you know it's going to hurt like hell.

In my case, it was filmmaker Kevin Smith who had me asking myself what my necessary speech was in my own version of "Chasing Amy." Did I ever even have one?

Men in Black

Directed by Barry Sonnenfeld
(July 2, 1997, U.S. Release Date)

Looking back at the summer of 1997, I cannot remember what attracted me to a movie like *Men in Black*. Was it because it was based on a popular comic book? Probably not. Comic books never did much for me. Was it because Will Smith would not only make me laugh, but would continue to prove that he had the stuff of a great action star he'd previously shown in *Bad Boys* and *Independence Day*? That's possible. Was it because I'd simply chosen to take the day off from work on a lovely summer day in New York City and decided to go to the movies in the middle of the work day when the theater would be empty? Most surely. But I think what finally did it for me was that I needed to revisit the innocent fun of watching sci-fi on the screen, something I hadn't had the pleasure of since *Star Trek: First Contact*. Much of the last six months was spent on the serious side of cinema with filmmakers like Anthony Minghella, Scott Hicks and David Lynch. I needed to have fun at the movies again.

Was *Men in Black* to be just another "Earth vs. aliens" story? Not exactly. In this case, the story followed two agents of a secret organization called Men in Black (MIB) who supervised extraterrestrial life forms living on our planet and concealing their existence from ordinary humans. The agency operated from an underground base at the Tri-Borough Bridge and Tunnel Authority ventilation station in Manhattan's Battery Park, and their members often used a device called a neuralyzer on witnesses' memories of alien sightings.

Agent K (played by Tommy Lee Jones) was the serious, by-the-book agent with no sense of humor, and whose job it was to find a brand-new recruit who could also handle the job. Enter New York City police officer-of-the-streets James Edwards (Smith) and soon-to-be Agent J who was cocky, arrogant, and had no respect for authority. In other words, he was *perfect* for the job.

It was during the interview scene between Smith and Jones that I took notice of a particular piece of dialogue. Anyone who knows me well enough in life knows what a cynical son-of-a-bitch I can be. A partial reason for my rather negative outlook on life and people may have come when this dialogue was spoken:

> *"Why the big secret? People are smart. They can handle it."*
>
> *"A person is smart. People are dumb, panicky dangerous animals, and you know it."*

Never in my life did I wholeheartedly agree with such a descriptive narrative. History may be filled with brilliant philosophers of the past, but it took a man like Tommy Lee Jones, in my opinion, to nail the human race right on its head.

Suspicious of why aliens were suddenly leaving Earth, the MIB investigated a farmer named Edgar who'd been acting strangely after an alien craft crashed on his farm. Edgar was killed and his skin was used as a disguise by a very angry "Bug" who was a member of a giant cockroach-like species at war with other alien races in the galaxy, including the Arquillians. From the tiny dying alien inside the giant's body, MIB learned that the galaxy was on Orion's Belt. What this meant, we didn't know yet. But if Earth didn't deliver the galaxy within one hour, the Arquillian battle cruiser hovering over our planet would destroy all human life. Turns out the galaxy was a tiny thing housed inside a necklace charm hanging around the neck of a cat whose name happened to be Orion (get it? Orion's belt). To those of us who knew the five boroughs of New York City, it was interesting to see the observation towers of the New York State Pavilion at Flushing Meadows in Queens (made famous at the 1964

World's Fair) secretly disguised as two flying saucers to be used by the enemy "Bug" to get away with his villainous deed. Since bad aliens almost never got away with it in the end, it was fun to watch to bug destroyed and the MIB win the day, and we as ordinary, stupid citizens of the world were all the better for never knowing what sort of cosmic danger we were really in the entire time.

For myself, I was satisfied in enjoying all of the textbook requirements for an enjoyable summer adventure film on a day off from work. However, an intelligent script, spectacular set pieces and charismatic performances from men like Mr. Smith and Mr. Jones make it something more entirely. Smith's arrogance is only matched by his outrageous sense of humor, and I think it's that humor that made *Men in Black* something more than just another fun sci-fi hit for me (despite its forgettable sequels, including the pale skank that was Lara Flynn Boyle in *MIB II*). What made it personal for me was that in embracing the comic wit and pacing of Will Smith, I realized I'd reached a turning point in my own life when the past of the 1980s, and my enjoyment of a young comic genius like Eddie Murphy in films like *48 Hrs.*, *Trading Places* and *Beverly Hills Cop* was now a symbolic torch that had been handed over to the new generation of the 1990s, and the man who accepted that torch was wisecracking Will Smith. I accepted it, and I loved him for it, even if he was guilty of firing a bullet into poor, little eight-year-old Tiffany's head.

Or does he owe us an apology?

Cop Land

Directed by James Mangold
(August 15, 1997, U.S. Release Date)

From the moment I saw the movie poster for *Cop Land* and its ensemble of Sylvester Stallone, Robert DeNiro, Harvey Keitel and Ray Liotta, I knew it was a movie I couldn't afford to miss. More than that, it brought together specifics in film I'd come to understand and appreciate over the years. Beginning with the police/crime thriller, which I'd been a fan of since I was old enough to watch them, my range of appreciation that included classics like *The French Connection* and *Serpico*, darker material like *Nighthawks, Manhunter,* and *Heat*, and popular franchise blockbusters like *Lethal Weapon* and *Die Hard*, which continued well into the '90s. This was also a time when I discovered the true star power of men like DeNiro, Keitel and Liotta thanks to films like *Goodfellas* and *Thelma & Louise* (while DeNiro was a star in his own right from as far back as the '70s, it took me a while to catch up).

Ultimately, what I think *Cop Land* was really about for me was getting to know Sylvester Stallone all over again. I've said before in my two preceding books that I consider *Rocky IV* the worst film ever made (and I hardly think Stallone's 2021 director's cut will change that opinion). Not just because of the film's content itself, but because it also represents the horrible degradation of a man whom I once considered a very credible actor in films like *Rocky, F.I.S.T.*, and even *First Blood*. However, the buzz on this new police thriller was that it was a true return to form for Stallone's acting abilities, which I'd all but given up on. I mean, how much faith can you have in a man who for years, put out such crap like *Cobra, Over the Top, Demolition Man*, and *Judge Dredd*? Perhaps this new film was the long-awaited remedy that would finally turn my negative feelings around for him.

Cop Land was, of course, about cops. NYPD cops who worked in Manhattan and created a life for themselves and their families just across the George Washington Bridge in the fictional town of Garrison, New Jersey. Many of these cops were bad to the bone, and led by Lt. Ray Donlan (Keitel). Stallone played Freddy Heflin, the quiet sheriff of Garrison, whose only real stretch of law enforcement was pulling over speeders and investigating who was illegally dumping their garbage bags on someone else's property. In other words, he was a simple town sheriff who knew his proper place among corrupt and racist cops, and didn't have the balls to stand his ground on anything (a very *anti*-Stallone character, indeed). Heflin was deaf in one year because as a younger man, he'd jumped into the icy water to save a woman from drowning in her car. That woman today was married to another cop, and Heflin still had a thing for her.

One late night on the George Washington Bridge, Donlan's nephew Murray Babitch (also known as "Superboy") was sideswiped by two black teens. One of them pointed what looked like a firearm at him (it was actually a black steering-wheel lock) just before Superboy's tire blew out. Thinking they'd just fired a gun at him, Superboy shot back and killed the teens in the ensuing chase. When other cops arrived at the scene, things were already in motion to cover up, plant false evidence, and protect Superboy. Worried about the consequences of his fatal mistake and its impact on his career, Donlan persuaded Superboy to fake his own suicide by making it look like he'd jumped off the bridge. Heflin, dumb as he was perceived by the rest of the town, knew that Superboy's suicide was orchestrated, and that the cops were hiding him somewhere.

Meanwhile, Lt. Moe Tilden (DeNiro) was an investigator for Internal Affairs. He approached Heflin earlier for information on the corrupt Garrison cops, but Heflin was too reluctant and intimidated to betray the trust the cops placed on him. After the Superboy incident, however, Heflin visited Tilden to try and cooperate, but it was too late. The Garrison investigation was shut down, and Tilden angrily dismissed Heflin's noble effort. Leaving the IA office, Heflin stole case files on the Garrison cops and, while reading them, discovered the extent of the town's mob-related corruption. Even while Superboy was living as a fugitive in Donlan's home, it became apparent that without a body, the case wouldn't stay cold. Donlan and his partners-in-crime would have to get rid of Superboy. They tried to drown him, but Superboy escaped and went to Heflin's house for help, but ran away when he saw Figgis (Liotta) there.

Figgis was leaving, having collected the insurance money after burning down his own house that inadvertently killed his girlfriend who was there without his knowledge. Heflin found Superboy and was prepared to take him in, even warning Donlan about it in advance as a courtesy to their friendship. It was during this scene when Donlan was making a long-winded speech to Heflin about the difference between men and boys, that I took notice of a particular line when Harvey Keitel said, "*You come to me with a plan to set things right—everyone in the city holding hands singing 'We Are the World'!*" I couldn't help but laugh more than others in the theater because it was the inclusion of this song title that genuinely represented my cynicism toward the world (thanks for that moment, Harvey).

On the morning Heflin and Superboy were prepared to cross the bridge into the city, they were ambushed by Donlan's team and one of them fired his gun next to Heflin's good ear, deafening him, and took Superboy. Almost totally deaf (we heard nothing but high-pitched ringing), he followed them on foot to Donlan's house, where he was suddenly joined by Figgis (like Han Solo suddenly appearing at the end of the Death Star battle in *Star Wars*) in a violent shootout, leaving all the bad guys dead. Heflin and Figgis made it into Manhattan and handed over Superboy to Tilden. The resulting police scandal was investigated and indictments were handed down. Justice was served, and those who lived across the river in New Jersey went back to work and their normal lives.

In its simplest form, *Cop Land* plays like a who's who of cop and mafia films, with some of the most well-known Italian American actors of our generation. Short of adding the great Al Pacino to the mix, it's almost perfect. What we ultimately have here is *Mean Streets* meets *Rocky* meets *Taxi Driver* meets *Goodfellas*, and it's great. But even with all of these Italian greats, I confess that all eyes are on Stallone. His performance builds itself at a steady pace all the way to its stunning payoff when, like Gary Cooper in *High Noon*, he decides to clean up his town in a final shootout for truth and justice. Freddy Heflin is a man who eventually awakes to his own potential, and it's exhilarating to watch not only the character, but Stallone himself revive themselves together in unison. The transformation is more than just physical. He looks spiritually beaten and terribly sad. In other words, he looks like a *real person* delivering his best performance since his work in the 1970s, in my opinion. Its best strength, however, is in its hard-edged, human portrayals, which intensely comes together during the film's dynamic opening scenes right up until the final climax. Everywhere we look, director James Mangold's camera turns in a tense and volatile drama, and it supplies enough interest for a heaping pile of conventional and traditional Hollywood content. The talent burns bright on the screen, thus minimizing whatever small limitations the film may possess.

Looking back at my time at the movies on that day in August '97, I felt I'd been given a second chance on how to perceive Sylvester Stallone. He'd redeemed himself not only as an actor, but in the sort of character he played, and this felt personally important to me after having endured so much of his screen crap in the '80s and '90s. Was this a comeback, and if so, how long would it last? In my opinion, it didn't last beyond *Cop Land*. Give a man enough time, and he'll inevitably return to what earns him the most money and success in a world of blood, guts and action. This exceptional police thriller may have been a welcomed diversion, but it eventually turned into more of what defined Stallone as the mindless action star he often was, including a new century of more *Rocky/Creed* movies and an entirely new franchise that is *The Expendables*.

Like I've said before, nothing lasts forever—nothing good, and nothing bad.

L.A. Confidential

Directed by Curtis Hanson
(September 19, 1997, U.S. Release Date)

Recalling the best years of my life also means recalling the movies (even just *one* movie) that stand out. In 1977, I experienced *Star Wars*. In 1987, I experienced *Full Metal Jacket*. In 1997, I experienced *L.A. Confidential*. But to tell the story of that experience, I'll divulge the twenty-four hours of my life that preceded it.

By September 1997, the annual summer season was over, and I enjoyed the peace of post-Labor Day weekend living in Westhampton Beach. The crowds were gone, but some clubs stayed open throughout the year. On a Friday night, I drove to one of these clubs in Hampton Bays to check out a local rock band and met a girl named *Ginger A.* We drank, talked, danced, and eventually got physical with each other. When it was time for me to leave, I didn't ask for her phone number. Instead, I tried something different and gave her my address in Westhampton Beach, telling her if she wanted to see me again, she was welcome to just show up the next morning. Driving home that night, I was convinced I'd never see Ginger again.

Sometimes life is full of surprises. The next morning, as I slept off the night before, I was awakened by a knock at my front door. Do I have to say who it was? In Ginger's hands were two cups of coffee and something I didn't expect—a bottle of massage oil. Without going into any inappropriate sexual details, it was hours before we realized how much time we'd spent in bed together. The day was half over and it looked like the sun wouldn't shine. Deciding to go to a movie, we set our sights on the new Kevin Kline comedy, *In & Out* playing in Southampton. Realizing the movie's start times wouldn't cooperate with us, we settled on seeing *L.A. Confidential* instead. In restrospect, it's hard to believe that I use a word like *settled* for an extraordinary film like *L.A. Confidential.*

Admittedly, I had my doubts about this film. This wasn't the first time Hollywood in the '90s attempted to revive classic neo-noir in cinema. Three previous attempts, *The Two Jakes, Devil in a Blue Dress,* and *Mullholland Falls,* failed to gain recognition with the public or the box office. This new project based on James Ellroy's 1990 novel (which I've never read) seemed risky because as I understood it from the media coverage on TV, the novel was considered difficult to translate to film. It also starred virtual unknowns at the time (Danny DeVito and Kim Bassinger being the exceptions). Still, unknowns often proved highly effective in generating quality films, so anything was possible. As Ginger and I sat through the opening screen advertisements waiting for the show to begin, I noticed a very familiar face walk into the theater. It was the late *Roy Scheider* and his wife Brenda. When I pointed him out to Ginger, her reply nearly knocked me out of my seat. She *knew* him because she'd been nanny to his kids when she once lived in Los Angeles while he was shooting his NBC TV series *seaQuest DSV.* Holy crap—not only was the great Roy Scheider in the theater, but *I* was sitting next to someone who actually knew him. Naturally, I asked if she'd introduce me to him after the movie, and she said yes. Now that I had high anticipation sitting on my shoulders, it seemed *L.A. Confidential* would probably be the longest movie of my life.

The film was set against the backdrop of Los Angeles in the year 1953, and told the story of a group of LAPD detectives and their involvement with police corruption in the time of Hollywood celebrities. Sergeant Ed Exley (played by Guy Pearce) was a good cop determined to live up to the reputation of his deceased father, also a famed L.A. detective. After a violent clash between police and Mexican prisoners at the station on Christmas Eve, Exley did what he considered to be the right thing and testified against fellow officers involved in the riot in exchange for a promotion to detective lieutenant, despite the disapproval of his precinct caption Dudley Smith, who believed Exley didn't have what it took to make hard decisions as a detective, like planting evidence against a suspect known to be guilty, or shooting a hardened criminal in the back to prevent him from being set free by the courts.

Officer Wendell "Bud" White (played by Russell Crowe), considered a mindless thug brought in as muscle against criminals, was obsessed with taking violent action against women-abusers. White hated Exley because of his testimony that got White's partner, Dick Stensland, fired. With crime boss Mickey Cohen imprisoned for tax evasion, White was brought in to torture and scare away out-of-towners seeking to gain a new criminal foothold in Los Angeles. It was at a liquor store that White first met Lynn Bracken (Bassinger), a high-class hooker who resembled actress Veronica Lake and worked for Pierce Patchett, whose service *Fleur-de-Lis* ran hookers cut by plastic surgery to look like famous movie stars (White later began a romantic relationship with her).

Sergeant Jack Vincennes (played by Kevin Spacy, whom I'd never forget as Keyser Söze from *The Usual Suspects*) was a narcotics detective moonlighting as a technical advisor for a popular TV show called *Badge of Honor* (a fictional knockoff of the popular real-life TV police drama *Dragnet*). Sid Hudgens (DeVito), publisher of the popular tabloid magazine *Hush-Hush*, often tipped Jack on celebrity drug activity to make high-profile arrests for Sid's magazine—a relationship that included a shameless fifty-dollar gratuity for Jack each time they made a deal.

A turning point occurred after a series of bloody murders at the Nite Owl café. Stensland was one of the victims, in addition to one of Patchetts hookers cut to look like Rita Hayworth. Exley and Vincennes arrested a group of African American men (known felons) for the crime. During Exley's interrogation of them, he realized they may not have been the guilty ones for the Nite Owl crimes, but they *were* holding a kidnapped Mexican girl as their personal rape victim. After the girl was rescued by the cops, the arrested felons escaped from the station, and were later killed by Exley in a shootout. Despite

Exley's despised reputation in the department as a snitch, he was now admired, respected and even decorated for his bravery.

Although the Nite Owl case appeared to be solved, Exley and White investigated further, and discovered evidence of police corruption involving drugs. Then the bodies started piling up—a struggling homosexual actor, Pierece Patchett, Sid Hudgens, and even Jack Vincennes when he was shot by Dudley Smith after revealing the evidence he'd discovered about the police corruption and the specific names involved. Now we knew Smith was the true bad guy. Before he died, though, Jack uttered the name "Rollo Tomasi", a name Exley had confided to him earlier in the film. It was a fictional nickname Exley secretly gave to the man who'd killed his father and gotten away clean. Exley's suspicions were aroused when Smith asked him if he'd ever heard of "Rollo Tomasi". Exley and White finally had to work together to properly solve the Nite Owl murders and nail Smith for his corruption. They deduced that cops and ex-cops were killed over a large supply of stolen heroin, and the Nite Owl killings were orchestrated to allow Smith to kill Stensland and take over the drug racket in L.A.

The climax lured Exley and White into an ambush at an isolated motel, where a group of Smith's police hitmen showed up for a gunfight. They killed the hitmen, but were both shot when Smith showed up. As Exley held Smith at gunpoint, Smith was prepared to explain the entire thing away when the good cops showed up at the scene, and he promised Exley another police promotion to keep his mouth shot. But in the end, Exley shot Smith in the back, proving he *did* have what it took to do what was necessary to stop a hardened criminal from escaping justice. While in custody, Exley didn't hesitate to confess the police corruption and name all those involved. The LAPD protected their stained image by claiming Smith died a hero in the shootout, and thus awarding Exley a second medal of honor for bravery. White and Lynn lived happily ever after when they drove off to her home in Bisbee, Arizona.

L.A. Confidential was over. I absolutely loved it, and would take the proper time to reflect upon it later. Right now, it was time for me to meet the man I'd grown up with in *The French Connection*, *Jaws* &

Jaws 2, All That Jazz, Blue Thunder, and *2010*. When Ginger and I approached Roy and Brenda, it played out like a reunion for the three of them, as they hadn't seen or heard from Ginger in years. After my introduction, and some pleasant words of small talk, I asked Roy what he thought of the film, and he said he thought it was very well made. I told him I thought it was the best police/crime thriller I'd seen since *The French Connection*. I didn't say that to flatter him, but because I felt it to be the genuine truth (I still do). He gave no reaction to the mention of one of his own films, but did seem genuinely impressed when I told him I was an architect. I'll never forget what went through my mind, and that was, "Holy shit! I'm standing here talking with the star of *Jaws* and he's impressed with *me!*" What can I say? That was one of my life's rare celebrity moments that I've never forgotten. Thankfully, I wasn't stupid enough to say, *"You're gonna need a bigger boat"* to him like some crazed fanboy.

Now let's talk about the film. One of the first impressions I walked away with was that it turned out the 1950s weren't as innocent as "the Beaver" led us to believe on TV. Hard realities of corruption, pornography, prostitution, murder and violence existed, but were well hidden from the general public in lieu of sensationalized stories and smear tactics of suspected communism in the age of Joseph McCarthy. As a traditional crime film, *L.A. Confidential* deals unusually with the psychology of its main characters, while still containing elements of traditional police action. It's brought to the screen in a more sharply clipped style and provides an exciting arena for personalities like the cops played so masterfully by Crowe, Pierce and Spacy to grab hold of our interest. But aside from the actors themselves, the city of Los Angeles shines as a big star in its own right. Much like Roman Polanski's depiction of 1930s L.A. in his 1974 film *Chinatown*, the atmosphere and closely detailed production designs are a rich element where the strands of its narrative form are obvious to those of us who can recognize the nostalgia of classic film noir.

This isn't always an easy film to follow because we have to pay strict attention to the double-crossing intricacies of the plot. However, the reward for the two hours plus we've invested is not only the dark and dirty fun, but also the undeniable satisfaction we feel for having been made a part of it all, and watching it come together in the end. Then like me, perhaps you buy the film on video and watch it again, and that's where the real love for an extraordinary motion picture like *L.A. Confidential* pays off.

Let me conclude by saying that while I have nothing but love and respect for James Cameron and *Titanic*, it's *L.A. Confidential* that I feel should've taken home that Oscar for Best Picture of 1997. It's also one of my top ten favorite films of the 1990s. As for me personally, I saw Ginger only one more time after that day we spent together, and it wasn't until a year later in the summer of 1998. But I'm grateful for having met her, and for having met one of my favorite actors of all time.

Thank you, Roy. You were truly one of the greats.

Good Will Hunting

Directed by Gus Van Sant
(December 5, 1997, U.S. Release Date)

Deciding to see *Good Will Hunting* presented a conflict for me. On the one hand, I wasn't too impressed with director Gus Van Sant so far. Films like *Drugstore Cowboy*, *My Own Private Idaho*, and *To Die For* failed to leave a positive impression on me. On the other hand, Robin Williams in a dramatic role practically spoke for itself. But there was something else at work here. This was a time when my own screenwriting ambitions were high, so I was constantly keeping my eyes open for new and exciting original screenplays on screen, as well as trying to understand what made a good script great. When I learned that this film was a first time writing effort for friends Matt Damon and Ben Affleck, I ignored my hesitations toward the director and concentrated on the writers and actors instead.

Damon and Affleck were still relative unknowns to me, the former being only familiar to me in *Courage Under Fire* and *The Rainmaker*, while the latter was more recognizable to me from his recent role in *Chasing Amy*. As Will Hunting of South Boston, he was a self-taught genius in mathematics, but got no further at Massachusetts Institute of Technology (MIT) than working as the janitor. When Professor Gerald Lambeau posted a difficult problem on the hallway blackboard with the hopes that one of his graduate students would solve it by the end of the semester, everyone was shocked to discover it had been solved overnight by an anonymous unknown. When he posted a more difficult problem, Will fled while caught in the act of solving it on the blackboard.

By night, Will hung out with his best friends, including Chuckie (Affleck). At a bar one night, Will met Skylar, a British girl about to graduate from Harvard University and then move on to medical school at Stanford in California. She was impressed with how Will could verbally hold his own against one of the arrogant young men competing for her attention. By the time Will called her, he was already awaiting sentencing for public fighting and attacking the arresting police officer. But Professor Lambeau arranged for him to avoid jail if he agreed to study mathematics under his supervision and to also see a therapist (enter Robin Williams as Dr. Sean Maguire). Will agreed, but not without treating it like a joke. Unlike previous therapists, though, Sean challenged Will's aggressive defensive mechanisms, even threatening Will after he disrespected Sean's deceased wife.

Will eventually opened up. He was particularly amazed by Sean's story of how he first met his wife in a bar in 1975 on the same night he and some friends had tickets to game six of the World Series, for which Sean was willing to miss to be with the woman who'd one day be his wife. Sean was a passionate man who deeply loved his wife, and regretting nothing about the time he spent with her, even when she was sick for years with cancer and then died. These stories of love and devotion encouraged Will to try and build his own relationship with Skylar, though he lied to her about his past and repeatedly kept her away from his rundown apartment and neighborhood.

What struck me as odd was Will's efforts to challenge Sean about not being able to move on from his wife's death. I may not know too much about psychology and therapy sessions, but I can make the educated assumption that no real-life therapist would open up about their own life to their patient, as Sean did to Will. This is perhaps where the audience was required to open its mind and suspend its disbelief of not only the profession of therapy, but also how far both participants were willing to go throughout the healing process.

What would become of Will's future was the big question. He ignored a number of job interviews by sending Chuckie in as his chief negotiator (a joke in which Chuckie was able to con his interviewers out of some cash as a retainer). Will also rejected a position at the National Security Agency (NSA) by severely criticizing the agency's moral positions. Skylar fell in love with Will and asked him to move to California with her, which he refused. During their first fight, he angrily confessed to her that he was not only an orphan, but had been physically abused by his foster father. He walked out on her, leaving her broken-hearted. Sean later revealed that because Will anticipates future failure in his relationships, he deliberately sabotages those relationships to avoid his own emotional pain.

I suppose that sort of professional diagnosis might've been considered textbook therapy, even to someone like me who only knew about this stuff through the movies. What caught my attention instead was a moment between Will and Chuckie, when Chuckie all-but threatened Will that he wouldn't permit him to spend the rest of his life in South Boston, working construction jobs and wasting his gifts of intelligence, believing it would be an insult to those of Will's friends who weren't blessed with such gifts and opportunities. This was a moment of selfless friendship and support I knew many of us would be lucky to have in our lives. It seemed the kind of friendship and support that only came with two childhood buddies sharing a couple of beers and being completely honest with each other. I think it was best summed up when Ben Affleck spoke these words:

> *Let me tell what I do know. Every day I come by your house and I pick you up, and we go out, we have a few drinks and a few laughs and it's great. You know what the best part of my day is? For about ten seconds, from when I pull up to the curb to when I get to your door, 'cause I think maybe I'll get up there and I'll knock on the door and you won't be there. No goodbye, no see ya later, no nothin'…you just left. I don't know much, but I do know that.*

During their last session together, Will and Sean learned they were both victims of child abuse. By repeating the words, *"It's not your fault,"* Sean helped Will to understand that he was a victim of his own inner demons, and to accept that which he couldn't control. Will broke down in tears, and the two of them hugged. This was the big breakthrough in Will's recovery, and he even accepted one of the jobs offered to him, though he never actually started the job. Instead, he did exactly what Chuckie wished for by getting into his car and beginning a long drive to California to reunite with Skylar, whom he finally realized he loved.

At the time I saw *Good Will Hunting*, I was dating a young woman who was pursuing a degree in psychology. I don't know if she ever achieved her goal, but I do remember her confirming my suspicions about the doctor-patient relationship in which the therapist didn't reveal their personal life to their patients. True or not, it was impossible for me not to recognize the talent potential in young men like Matt Damon and Ben Affleck after seeing this film (despite whatever I thought years later of their efforts as action-based characters Jason Bourne and Batman, respectively) that took on predictable clichés, including friendship, love, and hope (I suppose sometimes cliché is not only fitting, but even necessary). This was surely an attention-getter that found its way to the Oscars when Damon and Affleck won the golden statue for Best Original Screenplay, and like two years prior when Christopher McQuarrie won the same award for *The Usual Suspects*, I felt my own pride as a screenwriting hopeful in watching two close friends come together in such a great collaboration to take home the big prize.

As for Gus Van Sant, he was in my good graces for now with *Good Will Hunting*. But like I've previously said, nothing good lasts forever. A year later he shamelessly remade Alfred Hitchcock's *Psycho* in a pointless shot-for-shot effort that no half-witted film lover should ever waste their time with, in my opinion. I've also previously said that nothing bad lasts forever, either. Two years after that, he made *Finding Forrester* with the late Sean Connery, and he had my respect again.

Amistad

Directed by Steven Spielberg
(December 10, 1997, U.S. Release Date)

As I previously mentioned, if I'm already in a bad mood, then I'm likely to unfairly take it out on the movie I'm watching by attacking it for any reason. This happened in 2001 with *A Beautiful Mind*, in 1995 with *GoldenEye*, and it happened in 1997 over Memorial Day weekend with Steven Spielberg's *The Lost World: Jurassic Park*. By the time I watched these films again months later, my mood was better, and I gave them the fair and honest perspective and criticism they deserved.

When *Amistad* was released in December of '97, I hadn't yet rewatched *The Lost World*, so it felt like Spielberg was still skating on a thin sheet of ice with me, and it would take a strong act of Oscar-worthy redemption to make me forget what I'd considered (at the time) to be a pointless second go-around with the big dinosaurs on the forbidden island. I'd also never watched the miniseries *Roots* until I purchased the DVD set in 2001. When it first aired on ABC in January 1977, I was still too young to understand its cultural and historical impact (it still holds the record as the second-most watched overall miniseries finale in U.S. television history). Spielberg's new film of African slavery, based on a true story, would be the first and freshest look I'd get at that part of history without having the famed TV miniseries as a basis of comparison.

Aboard the slave transport ship *La Amistad*, a revolt and mutiny was about to erupt. The leader of the African slaves, Joseph Cinqué (played by newcomer Djimon Hounsou) broke loose from his chains and led a bloody takeover of the ship and their captors. They spared the lives of two Spanish ship navigators and ordered them to sail the ship back home to Africa. However, the navigators misdirected the slaves and instead sailed north to the east coast of the United States, where their ship was seized by the American Navy off the coast of Montauk Point on Long Island, and the surviving slaves were taken and imprisoned. Not speaking any English in this strange and unfamiliar country, the Africans were caught up in a legal battle between their status as cargo and property, and the charges of piracy and murder. President of the United States Martin Van Buren, seeking re-election, supported the claims of the Spanish government that the Africans were the property of Spain based on a treaty signed between the U.S. and Queen Isabella II of Spain, who was only eleven years old.

Local real estate lawyer Roger Baldwin (played by Matthew McConaughey) was hired by two slave abolitionists (one of them played by Morgan Freeman) to defend the Africans. He argued that the Africans had been kidnapped from Great Britain to be illegally sold in America. Through documented proof found aboard *La Amistad*, Baldwin proved that the African slaves were legal cargo that belonged to the Portuguese slave ship, the *Tecora*, and therefore, the Africans should be considered free citizens and not slaves. But because this was still a time in American history where the courts could be manipulated by the President and his staff, the judge sitting on this trial was replaced by a younger judge believed to be easily influenced and more impressionable.

Faced with a new trial and a new judge, Baldwin found James Covey, a former African slave who spoke both English and Mende. Cinqué relayed the full story of how he and his people were kidnapped by slave traders outside his African village and brought to the slave fortress of Lomboko, where thousands of African captives were held under heavy and cruel guard. He and others were sold to the *Tecora*, chained inside the brig of the ship and beaten and starved. During a purging of the ship one day, captors threw fifty of the Africans overboard into the water. Arriving later in Havana, Cuba, those slaves not sold at auction were taken to *La Amistad*, thus inevitably leading up the events that opened the film. Subsequently, Baldwin proved from the *Tecora*'s inventory that the number of African captives had been reduced by fifty, and that some slave ships were forced to get rid of their slaves as evidence of their illegal crime. During this second trial, as tensions mounted, Cinqué rose from his chair and repeatedly shouted, *"Give us free!"*

Despite the presumption that this younger judge would "play ball" with those in power, he surprised us all by ruling in favor of the African slaves. But after political pressure from South Carolina's Senator John Calhoun, President Van Buren ordered that the case and its ruling be appealed to the Supreme Court. It was here that Cinqué forced me (and perhaps others) to realize the insanity of governmental politics when he lashed out against laws that "almost" work in a country like ours. It was now that former President John Quincy Adams and trial lawyer (played by Anthony Hopkins) stepped in to assist with the new case. During the trial, Adams made a long and moving speech in defense of not only the African's release, but the undeniable lengths and nature of freedom itself. He was successful. The Africans were now free men. In an epilogue montage, the slave fortress Lomboko and its captives were liberated by the Royal Marines, followed by its destruction. President Van Buren lost his re-election campaign, and tensions between the North and South eventually led to what would become the Civil War.

Despite my negative feelings over the years for films like *The Temple of Doom*, *Hook*, and even *The Lost World* (temporarily), it was impossible for me to ignore that Steven Spielberg was a filmmaker that (more often than not) wouldn't let me down. *Amistad* was proof, because I couldn't help but be amazed at a cinematic talent who knew how to touch the heart of the world with breathtaking and groundbreaking stories. I also reminded myself that stories as this, based on historical fact, might be laced with historically inaccurate issues, nonetheless. Were the events of *Amistad* a genuine turning point in America's perspective on slavery, as the film suggests? Academic scholars may argue that they had nothing to do with slavery as an overall domestic issue. Someone like myself, unless I researched it, might not ever know the truth as being one hundred percent accurate. Perhaps the point was for me to simply enjoy historical film as entertainment from a very reputable artist like Spielberg.

Historical accuracy aside, *Amistad* remains an important and engaging story told with thrills, mystery, culture-clash and the inevitable courtroom drama in which a gifted actor like Anthony Hopkins gives a brilliant performance as John Quincy Adams with a passionate courtroom speech that easily rivals classic dramas as *Inherit the Wind*, *To Kill a Mockingbird*, and *Judgment at Nuremberg*. It's hard to believe the story of *Amistad* takes place *after* the United States Constitution was written—a document whose ideals and principles may have been worthless during the times of nineteenth-century slavery.

Deconstructing Harry
Directed by Woody Allen
(December 12, 1997, U.S. Release Date)

I've previously mentioned that I once had ambitions to be a professional screenwriter, even while making a living as an architect. This ambition included screenwriting and film appreciation classes at various Manhattan institutions where I often concluded the instructors had no idea of what they were talking about (remember the old saying? Those that can't do, *teach*). It was at one of these film classes where I caught a sneak preview of Woody Allen's newest film, *Deconstructing Harry*. I didn't know it at the time, but this turned out to be what I consider the last great film of Allen's career. I've seen nearly everything he's done since, and none of them have left me with any of the lasting impressions left by favorites like *Annie Hall*, *Manhattan*, *Hannah and Her Sisters*, or *Crimes and Misdemeanors*. For this film, though, it served as a way to continue my exploration of writing and original storytelling, even if it meant the inevitable writer's block.

Woody Allen was a successful writer named Harry Block (fitting name for a man who experiences writer's *block*) who drew inspiration from the people and events of his real life. These people read his work and were often very angry with him. Some of them, like his sister-in-law, with whom he based a story of an extra-marital affair with one's sister-in-law, became enraged and wanted to kill him. To distract her, Harry told her a story he was currently writing, which was a semiautobiographical story of a sex-obsessed young man who was attracted to every woman he came into contact with except his own wife, and after sleeping with a hooker, was mistakenly claimed by Death.

During one of his therapy sessions, Harry discussed a planned ceremony in his honor at the college that once kicked him out, and his sadness in having no one to share the event with. He asked his ex-wife (and therapist) if he could take their young son with him, but she refused to be flexible about it, citing that Harry was a bad influence on their son. She was also furious at Harry over his writing, in which a patient's marriage to his former therapist crumbles after the birth of their son, in which the wife became, as he put it, *"Jewish with a vengeance."* The fictional vision of this fact involved actress Demi Moore in the role of the Jewish therapist and her act of saying a Hebrew prayer before giving her husband a blowjob. I don't exactly know what the Hebrew words, *"Boray P'ree Ha blowjob"* signifies, but it's a miracle if you can convince a Jewish woman (even a married one) to willingly give you a blowjob.

Harry's final solution for taking his son with him to his university was to kidnap him. Also in the car with him was an old acquaintance with health problems, and a black hooker named Cookie whom Harry had just been with the night before. Unfortunately, Harry's friend died in the car, and Harry himself was arrested for kidnapping his son once he reached the university. Harry was bailed out of jail by his best friend who'd just married the woman Harry realized he truly loved. Harry reluctantly gave them his blessing, but still considered his best friend to be the Devil who left a trace of burning sulfur wherever he went. In a fictional account of Hell, Harry and his friend engaged in a verbal conflict as to who was truly the more evil of the two of them, all while enjoying drinks and the pleasure of air conditioning in Hell.

Back in the reality of his Manhattan apartment, a defeated and miserable Harry Block finally came to terms with who he was as a writer by fantasizing the ceremony that never took place with a room full of every character he'd ever created, played by every celebrity on the film's movie poster. He realized that he (like many writers) can only function in art, and not in life, and that now his block may be ending, allowing him to return to his writing.

After the film, I spoke with the young woman sitting next to me and confessed to her my writing aspirations, and the influence of Woody's latest film on myself at that moment. We went to lunch, and I was surprised at how much we agreed upon when it came to film criticism. We discussed character development, and how it was more than just something on a printed page. We got to see, firsthand, what Woody's characters looked like, their actions, and how each of them directly related to someone in his real life. Woody, like so many of his other characters, continued to be the pill-popping, dysfunctional man incapable of real intimacy with anyone other than his son, and also incapable of functioning in life, thus choosing fiction and the imaginary worlds surrounding it. We also spoke about how the R-rated *Deconstructing Harry* was probably the most racy and vulgar film of his entire career.

That aside, though, this was and remains an honest, sad and revealing film about a very creative writer. It's funny, witty, and also depressing as hell for someone like myself trying to be a writer. Fantasy, too, plays a major role here, though it may not necessarily be classified as fantasy. The parallels between Woody himself and the characters and plots he's created are more than obvious to those who know him well. I can't say I care much for the camera work of jerky jump cuts because I don't consider them worthy of the man's talents and abilities to film and tell stories about people. I'd expect this sort of cheap visual effects tactic from a director like the late Tony Scott or someone who's more interested in action and special effects.

This remains Woody's last great film, in my opinion. Like his 1980 black-and-white film, *Stardust Memories*, it too centers on an artist taking part in a ceremony in his honor, while he painfully reflects upon the failed relationships of his past while trying to mend the current ones. It also echoes Ingmar Bergman's *Wild Strawberries* in which an academic man takes a road trip to receive an honorary award from his old university while reflecting upon his past experiences. Let's also not forget Fellini's *8 ½* which is also about a misunderstood artist struggling with the relationships of his past and present as they intersect with dream sequences and fantasies.

While Woody Allen may not be accused of being the most original filmmaker of all time, that's okay, because it seems everybody copies everybody with homage. We can only decide for ourselves what sort of personal conclusions we walk away with from his work. This film told me to never stop writing and to never give my imagination a rest. Even if the rest of Woody's career hasn't spoken to me since, I can forever be grateful for the lessons I walked away with from *Deconstructing Harry*.

Titanic

Directed by James Cameron
(December 19, 1997, U.S. Release Date)

This is it—the big movie of 1997. It was released after months of delay and months of high anticipation that it would be the most epic event in the world of film entertainment, as well as bringing new depths to the common disaster film. It made international stars of both Leonardo DiCaprio and Kate Winslet, and it won all those Oscars. It was also the one and only movie Caren and I went to see when our friendship briefly rekindled itself. We went to see it the day after it opened at one of the largest multilevel multiplexes in Manhattan, and we had no doubt it would be spectacular.

In the process of my writing, I've often rewatched films to gain a fresh perspective. Some films, though, stand the test of time in one's brain that don't require rewatching. I hardly need refreshing with *Jaws*, *Star Wars*, *Raiders of the Lost Ark*, *E.T.*, and *Back to the Future*, and the same holds true for *Titanic*. I've seen it many times, and when it airs on any of the pay-TV channels, I always catch parts of it. Prior to its release, my only cinematic exposure to the sinking of the great ocean liner was the occasional airing of the 1953 film *Titanic* with Barbara Stanwyck and the 1958 British film *A Night to Remember* on Turner Classic Movies.

On the surface, *Titanic* was a spectacular disaster film, as well as a heart-touching love story between young adults Jack Dawson and Rose Dewitt Bukater (DiCaprio and Winslet) who met by chance on the luxury ocean liner days before it met its fate when it collided with an iceberg. It was a grand film of not only scale and size, but also a technological breakthrough in the world of film sets and CGI effects. But even as I watched this great story between two star-crossed lovers unfold, I couldn't ignore something greater taking place, and that was its depiction of social class relationships and conflicts, in which a passenger's place aboard the ship was solely dependent on what class level they fell under. Those of high-end wealth and privilege, as were Rose and her fiancée, Cal Hockley (played by Billy Zane), could afford to buy the best the ship offered, whether it was their spacious stateroom, the food they ate, the deck level of the ship they occupied, or even the right to take part in the Sunday church services. Those who couldn't afford such luxuries (like Jack) were placed in third class to dwell within the ship's depths, grouped together like rats.

The love between Jack and Rose was flanked by Rose's people (including her widowed mother) of upper-crust breeding who made no secret of looking down on, and even despising the lower class elements occupying the same ship as them. Even the ship's staff wasn't exempt from their "holier-than-thou" attitude, as they were considered just mere servants who didn't deserve proper respect. Because of Jack and Rose's social class differences, it seemed unlikely the two of them would even *meet* because they were each expected to occupy their own portions of the ship. But fate and Rose's failed suicide attempt intervened when Jack saved her life, and she was drawn to his free spirit and lust for life's daily pleasures.

This was an unavoidable attraction for her because we learned that she was a prisoner of her own life of stuck-up privilege, as she was expected by her mother to marry Cal as a matter of convenience, ensuring her family's name and financial security in high society's social order. Rose was the mail-order-bride, bought and paid for by a vicious man who believed he could possess anything he wanted in life simply because he had the means to do it. Jack, while falling head over heels for Rose, wasn't ignorant to the realities of their class levels and financial positions. By the time the ship collided with the iceberg and its destiny, the love story took full effect as Jack and Rose realized that disaster and the potential for one's own survival made their love for each other stronger and more dedicated. Even as the ship was in the process of sinking, Rose was forced to make the ultimate choice of surviving with the rich man she didn't love, but who'd give her everything in life, or the choice of not surviving that ill-fated night and remaining with the man she truly loved, thus declaring to Cal, *"I'd rather be* his *whore than your wife!"*

Upon having experienced the full three hours and fifteen minutes running time of *Titanic*, its audience (myself and Caren included) likely walked away with only the gratification that true love did, indeed, triumph against all odds and that even though Jack Dawson died in the icy waters of the North Atlantic, Rose never let go of his memory, and her heart did go on. In fact, when we left the theater, I remember thinking to myself, "Nobody will ever love me that much." (I never shared that thought with Caren). I also thought this just might be the greatest love story ever put on screen.

So… *Titanic*—you've seen it many times, I'm sure. You know the flawlessly crafted story, you thought all the performances were top-notch, you love that it won Best Picture of 1997, you know that James Cameron was *"King of the World,"* and if you're a red-blooded heterosexual male like I am, you probably built your own fantasies around watching Kate Winslet naked for the brief moment we're treated to it during the sketching sequence. And regardless of other motion pictures made about the legendary sinking, this is the version of *Titanic* my generation of film fans have come to love the most, watching it over and over again. Still, I'll continue to discuss this film a little outside of the box and describe further the social relations and conflicts on their socioeconomic levels. Don't think I can? Stay with me and we'll see.

When one is aboard the *RMS Titanic*, their class level is bought and paid for as commonly as any other commodity. Cameron makes a deliberate effort to distinguish both classes aboard the ship by first depicting the very elegant dinner of the first-class passengers with all the items of the table in their proper place and the very fine food and drink they dine on. Third-class passengers, however, eat cheap food, drink cheap beer, and dance themselves into exhaustion. These distinctions, by comparison, not only display the level of what's considered entertaining for each social class, but also makes a point that third-class people are apt to loosen up and enjoy themselves more than their stuck-up counterparts. But it's when the ship is slowly and progressively meeting its doom that we learn how far, and to what extent the order of social classes takes its toll.

Early in the film, we learn there aren't enough lifeboats to accommodate every passenger aboard the ship, should they be required. When the time comes that they *are* required, it's not necessarily the traditional law of "women and children first," but rather the more socially accepted law of the time when *first-class* women and children shall come first. The notion of all human beings having their own right to survival has just gone out the window simply because the ship's first-class passengers are deemed *"the better half,"* as Cal puts it. Even Rose's mother isn't shy about blatantly asking if the lifeboats shall be seated according to class. This is not only the social order of Cameron's film, but also the historical order of the time.

Many of the 705 survivors of the *RMS Titanic* were part of the first-class social order of the time and had the odds of survival stacked higher in their favor. The film deems this order as seemingly acceptable by not only the first class, but also among the third-class passengers, as well, because many of them don't bother to question the injustice of it. When asked by her little girl what's going on, her third-class foreign immigrant mother tells her the ship is calling upon first-class passengers to the lifeboats first, and will then eventually get around to the third-class passengers, and they'll want to be ready. Actress Jenette Goldstein's facial expression, however, tells us she knows differently and that she and her children, as well as all the other third-class passengers, are likely going to die. Such social orders of that time not only defined who had the right to live and die, but also that time and change would inevitably pass laws of ocean travel that would not only provide enough lifeboats on luxury liners for *all* passengers, but perhaps even do away with the factors of class existence and conflict that decide a person's fate in the face of disaster.

Personally, I've vacationed on a cruise ship only twice (*not* my preferred choice of vacation options. I'm more of a land lover). The first was in the year 2000 aboard the Disney Cruise Line. The second was two years prior in Egypt aboard the *Sonesta*, cruising up and down the Nile River. I'll never forget the band on the deck of that ship playing their own rendition of Celine Dion's famed song, "*My Heart Will Go On*" (I hate that song), and thinking how grossly inappropriate playing that song aboard a cruise ship was, for obvious reasons. Geez, that's like playing an *Airport* movie of the 1970s aboard a commercial jet airliner.

*****

This is the last film of 1997 I shall discuss in any great detail.

All in all, this was a great year defined by losses, gains, and new beginnings. I lost a job but gained a much better one very quickly. I regained occupation of the family beach house in Westhampton Beach and, thus, began a new chapter of memories there, including a brief time of sorrow over Labor Day weekend when I and a houseful of friends were shocked to learn of the death of Princess Diana of Wales when we turned on the TV for the first time that Sunday. I regained Caren into my life, which at the time was important for me to gain closure on our entire past relationship.

I also lost my stepsister, Michelle. Nothing tragic happened to her, but our close relationship ended as quickly as it began a year earlier when I found out she'd betrayed my trust by repeating to her father all the intimate details of my life I'd confided to her. He repeated those details to my mother, and she repeated them to *me*. You'd think any reasonable person would have the tact to keep what she knew to herself and not reveal themselves back to her own son, but my mother isn't always a reasonable person. Michelle's betrayal, by my own standards of decency, was an unacceptable and unforgivable offense. If she was deliberately trying to push me away from her, she'd succeeded. I immediately broke off my relationship with her, and she never bothered to inquire why I had. She and I were over, and she hasn't been in my life again since (like I said, nothing good lasts forever).

I suppose I never had much luck with women. Dating in the late '90s seemed an endless and disgusting process. How many drinks, dinners, and movies did I endure with women I ultimately didn't end up with before I inevitably met the one who'd become my wife? A girl once stopped seeing me because she was apparently turned off by the fact that I could name the '70s female porn stars making cameos in the film *Boogie Nights*. *I* stopped seeing a girl because she hated pasta (seriously, who hates *pasta*?). Sounds like something any number of characters on *Seinfeld* would've done. Perhaps this is why the latter part of '97 and the first half of '98 was a good time to (temporarily) have someone like Caren back in my life. She was my female companionship (though I sometimes wondered how her husband felt about it thousands of miles away—I *wondered*, but I hardly cared) and a good diversion to the New York City dating scene that constantly made me sick. Perhaps if I'd been trying to write a romantic comedy at the time, all of this would've made good story material.

Life continued to play out like a movie in my head. And like the Titanic itself, sometimes the ship sank without enough lifeboats to keep me afloat. Still, I kept breathing.

And that, my friends, was the year 1997 for me.

THE YEAR WAS 1998...

- The story breaks of President Clinton's alleged affair with White House intern Monica Lewinsky, eventually leading to his impeachment.
- The Kosovo War begins as a result of a massacre in Likoshane.
- Windows 98 is released by Microsoft.
- The bombings of United States embassies in Dar es Salaam, Nairobi, and Tanzania are linked to terrorist Osama bin Laden.
- First baseman Mark McGwire of the St. Louis Cardinals hits his sixty-second home run of the season, breaking the single-season record previously held by Roger Maris in 1961.
- Former astronaut John Glen returns to space aboard the STS-95 mission.

...AND THERE WERE MOVIES!

The '90s was almost over. By 1998, talk of the new millennium was already underway, though I cared little about that, as I was accustomed to taking the events of my life day by day, year after year. On January 1, after a night of New Year's Eve partying, my only intention for my day off work was to finally see the new James Bond film, *Tomorrow Never Dies*, and see it I did. It didn't disappoint me.

I've come to believe that one year going into the next is best if there are no significant changes, and thankfully for me, '97 into '98 was like that. The job was good, my social life was good (even if dating felt like crap), and I continued to look for new ways to take advantage of what living in Manhattan offered. But for the life of me, I couldn't understand why a new year brought out the most uninteresting movies Hollywood could offer. Looking through the entertainment section of the newspaper (still preinternet for me), titles like *Spice World*, *Blues Brothers 2000*, and *The Wedding Singer* left me scratching my head and wondering about better options. Such options, I suppose, are a matter of one's taste and opinions. Critics and audiences may have had their own reasons for dismissing films like Barry Levinson's sci-fi psychological thriller *Sphere* and the action spin-off to *The Fugitive*, *U.S. Marshalls*, but I found them to be solid entertainment, even if they didn't leave me with any "strictly personal" feelings.

The upcoming summer was on my mind more than ever. I looked forward to Steven Spielberg's new war film *Saving Private Ryan*, the *X-Files* movie, and perhaps even a new vision of *Godzilla* by the director of *Independence Day*. But I cringed at the thought of fourth *Lethal Weapon* movie and wondered what the outcome would be when Hollywood released two movies about our global destruction—by a comet in *Deep Impact* and a huge asteroid in *Armageddon*, in the same summer. Hey, at least there weren't any new comic book superhero movies coming out, which felt like a big relief after last summer's disgusting debacle that was *Batman & Robin*.

Despite the wide variety of movie possibilities on the horizon, this didn't drive me toward the oncoming summer. The summer of '98 would finally mark the first full season I'd have at the recently reacquired family beach house since the summer of '92. Six long years I'd waited for things to stabilize out there, and I'd been insanely patient through it all—patient through years of beach erosion and tropical storms, patient through months of bureaucratic and legal bullshit to retain the deed to the house in my family's name, and patient through my own demons of having to deal emotionally with having almost *twice* lost the house. That was all over now. Come late April, I'd reopen and I'd have the house to myself, as my father showed little interest, and my mother and Kevin lived in Los Angeles.

But getting back to the early movies of the year, let's remember that even though most of what's released is of little interest to me, there's always a few gems out there that just might surprise us if we keep our eyes open and look hard enough. For me, one of those gems came in the form of dark, neo-noir science fiction from the man who directed *The Crow* in 1994.

Dark City
Directed by Alex Proyas
(February 28, 1998, U.S. Release Date)

You've heard me say this before—I'll say it once again—I love intelligent, high-concept science-fiction films that often require multiple viewings to fully appreciate their artistic potential. The average Friday-night-multiplex moron likely doesn't have the patience, heart, or spirit to go for films like the silent classic *Metropolis*, *2001: A Space Odyssey*, *THX-1138*, *Blade Runner*, David Lynch's *Dune*, or even Steven Soderbergh's remake of *Solaris*, and that's a damn shame, because they're all considered great sci-fi classics in their own right. My interest in seeing *Dark City*, though, was hardly based on the reputation of its director, because I thought *The Crow* was only okay. Even if I had no idea of its plotline, it was the darkness and the mystery of the movie poster that drew me in, as well as the tag line that said:

> *They built the city to see what makes us tick. Last*
> *night one of us went off.*

The hero John Murdoch (played by Rufus Sewell) was an actor I vaguely recognized from Kenneth Branagh's four-hour version of *Hamlet*. At the beginning of the film, he awakened suddenly in a hotel bathtub amidst a strange and dark city, unable to remember how he got there or who he was. He received a mysterious phone call from Dr. Daniel Schreber (played by Kiefer Sutherland), urging him to leave the hotel immediately to evade a group of men who were after him. While still in the room, John discovered a murdered young woman, as well as a bloody knife. Fleeing the scene, he barely escaped a group of pale men in trench coats and hats, whom we later learned went by the name, "the Strangers" (I thought they bore a strong resemblance with similar collective consciousness to the "Borg" of *Star Trek: The Next Generation*).

Considered a suspect in the woman's murder, John followed a series of clues to not only learn his own name, but to also discover he had a wife named Emma (played by Jennifer Connelly) who sang at a local nightclub. Hot on his trail was Police Inspector Frank Bumstead (played by the late William Hurt) determined to catch him for a series of murders committed throughout the city, though John had no memory of ever doing so. Pursued by the police and the Strangers, John escaped them when he discovered he was telekinetic, with the ability to alter reality at his will. The Strangers also possessed this ability and called it "tuning."

Exploring the strange city, we (as well as John) discovered there were distortions in the chronology of time, and none of the citizens ever seemed to notice that it was *always* nighttime. At the stroke of midnight every night, the city's population fell asleep in the middle of whatever they were doing at any location…except for John. During this time of sleep, the Strangers physically rearranged the entire city, as well as changed people's memories and identities around like pieces in a jigsaw puzzle. John's memories were that of a child raised in a coastal town called Shell Beach—a town familiar to everyone in the city, though nobody had any idea of how to get there. Eventually, even Inspector Bumstead had his doubts about the nature of the city, while acknowledging that John might be innocent of the murders he was accused of.

John and Bumstead confronted Dr. Schreber, who finally explained that the Strangers were really extraterrestrials who used bodies of the dead as their hosts. Encompassing one collective mind, they experimented with humans to analyze their own individuality in the hopes that some insight might help their own race to survive. He also revealed that John was different, in that he inadvertently awoke in that hotel bathtub when Dr. Schreber was in the middle of imprinting John's latest identity as a murderer. The three of them then journeyed to find Shell Beach for themselves, but it existed only as a poster on a wall at the edge of the city. Angered, John and Bumstead broke through the wall to reveal outer space. The Strangers showed up to confront them, holding Emma hostage. In the ensuing struggle, Bumstead and one of the Strangers fell through the hole into space, revealing the city was surrounded by a force field and not part of Earth.

The Strangers brought John to their home beneath the city and forced Dr. Schreber to imprint John with their collective memory, believing John was the final peak of their experiments. In a surprise twist, Dr. Schreber betrayed the Strangers by instead inserting false memories into John that would artificially establish his childhood as happy years spent training his skills to learn about the Strangers and their machines. John awakened to fully realize his skills and his purpose to do battle with the Strangers high above the city and defeat their leader.

Following this victory, John learned that Emma was reimprinted and couldn't be restored. Using his newfound powers alongside the Strangers' machines, he created a real Shell Beach by flooding the area within the city's force field with water, forming beaches and mountains, as well. In an act of rotating the city toward the star in space, its citizens experienced sunlight for the very first time. Stepping into the new sunrise, John saw the woman he knew as Emma standing at the edge of a pier, now with a new identity and new memories as Anna. As they walked to Shell Beach together, their relationship was brand-new.

My immediate reaction to *Dark City* was that I could now add it to that category of intelligent, high-concept sci-fi films alongside those classic titles I mentioned earlier, which also meant I'd watch it again soon. Like *Blade Runner*, this echoed a 1940's style neo-noir film taking us deep into the mystery of a city easily comparable to a variety of similarly themed structures, including the murky, nightmarish German expressionist depiction of urban mechanism and human repression (think Fritz Lang's *Metropolis*), and the dreariness reminiscent of popular works by American painter Edward Hopper during World War II. There are details from different eras and architecture altered at will by the Strangers affecting city inhabitants who don't realize they're imprisoned and live their lives according to what the dominant higher intelligence has manipulated them into believing and experiencing. If this sounds like the 1999 sci-fi action film *The Matrix*, you're not wrong. But remember that *Dark City* came first.

The city itself is a confusing mish-mash of pieces taking place nowhere specific, and yet everywhere at the same time. Because the city's organic architecture is a mixed blend of styles and structures, you never really know where you are exactly, because at one section, it may look like a street in London, and in another it may look like a part of New York City. You're always an inhabitant, though you never know where you really are, and if you try to travel outside its walls, you'll be lost. The designs of the city are spiral that shrink when approached closely. There are clocks, but the hours other than midnight are nondefinitive. Even the cars the citizens drive are plain, and avoid anything personal that will distinctively identify one person to the next.

Atmosphere is the key word for *Dark City*, with a grand choice of words to describe its design—dark, grim, gloomy, stylish, visionary, dazzling, stunning, polarizing, ominous, and certainly noir-ish. We don't just passively observe its existence, but rather allow ourselves to get lost inside by plunging deep into its bizarre, always-changing skyline of structure, and along the way, we're caught up in the mystery of John Murdoch as the protagonist trying to understand where he comes from and why the sun never shines. During this journey, we allow our own imaginations to be visually stirred, while taking part in strange and complicated twists of reality and fantasy. This is perhaps best described as director Alex Proyas's trademark signature. You need only watch *The Crow* and *I, Robot* to understand. He offers bewildering experiences that we can't take our eyes off of, and in the process, we're able to understand his own artistic world that originated in comic arts. Perhaps that's why some of his work often reminds me of the dark and dreaded gothic nightmare of Tim Burton's *Batman*.

Dark City continues to remind me to never take the easy way out when appreciating complicated cinema. It's easy enough to walk away from a film with solid clarity and no sense of confusion. But if we're faced with more questions than answers, it means the film has successfully penetrated our desires to know more and understand beyond what appears on the surface, especially in science fiction. Complexities like these would surely make men like George Orwell and Franz Kafka proud, and ultimately, as the movie poster suggests, they're what makes us tick.

Primary Colors
Directed by Mike Nichols
(March 20, 1998, U.S. Release Date)

The timing of the release of *Primary Colors* couldn't have been stranger…about as strange as the release of *Kramer vs. Kramer* and *The War of the Roses* ten years apart just as my own parents were splitting up…*twice*. This politically motivated film, based on an original book documenting Bill Clinton's 1992 presidential campaign and written by an author simply known as "Anonymous" (though it's since been revealed to be journalist Joe Klein who was with Newsweek Magazine at the time), was released less than two months after the real-life scandal of Clinton and Monica Lewinsky broke the nation's headlines. Of course, I didn't realize this immediately, because before going to see Mike Nichols's' new film, my only real knowledge of Bill Clinton back in '92 (other than the election itself) was when he infamously played his saxophone on *The Arsenio Hall Show*.

John Travolta's role as presidential candidate Jack Stanton may have been fictional, but it was impossible not to acknowledge the resemblance between himself and Bill Clinton—not just his physical appearance, but the mannerisms and the Southern accent, as well. The same could be said for actress Emma Thompson as his wife Susan and her similarities to Hillary Clinton. Accurate or not, I knew I'd enjoy all of this, whether I chose to interpret it as a serious political story, or a farce supposedly "based on a true story." One thing's for sure, and that's the film's content would warrant comparison to real (or not real) history that many of us may or may not recall for ourselves.

Jack was an idealist with the capacity to make voters and his own campaign staff truly believe in what he said, thought, and felt about our world and our future. Like John F. Kennedy decades before him, he made those believe because they *wanted* to believe. They wanted to believe that tough times in our economy and our lives could be made better by his political efforts. They wanted to believe in bullshit that was endlessly spewed about good, old-fashioned family values and ethics that came complete with harmonizing group songs of love and Thanksgiving turkeys shared with the homeless. They wanted to believe in love, honor, and the possibility that all was well, and we were safe on our own home front (guess what, people—it ain't like that).

Jack repeatedly demonstrated his belief in the power of say-ing "Yes" to all good things in life that would assure his people of peace and serenity. But like most people, he couldn't say "No" to life's unavoidable temptations, whether it was harmless issues like extra Krispy Kreme donuts or more serious stuff like dirty political backstabbing, or indulging in underage sex with a black teenage girl and falsifying the results of a pregnancy test to ultimately determine if he was the father. In comparison to something like *that*, the accusa-tions against Jack for his arrest in 1968 following an antiwar protest rally in Chicago seemed harmless. Such allegations and accusations were investigated and spearheaded by the Stanton's old friend Libby Holden (played by Kathy Bates) who was tough and damn good at her job (but also unbalanced), and whose purpose was to protect the Stantons against anyone who'd use such accusations against them during the election.

As they fell behind in the polls, Jack desperately tried to gain votes with the elderly in Florida by defending the state of Israel and casting his votes against cuts in Social Security and Medicare. During a radio talk show against his opponent Senator Lawrence Harris, Jack confronted these issues without mercy, and Harris suffered two heart attacks as a result, thus eliminating him from the presidential race. But he was quickly replaced by his friend, former Florida governor

Fred Picker (played by the late Larry Hagman), whose straight-talking, wholesome image proved threatening to the Stantons. But even *that* threat was short-lived when it was discovered that Picker had a cocaine addiction in his past which led to the end of his first marriage (he also had a homosexual affair with his cocaine supplier).

Still, Jack proved he still had some humanity left in his soul when he chose not to use the information against Picker following Libby's shocking suicide. Despite all of these tragic turns, though, it seemed nothing would stop the Stantons from reaching their historical goal all the way to the White House, which they did. Jack Stanton was now President of the United States.

Despite *Primary Color's* ill-timing with the Monica Lewinsky scandal, it's important to note that principal shooting was already completed before the scandal surfaced. This leads me to ask the question if the film's (and the book's) allegations on the fictional Jack Stanton allegedly based on the real-life Bill Clinton are considered true or false? Did ol' Billy really screw around before and during his '92 campaign or not? Did Hillary really take it and bear it to see her husband reach the White House so she could take her honored place as First Lady? True or false, Mike Nichol's film may be more than a fair and viable look inside the world of American politics and all the ugliness that goes with it. Whether or not a prospective voter chooses to take any of this crap seriously is up to them, but it's enough to make one take notice of real-life political candidates, and what they're capable of, good or bad.

Travolta and Thompson, in their portrayals of more than obvious real-life political figures, take their respective roles and have fun with them, particularly Travolta. Just look at that boyish smile on his face and tell me he's not indulging himself in the opportunity to lend his own creativity to the ultimate public figure, perhaps even a man he admired himself. And while our politicians and would-be presidential hopefuls are making spectacles of themselves in public and private life, there are those who support their journey with all their naive innocence, only to be disappointed and let down in the end (that's politics for you). It's fun and delightful fiction, but nonetheless, we may still ask ourselves, "Did Bill Clinton really do all that?"

As a general cynic of all politicians (both parties), I have no reason to doubt that any of it is false, even if it's dressed up for the benefit of Hollywood storytelling.

If we look back at the era when Clinton was president of the United States, we must consider that the only real life-changing event during those eight years was a series of blowjobs given by an overweight White House intern and the cum stains on her dress. The fact that Bill confessed to receiving those blowjobs makes it more than plausible to believe he may have scored some pussy outside his marriage before taking office. When we consider how much the world went to hell during the years of George W. Bush and Donald Trump, it seems, in retrospect, that blowjobs and cum stains weren't such a bad thing (and I suspect being married to Hillary Clinton doesn't exactly make for a wide range of sexual excitement in the bedroom). Can we honestly blame Bill for getting his knob polished by *anyone* of the female species who was willing to do it to him? It could even be argued that a good blowjob once in a while may produce a more relaxed president…and a more relaxed president might do a better job for the people.

It's a theory I'm willing to consider.

Deep Impact

Directed by Mimi Leder
(May 8, 1998, U.S. Release Date)

Here's another theory to consider—I believe an era has a tendency to repeat itself every twenty years. Think about it. In the 1970s, movies like *American Graffiti* and *Grease*, and TV shows like *Happy Days* glorified the music and pop culture of the 1950s. In the 1980s, a string of films like *Platoon*, *Full Metal Jacket*, and *Hamburger Hill* brought the Vietnam War to the light of cinematic pop culture, as well as glorifying the music of its time. In the 1990s, disco music made a big comeback (I know because I was on the dance floor at the clubs when it happened), and films like *Daylight*, *Turbulence*, *Dante's Peak*, and *Volcano* attempted to revive the genre of the disaster movie (unsuccessfully, in my opinion). The success of *Independence Day* in 1996, however, jumpstarted Hollywood's madness into looking for new ways to destroy our planet. In fact, looking back at the summer of 1998, our cities were destroyed on the big screen three times over—Roland Emmerich's new form of *Godzilla* wreaked havoc in New York City, and two major studios competed with their own oversized outer space rocks destined to collide with Earth, the films being *Armageddon* and *Deep Impact.*

When *Deep Impact* was released in May of '98, I'd just reopened the beach house for its first full season since 1992. My mother and Kevin were in Los Angeles and my dad only occasionally showed up at the house. Basically, I was alone out there with a four-bedroom house to myself. Not that I minded, as I constantly had friends spending many weekends with me. But early in May before the official season began, it was quiet out there, and the film's opening weekend was a grey and dreary one. I went to see it the night after it opened in the small town of Hampton Bays. My strongest interest from the film's trailer was that Morgan Freeman played the first African American president of the United States in the history of the movies. Seems we made some headway in the world of American politics and race ten years before Barack Obama made history for real.

Beginning with teenage astronomers at a star party, Leo Beiderman (played by a pre-*Lord of the Rings* Elijah Wood) discovered an unusual object in the night sky while looking through his telescope. He sent a picture he took of it to astronomer Dr. Marcus Wolf, who upon realizing the picture was of a dangerous comet on a collision course with Earth, panicked and died in a car crash while recklessly racing to tell the world. One year later, MSNBC journalist Jenny Lerner (played by Téa Leoni), while investigating the connection between the Secretary of the Treasury and a mistress named "Ellie," inadvertently learned after she was apprehended and interrogated by the FBI, that "Ellie" was in fact the acronym "ELE," which stood for extinction-level event. Two days later, President Tom Beck (Freeman) went on television and announced to the world that the Wolf-Beiderman comet was headed for Earth and could result in humanity's extinction. To try and stop the comet, the United States and Russia constructed a spacecraft in orbit called the *Messiah* to attempt to alter the comet's path away from Earth by detonating nuclear weapons drilled into the comet's core.

The *Messiah* failed when it lost contact with Earth and the comet wasn't destroyed but, instead, broke into two uneven pieces, both still heading for our planet. The president then announced a computer-based lottery to randomly select 800,000 Americans to join 200,000 preselected individuals to be placed in a series of underground caves in the state of Missouri. Jenny Lerner and the entire Beiderman family were preselected, but Leo's girlfriend Sarah and her family were left behind. Despite their very young age, Leo and Sarah were married in vain to try and save her family, though Sarah refused to leave them behind. Leo inevitably left his own family to find her. A last desperate effort with a series of intercontinental ballistic missiles launched at the comets failed, and there was no stopping them now. Leo and Sarah took off together with her baby brother to try and get to safety. Jenny gave up her seat on the last evacuation helicopter to her friend and boss Beth and baby daughter. With the last remaining time of her life, Jenny headed to the family beach house in Virginia to reconcile her estranged relationship with her father.

Finally, the moment was at hand. The first smaller comet made impact with the earth and created a megatsunami that destroyed much of the East Coast of the United States, including New York City, resulting in millions of human fatalities, including Jenny and her father as they stood on the beach waiting for the enormous tidal wave to hit them. Leo, Sarah and the baby survived when they made their way up to higher ground on the Appalachian Mountains. All of this was just from the first comet. The second one was still on its way to Earth. But in a suicide mission, the surviving crew of the *Messiah*, after saying a final goodbye to their loved ones, flew their ship into the deep crevasse of the comet to detonate the remaining four nuclear warheads to blow it into smaller, harmless pieces burning up in the earth's atmosphere. The waters receded, the rest of humanity was saved, and the first black screen President reminded us all that what was lost would be rebuilt again.

So much went through my mind when it was over. I'll begin with the film itself and then tell you how I felt when I got home later that night. My first thought was that *Deep Impact* certainly lived up to its title, not only in its physical impact with our planet, but its impact on human lives. It's a disaster film that can choke you up at certain moments. For myself, when Jenny was in her father's arms on the beach in front of the house she grew up in and she said, *"Daddy"* just before the fatal wave destroyed them both, I couldn't stop the lump that developed in my throat.

Like *The Towering Inferno* more than twenty years before it, this was a disaster film that dared to be *human*. When you think about it, the concept of spending the better part of a year preparing yourself for a comet that's going to collide with Earth isn't exactly a fun or exciting prospect. It's a frightening thought. How will you spend the remaining part of your life? What will you accomplish and who will you care about it? Who will you reconcile with before the end comes? Who will be selected for survival in the end? These are questions surrounding characters you come to care about as the story builds to its disastrous climax. In fact, during those final moments of human panic before the first comet hit, I felt a dreaded sickness I hadn't experienced since watching the final moments of panic before the nuclear warhead struck our world in the 1983 ABC TV movie *The Day After*.

When I got home later that night, it was dark and there was a bright moon in the sky. I spent hours walking alone on the beach, contemplating not only *Deep Impact*, but my own life, as well. The family beach house was twenty years old, but where was the *family*? My parents and brother were scattered to the wind in different directions and now it was just *me*—the only one left to carry the torch and keep the light burning in the home that once held us together. The only woman I'd ever loved up until then would soon become a faded memory when she left New York to join her husband in Las Vegas. In those moments of personal reflection on a deserted beach under the moon, I'd never felt more lonely in my entire life. Despite my sadness, though, I couldn't help but feel fortunate to be standing where I was at that moment. As I gazed up at the night sky, I thought to myself, "Like Jenny and her father, if the end comes today, there's nowhere on Earth I'd rather be except at my beloved beach house."

In the years that followed, particularly after the events of 9/11, I thought Hollywood might calm down a bit and take a more sensitive approach to our global destruction. No such luck. If anything, it's gotten much worse. This planet of ours has been subjected to every form of phenomenal weather event (*The Day After Tomorrow* and *2012* also from Roland Emmerich) and every form of alien invasion dreamt up. Honestly, who could deny this sort of screen insanity hasn't possibly inspired global terrorists to inflict their own evil on the United States of America and the rest of the world?

It's any argument, anyway.

The Horse Whisperer

Directed by Robert Redford
(May 15, 1998, U.S. Release Date)

Someday I'd like to visit the state of Montana, and it's all because of Robert Redford (mainly his 1992 film *A River Runs Through It*). I didn't grow up with the films of John Ford. I'd only heard about his filmmaking style and technique for capturing the great, American open landscapes when I got older and developed my appreciation for classic cinema. For my generation, it was director Redford who exposed me to some of America's most wonderful open country. There are visual moments Redford has captured that demand I get out there and head out to Montana. By this time, his films were a good three out of four for me, *The Milagro Beanfield War* being the only one I couldn't sit all the way through. His directorial record was good enough, though, for me to take a strong interest in *The Horse Whisperer*.

I'm not a horse lover. I mean, they're pretty animals, but I have no passion for them the way some people do. I rode a pony at day camp when I was a child and went horseback riding once when I was in high school, but that's it. Still, I was caught up in the opening credits of the film with the visual beauty and spirit of the galloping horse. In the opening shots of winter's morning, teenager Grace (played by a then-unknown, pre-*Avengers* Scarlett Johansson) and her best friend Judith went for an early morning ride together on their horses, Pilgrim and Gulliver. As they tried to make their way up an icy slope, Gulliver slipped and hit Grace's horse Pilgrim. Both horses fell, dragging the poor girls onto the road where they were hit by an oncoming tractor-trailer. Judith and Gulliver were killed, while Grace and Pilgrim suffered severe injuries.

Grace had part of her right leg amputated, leaving her angry and withdrawn. It was suggested that Pilgrim be put down after the accident, as he was left enraged and traumatized, and with large portions of his skin left severely bleeding. Grace's mother Annie (played by Kristin Scott Thomas) was an independent and strong-minded workaholic and refused to allow her daughter's beloved horse to be put down, believing Grace's recovery was dependent on Pilgrim's. Desperate to heal both daughter and horse, Annie tracked down Tom Booker (Redford) in the remote mountains of Montana, a man known as a "horse whisperer." Reluctantly, Tom eventually agreed to help on the condition that Grace herself participate in the healing process of her horse. She agreed, and she and Annie also agreed to stay at Booker's ranch where he lived with his brother Frank and his family.

Over time, as Grace and Pilgrim slowly overcame their traumas, we gazed upon some of Montana's most beautiful glories, from the wonders of the landscape to the majestic spirits of horses in action. Oh yeah, Tom and Annie fell for each other too. Still, she was a married woman and he'd had his heart broken by his first wife, so they were reluctant to act on their romantic feelings. Tom also got Grace to finally open up and tearfully describe the accident that happened to her and Pilgrim on that fateful night to fully understand what Pilgrim was experiencing emotionally. But even as Grace and Pilgrim continued to heal, the tension between Annie and Tom got worse when Grace's father Robert (played by Sam Neil) showed up unexpectedly at the ranch. Annie was torn by her new feelings of love for Tom and the love and loyalty toward her family. Somehow, though, everyone's personal conflicts came to terms when Grace finally summoned to courage to work through her injuries (emotional and physical) and mount Pilgrim to successfully ride him again.

Preparing to return home to New York, Annie and Robert acknowledged the fact that he always knew he loved her more than she loved him, but he felt that as long as he was a good husband, father, and lawyer, that it ultimately wouldn't matter because *that* was all he required in their marriage. He knew Annie was unsure of her feelings toward him and that she'd have to make a choice, and that she should drive home by herself to be sure of what she wanted (what an emotional soap opera). Although Annie wanted to stay on the ranch with Tom, she also knew that her life belonged back home in the city. She left, while Tom watched her drive away from the top of a hill sitting on his horse.

Leaving the theater, I was conflicted on how to feel about *The Horse Whisperer*. Sure, it was a great drama with solid performances, but what did the film personally do for *me*? My first recall was Harrison Ford in *Witness*, not only because of the unspoiled American terrain, but also of a tense-filled love scenario destined never to be. Frankly, I wasn't convinced the love between Tom and Annie was genuine, and that it only existed to round out the overall story's need for love interest. What I focused on instead was the simple story of a man and a horse. This was a well-crafted American story that could've likely only been successfully tackled by a man like Robert Redford, who's not only as solid an American as they come, but a man who also truly loves the American landscape (Clint Eastwood is perhaps the only other American director I could associate with this project).

Ultimately, what this film did for me was to appreciate the peace and serenity that comes with the love of the land, but also that which comes from our spiritual love and understanding of animals. This doesn't mean I ran out and bought a dog as soon as I saw the film, but perhaps I learned to take a deep breath once in a while to appreciate the simpler elements of my life amidst my own versions of routine, stress and chaos. I may never know what the true meaning of "horse whispering" is, but I think I can understand what it means for someone like me to "lower my own voice" in life and try my own form of "whispering." It'll never involve a horse, but it sure beats my trying to do yoga (or something like that), and in the process, not falling victim to the advice Tom Booker gives Grace, *"Don't you disappear. You do whatever you have to do to hold on."*

Thanks, Robert. I'll take that advice, and perhaps someday I'll visit the state of Montana.

The Truman Show

Directed by Peter Weir
(June 5, 1998, U.S. Release Date)

I hate, loathe and despise reality TV. I also have a somewhat low opinion of people who enjoy it. But back in the summer of '98, two years before CBS TV's *Survivor* premiered, the concept of following one's life and activities on television seemed an alien concept that could only be the stuff of the movies. I knew that reality entertainment existed in the past before director Peter Weir's sci-fi comedy-drama was released, but it felt impossible for me to come to grips with the possibilities of reality (past, present and future) until I witnessed it for myself on the big screen. Yes, I wanted to see *The Truman Show*, but it's the particular day I experienced in the Hamptons that summer which led to my walking into the movie theater that I'll never forget.

I'll mention again my period of black-and-white photography of Manhattan movie theaters. This hobby also extended to Long Island or anywhere else I could fine old neighborhood theaters still standing. It was on a grey and gloomy weekend in June that I spent the day driving east from Westhampton Beach to Montauk Point, stopping along the way at each town with a movie theater worthy of my camera. *The Truman Show* played at the small theater in Montauk (closed in 2014), but it wasn't until I reached the town of Southampton on my way home that I decided to treat myself to Jim Carrey's new film on such a dismal afternoon—a film already hailed as a dramatic breakthrough for his career, which up until now was dominated by comedy.

On the surface, Truman Burbank was a lot like Jim Carrey himself—cheerful, friendly, and always ready with a witty comeback when greeted by one of his fellow neighbors. Little did Truman know, however, that he was the unsuspecting star (or victim) of a reality TV show called *The Truman Show* in which state-of-the-art technology and thousands of hidden cameras filmed his every move (even his sleep) twenty-four hours a day and broadcast to a worldwide audience. The show's creator and executive producer named Christof (played by Ed Harris) sat high in the makeshift moon above the world and captured Truman's everyday emotions, making him relatable to his audience.

Truman was selected from a variety of unwanted pregnancies, and he was adopted by not only the network, but by the world watching him grow up on in his hometown of Seahaven Island, which was no more than an elaborate TV set built within a gigantic dome and populated by actors pretending to be real people in Truman's life, including his own wife Meryl (played by Laura Linney) and best friend Louis (played by Noah Emmerich). Christof controlled every aspect of Truman's existence, including the daily weather. To psychologically prevent Truman from ever leaving the island or discovering his false reality, a series of scenarios were created to dissuade his desire for exploring the outside world, despite his inner longings to break free and discover the country of Fiji. But Truman already feared the water because of the supposed "death" of his TV father in a boating accident, leading him to believe he lacked the courage to face the water as well as the potential dangers of traveling, thus paralyzing him with the virtues of staying put at home.

It was the moment when a spotlight mysteriously fell from the blue sky one morning that Truman suspected something wasn't right about his life, and took actions to figure out what was going on. Despite having fallen for his beautiful college classmate Sylvia (an extra on the show), he was intended to fall in love with and marry Meryl instead. When Sylvia attempted to tell Truman the truth about his fake reality, she was kicked off the show and believed to be living in Fiji with her (fake) father, thus justifying Truman's desire to flee to that country to find her again. Now exiled outside the show, Sylvia was part of a campaign to free Truman from his fake life, thus accusing Christof of destroying Truman's life (which he denied). As time and the show went on, mounting evidence, including a radio frequency following his car, and rain showers falling only on *him*, led Truman closer to the truth. Even the sudden return of his deceased "fake" father, intended to return Truman to a more controllable emotional state, couldn't deter him from discovering who and what he really was.

Finally taking action, Truman went to sleep in his basement after Meryl left him. It wasn't long, though, before the TV production crew realized his sleeping body was out of their sight, and that something was wrong. Truman was gone, and Christof ordered the show's transmission cut while a citywide search for him began, thus leaving audiences around the world on the edge of their seats wondering what would become of their ignorant TV hero. He was eventually discovered sailing on the fake waters of Seahaven, determined to conquer his fear of the water. Despite the fact that Truman might drown on live television, Christof ignored all warnings and attempted to stop him with various tricks of controlled weather. Truman persisted, though, and sailed his boat into the wall of the makeshift dome and eventually located an exit door.

Desperate to save his TV show, Christof made his presence known and spoke directly to Truman through a giant speaker system, attempting to persuade him to remain by telling him that truth doesn't exist in the real world, and that only by staying inside his own artificial world, would Truman be safe. Tempted for a brief moment, Truman then took a bow and exited the dome, thus sending much of his audience into a cheering frenzy on his behalf. The show was over, and it was time to turn the channel to see what else was on TV.

It's almost impossible for me to reflect on my reactions to *The Truman Show* when I first saw it in 1998. Back then, I simply would've commented on how funny, emotional, dramatic and thought-provoking the whole premise was, particularly on the subject of celebrity culture, satire, and their impact on the everyday television viewer and their ordinary lives. I would've easily compared Jim Carrey's performance of blissful innocence to James Stewart in *Harvey*, Peter Sellers in *Being There*, and Tom Hanks in *Forrest Gump*. Those feelings seem irrelevant compared to how I view the film today. Back then, I never would've imagined the film becoming an unfortunate prelude to an onslaught of reality TV that has plagued the twenty-first century with shows like *Survivor* and *Big Brother* (just to name a couple).

Think about it, and you may also realize that in the real world, there's virtually nothing *real* about reality TV. Whereas Truman Burbank's reality is real to *him* on the fictional screen, everything that's supposed to compose reality on TV is false. None of what you watch on so-called reality TV is actually *real* because it all has the potential to have been scripted and rehearsed before it ever airs. None of the idiots you've watched on *Survivor* since its debut in May 2000 have ever been in any real danger, and the reason is because there's a camera crew (and probably a staff doctor) there on the island with them. In *real life*, there's no one there to save you if you get into trouble on a deserted island. Still, even as fiction, Truman's story illustrates the powerful hold the media has over the average moron who's willing to be controlled by the crap they watch on TV.

Finally, I'm sure it's no accident that the name *Christof* is so close to *Christ*, thus giving Ed Harris's character a representative quality of Jesus Christ or even an Antichrist (say it with me—"Christ-*off*") who seeks to control the minds of his many followers—in this case, the TV audience with an insatiable lust for the private details of the lives of (so-called) ordinary people in a world filled with too much celebrity pop culture.

Any way you look at it, it's easy to see why I prefer *movies* over television any day of the week. Thank goodness for that, because my books might not exist, otherwise.

Saving Private Ryan
Directed by Steven Spielberg
(July 24, 1998, U.S. Release Date)

In 1997, I purchased the latest Director's Edition VHS tape of *Close Encounters of the Third Kind*. Following the film, the tape featured a retrospective interview with Steven Spielberg and I noticed what appeared to be a battleground setting behind his director's chair. Nothing was said to this effect, but I knew this interview took place on the set of his latest film, *Saving Private Ryan*. That was anticipation number one. Number two was…well, did I really *need* a number two? This was *Spielberg*, and after his last film *Amistad*, I was determined to follow his career more closely than ever before. I went to see his new World War II film at the Hampton Arts twin movie theater in Westhampton Beach the night it opened in the summer of '98 amid a season of blockbusters that included comets, asteroids and a giant lizard destroying our cities. My moviegoing experience that night was far from perfect, but I'll describe that later.

Following the opening sequence of an elderly World War II veteran (whom we'd learn at the end of the film was James Ryan in the present day) and his family visiting the Normandy American Cemetery and Memorial in France, we were taken back in time to June 6, 1944 to the battle of Omaha Beach during the Normandy invasion, and the American soldiers who fought it. It was immediately obvious that this was no black-and-white John Wayne movie. Combat was neither glorified, nor was it exciting. From the moment the doors opened on the assault carrier, many of our young boys barely made it off the craft before they were shot to pieces by the unseen German infantry and their artillery fire on shore.

The first wave of soldiers was led by Captain John H. Miller (played by Tom Hanks in his first role with Spielberg). Though Miller and some of his men survived the bloody onslaught, too many heavy losses were suffered, and Miller was haunted and horrified by the extensive, violent casualties around him (Spielberg effectively used slow motion action to emphasize this). Eventually, Miller's team penetrated the German defenses and established victory for the great invasion, which history would record as a major successful turning point for the American foothold in the war. This opening battle sequence was nearly thirty minutes long, and although it was sometimes difficult to watch, I realized it was essential to tell the tale of such an important piece of American history that no textbook or previous war film could ever do (not even my favorite war film of all time, *The Longest Day*, could do that). When it was over, somewhere on the beach, there lied a dead soldier face-down in the bloody surf, and his pack was stenciled with the name *Ryan, S.*

Back home, the U.S. War Department in Washington, D.C. discovered that three of the four brothers named Ryan were killed in action and their mother in Iowa was due to receive all three telegrams of her son's death on the same day. The fourth brother James Francis Ryan (played by Matt Damon) was still missing in action and presumed alive somewhere in Normandy. John Miller and his team were assigned the mission to find Private Ryan and get him home to his mother. The idea of risking the lives of many to save the life of one man seemed illogical. In fact, I couldn't help but recall Spock in *Star Trek II: The Wrath of Khan* when he said, *"The needs of the many outweigh the needs of the few, or the one."* However, I understood the unique example of the human spirit and sacrifice behind such a mission, as well as the genuine empathy for a mother who'd lost three of her sons to war. This was a necessary feeling, as we journeyed with these soldiers to find one man, essentially *"a needle in a stack of needles,"* as Miller put it.

Along the way, there were more battle sequences and moments where the humanity of the American soldier was tested. When was it better to take a little girl away from the comfort of her family to assure her safety? When were they justified in shooting a German soldier who fearfully surrendered himself to them? When was it simply "an eye for an eye" form of justice? These were questions someone like me could never answer, but only true men of war. I could only watch and try to understand and appreciate the moral dilemmas and paradoxes that existed for such men on the battlefield.

Predictably, when they finally located Ryan, he refused to leave the men he considered to be the only brothers he had left. James Ryan himself, despite his rescue being at the heart of the film's story, wasn't someone we'd know or understand too well, other than a brief story he told Miller of the last wild night he spent with his brothers before they were separated by military enlistment. His character seemed no more than the means to the end in which Miller and his men would meet their ultimate destinies in the final battle of the film, be it life or death. Even the tough-as-nails soldiers (including Vin Diesel) couldn't withstand the power of the German bullet. Others like the simple interpreter who proved to be a coward in the face of danger, would survive. There seemed little comprehension for such coward-ice, even when this man justifiably shot the same German soldier he sympathized with earlier, and helped to survive the vengeance of the American soldier. War was confusing and complicated, even to the mere watcher like myself.

Perhaps the best aftermath of war was Miller's simple words he spoke to James Ryan before he died, when he told him to *earn it.* When that final moment transitioned back to the present-day Ryan, who stood in front of Miller's grave expressing his gratitude for the sacrifices he and his unit made for him, we could only try to relate to the question of whether he had "earned it" by simply being a good man and living his life to the best of his abilities. Then, like Ryan, we salute the graves of those who died in war. When the film ended, I and the entire theater could only take a moment to breathe and try to understand what we'd just experienced. I was a younger man, so I experienced nothing. It was the elderly gentlemen I overheard around me exiting the theater who spoke their own thoughts and memories of a war they likely experienced firsthand. *They* were the ones who mattered most.

Getting back to that night in Westhampton Beach, I had the terrible misfortune of sitting in front of two elderly women who continuously made verbal noises of shock and dismay throughout the entire film. Although I repeatedly asked them to be quiet, they had the audacity to react as if *I* were the problem—as if *I* was being rude to *them*. But even as I tried to tolerate these women behind me, I couldn't help but wonder what these two old bats honestly expected from an R-rated war film? Even if the internet and social media were not yet effective tools of researching the content of a film, they *had* to have known that a war film wouldn't be a pretty day at the beach. Modern war films of the '90s have blood, guts, and violence, ladies. If you can't handle that, then don't go to the movie. And if you *do* go to the movie, don't sit near *me*!

Years ago, I read a book entitled *Five Came Back: A Story of Hollywood and the Second World War* by journalist Mark Harris, which tells the story of Hollywood filmmaking during World War II. Key points consistent throughout the book is not only the timing of feature films and documentaries, but also their content. How much was too much, and how much was too realistic for American audiences to be exposed to during those war years? What would directors of American propaganda and war dramas, as well as the United States government and Hollywood big shots, have thought of *Saving Private Ryan*, possibly the most realistic and graphically detailed movie about combat ever made? Such a graphic and disturbing film would never have gotten the green light back then.

It's with this film that I've tried to understand who Steven Spielberg truly is in the world of movies and reality. My conclusion is that he's not just a filmmaker, but one who's spoken for those who need speaking for through his cinematic artistry. As *Schindler's List* spoke in the name of the countless Jewish Holocaust survivors, and *Amistad* spoke for those who'd not allow us to forget the tragic past of black slavery, *Saving Private Ryan* brings World War II to the big screen for our generation to fully understand the depth and perception of those brave American soldiers on the battlefields facing unspeakable German evil. He spoke for them successfully. So much so that many combat veterans of the war left movie theaters early, rather than continue watching the disturbingly realistic opening of the Normandy invasion. Their visits to counselors treating posttraumatic stress disorder rose in high numbers following the film's release. The Department of Veteran Affairs set up a nationwide hotline for war veterans affected by the nature of the film.

Finally, I'd just like to say to the Academy of Motion Picture Arts and Sciences, and those who deemed *Shakespeare in Love* worthy of the Oscar for Best Picture of 1998 over *Saving Private Ryan*, a sincere and heartfelt *fuck you*! There's no way that shameless piece of fluff deserved the big prize over Spielberg's war masterpiece. I'm glad he won the Oscar for Best Director, but it wasn't enough. It was just another example of the same royal screwing he got when *Out of Africa* beat *The Color Purple* for Best Picture of 1985.

So once again, fuck you!

Life Is Beautiful
Directed by Roberto Benigni
(October 22, 1998, U.S. Release Date)

Once upon a time, there was a young man who lived in New York City in the 1990s and had spent the better part of the last couple of years of his life going on *so many* first and second dates, his head was spinning from frustration because too many of these women he'd wasted his time and money on were nothing more than immature girls with the mental capacity of a common twit, and he was on the verge of never dating again—or at the very least, never dating women under the age of twenty-five years old again.

Then on Wednesday December 2, 1998, he participated in a product presentation from an outside vendor directly associated with the architectural firm he worked for. Assisting in that presentation was a young *twenty-three*-year-old woman named *Beth*, and he was undeniably attracted to her. Following the presentation, Beth handed out her business card to everyone in his office, and he was left with a hard decision to make—throw the card away and forget he ever saw her, or take a chance and give the possibility of dating one more try. He went with the latter. But wait—were there any moral or ethical issues involved in calling a total stranger at her business number? Surely, he didn't want to be accused of any sort of professional misconduct. On the other hand, Beth didn't work for *his* firm, so what could it possibly hurt to ask her out. "What the hell," he decided.

That night, he wrote down the exact message he'd leave with her business number. Once he finally got the words right, he got up the balls to call Beth's number and read his message to her (word-for-word), asking her out on a date. To his surprise, she responded days later with a message left on his home answering machine, accepting his offer. On Saturday December 5, 1998, they met for their first date, with drinks and dinner at a popular bar and grille on East Eighty-Fifth Street. To their surprise, the evening extended itself past dinner, until they eventually ended up at the Paris Theatre on West Fifty-Eighth Street (the same theater he'd last been to in 1996 to see *Hamlet*) for a late movie. Playing there that night was the Italian film creating a huge, international buzz with critics and audiences everywhere. The film was *Life Is Beautiful.*

(I'll now return to the first-person narrative for the time being).

By this time, my only knowledge of Italian actor and filmmaker Roberto Benigni was his role as a Roman cab driver in Jim Jarmusch's 1991 film *Night on Earth.* I'd also heard of him playing the son of Inspector Clouseau in *Son of the Pink Panther*, but why would I waste my time with a piece of crap like that? It was on this night I'd discover the man's comic and dramatic talent as writer, director and star. He played Guido Orefice, a Jewish man who'd just arrived in the city of Arezzo in Tuscany in the year 1939, where his uncle Eliseo worked in the restaurant of a local hotel. Guido was a comical man with the sharp wit to attract the Gentile teacher he'd fallen for, Dora. He was repeatedly and "coincidentally" running into her (sometimes physically) all over town and amazing her with his irresistible charm and magical personality. His repeated greeting of affection, *"Buongiorno Principessa!"* to the woman he loved never got old with me. Just like the spirit of Charlie Chaplin (who Benigni seemed clearly influenced by), it was joyful to watch this simple man win the heart of the beautiful woman whom other men sought, as well. Unfortunately, she was engaged to a rich and arrogant governmental official she didn't love (perhaps that was *fortunate*). It was at her own engagement party that Dora finally realized she loved Guido, and allowed him to carry her away on a horse, thus humiliating her fiancé and mother. Arriving at his home, they joined as lovers.

Five years later (continuing the same shot), Guido and Dora were married, owned a local book shop, and had a five-year-old son named Joshua. He was adorable and brought the entire theater to an emotional level when he burst out of a small side table and shouted, *"Buongiorno Principessa!"* to his mommy. It was 1944, and Northern Italy was occupied by Nazi Germany. It was Joshua's birthday when he, Guido and his uncle Eliseo were captured by the Nazis with other Jews, forced onto a train and taken to a concentration camp. Dora demanded that a Nazi guard put her on the train so she would be near her captured family.

To protect little Joshua from the horrors of what was happening to them, Guido was forced to employ his fertile imagination by creating the illusion that their world around them was a well-planned, organized and complicated *game* meant as a birthday present for Joshua. He explained the tasks Joshua had to perform to earn daily points, and whoever got to one thousand points first would win the grand prize of a real tank. But if Joshua complained, cried that he wanted his mommy, or asked for food, he would lose points, while the quiet children who hid from the prison guards would earn those extra points. Reluctant to follow these rules, Joshua really wanted that tank, nonetheless.

Guido maintained this elaborate fiction right until the end, when in the chaotic frenzy of eliminating the camp and its prisoners during the approach of the Allied forces, he told Joshua to hide inside a box until everybody was gone and it was quiet, this being his final task of the game to win the tank. Guido went searching for Dora within the camp, but was caught by a German solider. In his final effort to keep Joshua convinced it was all a game, Guido marched in a comical form while led by the armed soldier past his son's hiding place, and winked one final time before he was shot dead in an alleyway, far from Joshua's attention.

The next morning, the camp deserted, Joshua emerged from the box as a U.S. Army unit led by a Sherman tank arrived to liberate the camp. Joshua was overjoyed to see a real tank before him, believing he'd truly won it (unaware his daddy was dead). While riding in the tank to safety with an American soldier, he was reunited with his mother, excitedly telling her about how they'd won, his still believing it was all the game his father had promised. In the end, during a voiceover monologue, an older Joshua reminisced on the ultimate sacrifice his father made for him.

This was (and still is) one of those rare films that has since taken on a new and different meaning for myself since becoming a father. To witness the extents a loving father would go through to shield his son from terrifying evil is intriguing to witness. For this situation, love, family and the power of one's active imagination serves as the ultimate weapon against forces seeking to destroy all that is good. In the end, Joshua survives the Holocaust and will eventually grow up to manhood, having no memory of the same events that will make world history…and life will be beautiful.

For ourselves, though, we must consider just how "beautiful" life should be when we're dealing with the Holocaust. Like so many critics, let's ask ourselves where humor belongs in connection with one of the darkest times of humanity. Should the art of the human spirit and ingenuity be considered offensive? The film is, of course, dealing with a very sensitive subject matter, and Roberto Benigni is undeniably softening things up for not only the benefit of his son, but for our benefit of the comic cinematic journey into what is otherwise a terrible nightmare.

Still, *Life Is Beautiful* isn't necessarily about Nazi Germany and their fascist regime. What is real and what isn't must be suspended in our mind for this film. In real life, a man like Guido wouldn't last long enough for his "game" to succeed with his son. But if we suspend reality real long enough, then the human spirit succeeds in rescuing that which is good and hopeful from our damaged lives and dreams, and provides a sense of hope for not only surviving evil, but finding what is considered beautiful in a world of self-created delusions to ensure that survival. In the end, it's an effective tribute to our love, innocence, and vivid sense of imagination even in the most horrifying of circumstances, and reminds us to remember that every once in a while, *life is beautiful.*

(I'll now return to the third-person narrative once again).

When the movie was over, the young man and Beth completed their first date, which managed to last about six hours. They spoke little of the film they both loved (I think he would've been very put off if she *hadn't* loved it), as it was late, and they both had to get home. They had a wonderful time, agreed to see each other again, and kissed each other good night. As the young man walked from West Fifty-Eighth Street back home to his apartment on East Eighty-Sixth Street, thinking about the extraordinary Italian film he'd just experienced at one of the most upscale movie theaters left in Manhattan, he also hoped Beth wouldn't turn out to be another waste of his time like so many before her (she wasn't). The rest, as the future would eventually say, was history. You know the old story—guy meets girl, guy takes girl to dinner and a great Italian film, guy cooks dinner for the girl on their second date the very next night, girl brings over her toothbrush, girl sleeps over *every* night, girl moves in, then comes love, then comes marriage, then comes me pushing his baby boy in a carriage—yada, yada, yada.

"*I love you, Beth.*"

The Thin Red Line
Directed by Terrence Malick
(December 25, 1998, U.S. Release Date)

I'd never heard of Terrence Malick. I knew nothing of his 1973 debut film *Badlands* and only knew of *Days of Heaven* from newspaper ads back in 1978. But when I saw the original trailer for *The Thin Red Line*, its director seemed of little importance to me. Released just months after the enormous success of Spielberg's *Saving Private Ryan*, I was ready, willing and able to embrace another look at World War II through the eyes of the fighting soldier. I'd soon realize, though, that to dismiss a film's director so easily was not only wrong, but practically irresponsible in this case. For I'd soon learn what sort of filmmaker Terrence Malick was.

By this time, I'd seen what I considered to be a wide array of World War II combat films: from the great screen epics like *The Longest Day, Battle of the Bulge*, and *A Bridge Too Far*, to an endless assortment of smaller budget black-and-white films on Turner Classic Movies. During that time, I discovered that one of the most distinguishable things about war films is that the action and drama of combat almost never changed. It was blood, guts and glory all the way, particularly for World War II and our brave fighting men in the Pacific. At its heart, *The Thin Red Line* wasn't too different, as its mission was the straightforward arrival and departure of American soldiers off an island in the South Pacific, with the sole objective of securing a field held off by the Japanese. This mission would be a slow and tedious one, with many human casualties along the way.

I realized that while still a combat film, it was a *Terrance Malick* combat film, which was defined by narrated human thoughts and emotions and felt in conjunction with the horrors of war and the salvation of trying to find peace. When the film opened, life was calm and peaceful for a U.S. Army private gone AWOL (away without leave) from his unit, and living among the carefree natives of Melanesia. We heard his thoughts and felt his feelings of joy and contentment, but this lasted only until he was inevitably found and imprisoned on a troop carrier by his superior sergeant Edward Welsh (played by Sean Penn) and eventually thrown back into the mix of his unit.

These men of C Company arrived on the island of Guadalcanal as reinforcement in the campaign to secure Henderson Field and seize the island from the Japanese. Throughout their ordeal and their fears, the men contemplated the pending invasion and the meaning of their lives. On the one hand, it was hard to digest such deep, personal dialogue of the soldiers during the course of their intended survival. On the other, there was a certain brilliance to this sort of characterization in the art of filmmaking. Although a completely different genre, I couldn't help but think of David Lynch's 1984 sci-fi epic *Dune*, in which character thoughts and feelings were a constant throughout the film. And while I certainly wouldn't compare the artistic styles of both Lynch and Malick, it was impossible not to consider the similarities.

As their attack commenced and they stormed the hill, they were repelled by the enemy's heavy machine gun fire. Many men were scattered during the carnage (including Woody Harrelson carelessly blowing off his own ass with a grenade), with some of them hiding behind a safe knoll from enemy fire to await necessary reinforcements. As they were continuously fired upon, Lt. Col. Gordon Tall (played by Nick Nolte) repeatedly ordered over the radio for Captain James Staros, the sensitive company commander, to advance and capture the bunker by a frontal assault no matter what the cost. Staros repeatedly refused, declaring that he wouldn't commit his men to what he determined to be a suicide mission. Furious over his refused command, Tall ventured himself up to the men's position only to find the Japanese resistance had lessened in the last five minutes. Still, another battle ensued, but with the American forces victorious, the hill captured, and the men given a week's leave for their efforts, though there was little joy in the aftermath of their intense fighting. Tall relieved Staros of his command, deeming him too soft for the pressures and decisions of combat, and stressing that he apply for reassignment to practice law in the Washington, D.C. JAG Corps.

Throughout the film, we witnessed flashbacks of Private Jack Bell and the intense love he felt for his wife back home (she being the only woman in this film). It felt not only heartbreaking, but also infuriating to watch him receive a letter from her in which she informed him that she'd fallen in love with another man back home and wanted a divorce. Narrated words weren't necessary to express the pain and sorrow a man must feel when the woman he loves tells him it's over. I could personally feel the anger of such a harsh betrayal by a woman, having lived my own version of it, but hardly something that compared to a man fighting for his life among the horrors of war. Sometime later, the company was sent on patrol up a river, as Japanese artillery fire reached their position and their communications were cut off. Danger didn't stop those brave enough to volunteer to advance their position. Japanese soldiers were killed in that great, American heroic style that make war films ring true for those who honor them, but our own men were killed in moments where it was better to die than be captured by the enemy.

Throughout *The Thin Red Line*, Malick's narrative style felt contagious. I found myself thinking my own personal thoughts during the course of the film, though not nearly as deep and complex as the soldier's. Beyond my mild comparisons to David Lynch, I couldn't help but think thoughts such as these:

> "Nick Nolte reminds me of George Macready's character in Kubrick's *Paths of Glory* and Robert Duval's in Coppola's *Apocalypse Now*."
>
> "It's hard to believe that Sean Penn every played Jeff Spicoli. He's so damn good in every dramatic role he's had since."

"This is the first time I've seen John Savage since *The Godfather-Part III*."

"I wish John Travolta and George Clooney had bigger roles in this movie."

"Why does Woody Harrelson always manage to sound like an uneducated moron in every role he plays?

This is where *my* mind drifted, and I realized I did this sort of self-contemplation more often than I thought. For the film's settings, though, it's easy to consider them a virtual "Eden" or a "Paradise Lost" which is raped and pillaged by the poisons of war. Combat is bloody, but there are often camera shots that avoid excessive gore and focus instead on the explosion of a tree, the shredding of vegetation, or even the close-up of an exotic bird or alligator. Malick's unconventional filming styles and techniques also include the beauty of a bright, sunny morning with the majestic glory of tall trees, or the simplicity of a tree branch or a parrot.

As a World War II film, though, it's a daring, if not philosophical journey in its approach to what makes the American solider tick in a time of global crisis and uncertainty. Sometimes it's confusing, even while it fascinates us. The battle scenes are masterful in their own right, though it may evoke similar comparisons to *Saving Private Ryan*, as well as Oliver Stone's 1986 Best Picture winner *Platoon*. Truth, or whatever we consider to be the truth, is hardly based on the facts of war, but rather the emotions expressed by the human heart and the mind's wisdom. Out of death and destruction, we're meant to believe and understand that life, love and the power of creation can ultimately grow, even in war when, as Sean Penn puts it, *"The whole fucking thing's about* property!"

The Longest Day will always be my favorite war film of all time, and like that classic film, the players of *The Thin Red Line* are extensive ones, while avoiding too much attention to making any particular actor like Sean Penn, Nick Nolte, Jim Caviezel, Ben Chaplin, John Travolta, George Clooney, Woody Harrelson, or John Cusack, the star of the film, though we easily take notice of principal players like Penn and Nolte who maintain their own perfect tone and rhythm for scenes that may not last more than a few minutes. Everybody's a big star in our minds, but on the screen and in the jungles, these bright stars may also be interpreted as fallen angels… who just happen to be men who are big stars. It's these elements that made Malick's third film (and *Saving Private Ryan*) two of the best war films of the 1990s. It was disappointing, however, to learn in the course of writing this book that *The Thin Red Line* is the *second* film following a previous 1964 adaptation of James Jones's original 1962 novel. I generally frown at remakes, but I suppose exceptions can be made at every turn, for anybody, for any reason. I'll make that exception for Terrence Malick, and I'll thank him for an impressive film-making career that's also included *Days of Heaven*, *The New World*, and *The Tree of Life*.

Thank you, Terry.

*****

This is the last film of 1998 I shall discuss in any great detail.

I didn't realize it immediately, but the end of this year changed my life forever. Regardless of how Beth and I eventually turned out, it was impossible to recognize any potential this new relationship had in the beginning. We'd only dated a few weeks, and even though things progressed quickly, part of me still waited for the "other shoe to drop" on the whole thing. I'd been through too many failed attempts at dating and relationships over the past year and a half for me to allow myself to get too comfortable with anyone too quickly. I simply took things one day at a time and convinced myself that I wouldn't eat my heart out if it all inevitably fell apart. Well, it *didn't* fall apart. Beth and I were a confirmed couple, and that was a welcomed and wonderful change for me. Every moment, every activity, every dinner, and every movie felt different because I was finally sharing it with someone I was slowly falling in love with. It wasn't just merely falling in love; it was that I fell in love for the second time after such a damaging first attempt at love many years earlier. It was these emotions that allowed me to retain and cherish memories of our first movie date together, *Life is Beautiful* and even the ones that immediately followed, *Stepmom* and *Star Trek: Insurrection* (okay, maybe not *that* one).

It was also at the conclusion of '98 that I realized what an eye opening year it had been at the movies for me in its depiction of World War II. Within six months, men like Steven Spielberg, Roberto Benigni, and Terrence Malick had each in their own fashion, given my generation their own tale of the horrors of war and its ultimate impact on our emotions and spirit, far beyond anything any classroom or text book ever did before. Books and professors can only go so far, in my opinion. Those who don't understand the experience of war can perhaps better understand through the use of cinema as an effective media form. Whether we accept that or not, we are too often a race of human beings who only feel something when it's up on the big screen.

Spielberg understands that, I think, and succeeded in reaching our hearts and minds with *Schindler's List* and *Saving Private Ryan*. Malick understood too, and took it a step further by provoking us into our contemplations of life's meanings in *The Thin Red Line*. Benigni understood too, and I think even though he'll forever face the negative backlash of not taking the Holocaust seriously enough, he succeeded in suggesting that even the most horrible circumstances in life can be met with a spirit and beauty that's necessary to protect those we love, and that it's also necessary to remember that life can always be beautiful. I think *I* understood all of this because like so many others, I looked to the movies to continue expanding my mind, heart, and understanding of life, love, history, and even the deeper meanings behind war. It happened to me three times in '98, and it didn't happen again until 2001 with the HBO miniseries *Band of Brothers* and then again in 2017 with Christopher Nolan's *Dunkirk*. I wonder if it will ever happen to me again?

And that, my friends, was the year 1998 for me.

THE YEAR WAS 1999...

- U.S. president Bill Clinton is acquitted in the impeachment proceedings for his denial of a sexual relationship with White House intern Monica Lewinsky.
- For the first time, NATO attacks a sovereign state by launching air strikes against the Federal Republic of Yugoslavia.
- At Columbine High School in Littleton, Colorado, teenagers Eric Harris and Dylan open fire, killing twelve students, one teacher, and then themselves. At the time, it is the deadliest high school shooting in U.S. history.
- George W. Bush announces that he will accept the Republican Party's nomination for president of the United States.
- John F. Kennedy Jr., his wife Carolyn Bessette-Kennedy, and her sister Lauren Bessette are killed when the plane he is piloting crashes off the coast of Martha's Vineyard.
- Across the world, millennium celebrations take place to mark the end of the twentieth century. Consequences of the Y2K scare are minor.

...AND THERE WERE MOVIES!

This is the final year of this book.

This was the last year of the 1990s and the final year of the twentieth century. There was so much to consider and contemplate. What would the future and the new century bring? Would we proceed down a road of potential and improvement, or would we simply continue along our long path of human flaws, hypocrisy and bullshit?

For myself, I was taking my new relationship with Beth more seriously, and by the third or fourth month, was seriously considering the possibility of her being my future wife. I hadn't had thoughts like these in many years, and they were unnerving, as well as exciting. Still, I wouldn't allow myself to take things any further than just one day at a time—with love, life, and the prospects of the future. For right now, things were good. The job with my current architectural firm was good, my love life was good, the beach house was good, my enthusiasm for trying to get some serious attention toward my screenwriting was good, and the oncoming summer blockbuster season looked good, as Stanley Kubrick's next film, as well as the first *Star Wars* film in sixteen years, lay ahead.

One thing unchanged was my low expectations for movies of the late winter and early spring, and it seemed there was more for me to judge and scrutinize, as I went to the movies more often now that I had Beth in my life. Too often, movies that I got dragged to that I had little interest in, like *At First Sight*, *Blast from the Past*, *Message in a Bottle*, and Ron Howard's *EDtv* were at best, the kind of unavoidable fluff you had to occasionally sit through to make your girlfriend happy. Even potentially promising material (promising to *me*, anyway) like the late Joel Schumacher's *8mm* with Nicholas Cage and Clint Eastwood's *True Crime* (the last movie I ever saw with Daniela, by the way. We haven't been to the movies since) failed to deliver any real, substantial thrills. On the other hand, I was pleasantly surprised with the successful comic chemistry between Billy Crystal and Robert De Niro in *Analyze This* and was pleased to discover a new directing talent in Guy Ritchie with *Lock, Stock and Two Smoking Barrels*.

In effect, the final year of the '90s for me was starting off as a leveled balance of promise, as well as the same 'ol, same 'ol. Perhaps

George Lucas and the new *Star Wars* movie would jump-start things come summertime. Before that happened, however, there'd be a new step in science fiction and the questions of reality that would really shake things up by, brought to us by a couple of siblings I'd never heard of before known as The Wachowskis.

The Matrix

Directed by The Wachowskis
(March 31, 1999, U.S. Release Date)

Despite the fact that I lived in New York City for more than ten years, I never cared for it much. The pulse and hustle and bustle of Manhattan may be just what some people need, but it never agreed with me. I was raised a suburbanite who enjoyed the quiet, and I'll always remain one. One thing I *did* love, however, was the convenience and close proximity to my apartment on East Eighty-Sixth Street with which Beth and I could go to the movies, with little-to-no planning. This was the pleasure of living within a short walking distance of four movie theaters, affording us various opportunities to see just about every new release. While most hot movies on our must-see list were planned in advance, there was always that restless Saturday night after dinner when we both wanted to just get out and go to a movie…any movie.

On one of those Saturday nights, anything was possible, particularly because back then I still kept an open mind when it came to Hollywood's mainstream movies. Therefore, a new sci-fi movie with a real cool movie poster ad in the New York Times called *The Matrix* seemed just as promising (or disappointing) as anything else. What the hell—it was a short walk just down the street and the next show time was conveniently very soon. It hardly mattered to me right now, considering the only movie I focused my concentration on during the spring of '99 was the return of the new *Star Wars* movie called *The Phantom Menace*. So really, *The Matrix* could potentially blow me away or it could really suck. It didn't matter. I just wanted to get out of the apartment for the night.

From the moment *The Matrix* began at an abandoned hotel in a major city on a dark night, I immediately felt like I'd been here before. I had—a year ago with *Dark City*, and the same dark, dystopian, neo-noir tone and visual culture. Still, I told myself to keep an open mind and wait for something different to happen, which it did. In the hotel, a squad of policemen cornered a beautiful woman dressed in black leather named Trinity, who easily overpowered them with her uncanny superhuman fighting abilities. This wasn't traditional screen fighting, though. There was slow-motion, freeze-frames and spinning camera work involved, adding a level of fantasy to what could've easily been just another fight scene. Fleeing the scene, Trinity was pursued by the police as well as a group of well-suited Agents wearing shades, capable of the same superhuman abilities as her. She made it to a ringing public telephone and disappeared just before an Agent driving a truck crashed into the phone booth.

Enter now the ordinary computer programmer Thomas Anderson (played by Keanu Reeves of *Point Break* and *Speed* fame), also known by his alias as a computer hacker "Neo." Awakened by a troubled sleep, he was confused by repeated online communications with the phrase "the Matrix" attached to them. At a night club, Trinity informed him of a man named Morpheus who possessed the answers Neo was seeking (what were the answers? What were the *questions*, for that matter?). The next day at his office, Neo was contacted by Morpheus, who warned him that he was about to be arrested by a group of Agents. Although he tried to guide Neo to safety, he was arrested and coerced by the lead Agent Smith into helping them locate Morpheus, whom they considered a terrorist. Neo refused, and as a consequence, was deprived of the existence of his mouth and injected with a mechanical "bug" in his stomach. He then awoke from what appeared to be only a dream, but later learned the dream and the "bug" was real when Trinity took him to meet Morpheus (played by Lawrence Fishburne), who offered Neo the choice of swallowing two pills: the blue pill would return Neo to his former ordinary life, while the red pill would reveal the truth.

Neo chose the red pill and his sense of reality disintegrated, as he awakened to find himself naked within a liquid-filled pod among endless human beings attached to a mysterious and complex electrical system. Retrieved and awakened, he was brought to Morpheus's flying ship, the *Nebuchadnezzar* (wow—I had to look up how to spell that correctly).

Morpheus revealed to Neo (and to us) the history of their current situation: sometime in the early twenty-first century, a war broke out between humanity and the artificial intelligence of the machines (echoing mankind's fate in *The Terminator* and *Terminator 2*). Following the machines denial of solar energy by the humans, the machines struck back by capturing humans and harvesting their bio-electric power, while keeping their minds under the simulated reality of the Matrix, modeled after the world as it was in the year 1999. The machines were victorious, and the underground city of Zion was the last known refuge for free human beings. Morpheus and his crew were a group of resistance fighters who hacked into the Matrix to free enslaved humans by "unplugging" and recruiting them to join their fight. Understanding how the Matrix worked meant allowing those inside it to defy the laws of physics with the same supernatural abilities displayed by Trinity at the beginning of the film. But should one die in the Matrix, then the physical body itself would die, as well. The Agents were actually computer programs meant to eliminate threats to the system.

This was a lot of information and theories to take in. Not that I ever denied myself the mind challenge of a sci-fi think piece, but right now I thought I was simply getting out on a Saturday night. One had to now ask what the true nature of reality was in our minds. Perhaps Morpheus explained it best when Neo questioned what was real:

> *What is real? How do you define "real"? If you're talking about what you can feel, what you can smell, what you can taste and see, then "real" is simply electrical signals interpreted by your brain.*

That made some sense to me, and at the same time, it frightened me, because it opened up the possibility that anything we as humans deemed as "real" could easily be a self-induced illusion like in some black-and-white Italian Fellini film. Hell, for all I knew, I wasn't *really* sitting in a movie theater right now next to the girl I loved. Okay, maybe I was taking my contemplations a little too far right now. Best to just clear my mind and enjoy the rest of the movie.

During Neo's virtual physical training that included Jujutsu techniques, high jumping from one building roof to another, and dodging bullets, Morpheus declared his immovable belief that Neo was the human prophesied to free humankind from its virtual slavery, or "the One." The group entered the Matrix to visit a kind black woman known as the Oracle, a prophet who predicted the rise of the One. She informed Neo that he *wasn't* the One and warned that he'd eventually have to choose between his own life and Morpheus's. But before they could leave the Matrix, the Agents led by Smith and the police ambushed them (tipped off and betrayed by a disgruntled member of Morpheus's own crew named Cypher) and captured Morpheus, while other members of the crew were murdered by Cypher as they lied defenseless and connected to the Matrix. But before he could kill Neo and Trinity, Cypher was killed himself by another crewman.

While the Agents interrogated Morpheus to learn of his access codes to Zion's mainframe computer, Neo and Trinity returned to the Matrix to rescue him. During a very intense battle of guns and violence, Neo came to a full understanding of his abilities and his untested potentials, as he performed feats capable of battling the Agents. Trinity and Morpheus exited the Matrix, but Agent Smith appeared to kill Neo before he could escape. Trinity professed her love for Neo, and revealed that the Oracle told her she'd fall in love with the One. Neo returned from his apparent death with newfound abilities believed to control the Matrix, thus defeating Agent Smith. Now believed to be the One, Neo made a final phone call to promise the machines that he'd show the slaves a new world where anything was possible, and then like the new Superman he was, he flew away.

When Beth and I left the theater later that night, I said to her the one word most often repeated by actor Keanu Reeves in several of his movies, and that word was *Whoah!* This turned out to not just be another Saturday night at the movies, as *The Matrix* not only provided some incredible and spectacular action, but also *influential* action, as it introduced us all to a new level of filmmaking effects that hadn't been seen before. As I'd later learn, the film incorporated something known as *wire fu* techniques, including the involvement of top fight choreographers with backgrounds in Hong Kong action cinema, affecting the approaches to fight scenes taken by other Hollywood action films and steering them toward more Eastern cinematic styles (these sophisticated techniques from such choreographers would later influence one of the best modern Chinese films of the new century, *Crouching Tiger, Hidden Dragon*). The moments known as the "bullet time" effect on the screen during the sequence of spectacular shooting was particularly striking as a visual effect without being cheesy. In fact, as a purely surreal and visual film, *The Matrix* clearly speaks for itself.

But what about the story? Can we honestly claim that the concept of the postapocalyptic world of tomorrow is anything new? I say *no*. Can we honestly claim the world of tomorrow where human beings are dominated by artificial intelligence or machine technology is anything new (again, *Terminator* movies)? Hell, just look around the real world of today and you'll see that the majority of the human race have become helpless slaves to everything ever invented by the late Steve Jobs. But beyond the inevitable sci-fi concept of humanity versus machine intelligence, *The Matrix* also offers high concepts in the world of dreams versus reality. As Morpheus asks, *"Have you ever had a dream that you were so sure was real? What if you were unable to wake from that dream? How would you know the difference between the dream world and the real world?"* As a man in the real world who has his share of bizarre dreams, I can only state that such a concept is more than thought-provoking…it's downright frightening.

However, if the world of what is roughly the year 2199 is scorched beyond recognition by the inevitable nuclear fires, we should ask ourselves if ignorance is not indeed truly bliss in this case?

Would human beings choose the dark, grim and desolate world of reality's truth instead of the blissful world of simulation? Would we rather not be seated at the table of a fancy restaurant eating a thick, juicy steak and drinking a glass of fine red wine instead of fighting for our lives against the deadly machines of the underworld?

I suppose what I'm ultimately saying is that I would've chosen to swallow the *blue* pill. In fact, in *my* simulated world, *The Matrix* would've began and ended with the first film and without the pointless continuation of its three sequels, leaving us with a classic stand-alone film that ultimately proved itself as something far greater than a Saturday-night filler while waiting for *The Phantom Menace* to come out.

Star Wars: Episode I— The Phantom Menace

Directed by George Lucas
(May 19, 1999, U.S. Release Date)

History has a way of dictating itself. It was now sixteen years since *Return of the Jedi.* Boys and girls were now men and women. The President of the United States was once again a Democrat, the 1980s were now the years at the dawn of the new Millennium, and George Lucas was back in the director's chair for the first time since *Star Wars* in 1977. In November 1998, I was one of the few people *not* willing to sit through *Meet Joe Black* just so I could see the long-awaited teaser trailer for *Star Wars: Episode I—The Phantom Menace.* I was patient and waited until I finally watched it on a weekly cable TV show featuring new movie trailers (before you could easily watch them on YouTube). In fact, I taped the episode and watched the new trailer multiple times to the point of obsession. Then I went to Toys "R" Us and bought some new action figures (Darth Maul, Jar Jar Binks, and a battle droid, still mint-in-package today) in the same spirit in which I purchased those classic Kenner action figures when I was a boy. I was reliving a personal and nostalgic period of my childhood again at the age of thirty-two, and I hadn't even seen the movie yet.

When May 1999 finally arrived, I was also *not* one of those people who camped out overnight for tickets, nor did I obsess about advanced tickets days or weeks before the new movie opened. I didn't need to see *The Phantom Menace* on its opening day, or even days after. My philosophy was to wait a couple of weeks until the madness subsided and then see it at my own convenience. As it turned out, I didn't have to wait that long. After Beth and I went to a week-night showing of *The Mummy* (it sucked), we unexpectedly walked to another movie theater where *The Phantom Menace* was playing. There was another show starting in just under an hour, and tickets weren't sold out. Without thinking, we bought tickets and secured our right to see the new movie without waiting any longer. In one night, two movies at two different movie theaters (we didn't sleep much that night).

Even as I felt a small sense of triumph in having scored tickets so easily and unexpectedly, I realized George Lucas had a lot to live up to after so many years. He'd already alienated many fans with his Special Edition release of the original trilogy back in '97, and apparently, the word was already out that some fans thought *The Phantom Menace* sucked. Sucked? Was that even possible for a *Star Wars* movie? Even with all my negative feelings toward *Jedi*, I never went so far as to say it sucked. I had to see how this would turn out as quickly as possible, and my patience was already wearing thin from what seemed like an endless barrage of screen commercials and trailers.

So here we were—the world of a galaxy far, far away, a long time ago, more than thirty-two years before the events of the first *Star Wars* movie. Following the comfort of the classic opening scrawl accompanied by John Williams's' classic opening score, I had a smile on my face a mile wide, and the story hadn't even begun yet. Set during the time of the Galactic Republic, it was a period of turmoil because of the Trade Federation's blockade of the planet Naboo in preparation for a full-scale invasion by an army of battle droids. Two Jedi knights, Qui-Gon Jinn and his young apprentice Obi-Wan Kenobi (played by Liam Neeson and Ewan McGregor, respectively) were dispatched by the leader of the Republic to negotiate with the Trade Federation Viceroy in this matter. The Sith Lord Darth Sidious ordered the Viceroy to kill the two Jedi knights and begin the invasion, but the Jedi escaped and fled to Naboo. On the planet's surface, Qui-Gon saved the life of a Gungan named Jar-Jar Binks, who spoke with an irritating distortion of the English language. Indebted to Qui-Gon, Jar Jar led the Jedi duo to his home in an underwater city. After failing to get assistance from the Gungan leader, the Jedi and Jar Jar were on their own to survive the underwater sea monsters until they finally rescued Queen Padmé Amidala (played by Natalie Portman) from captivity and escaped aboard her royal starship, bound for the Republic planet of Coruscant.

Penetrating the Federation blockade, the ship was fired upon, and despite the efforts of a very capable and familiar droid named Artoo-Detoo, its hyperdrive was damaged. The ship landed on the desert planet of Tatooine to repair its damage. Qui-Gon, Padmé (disguised as one of her handmaids), Jar-Jar and R2-D2 visited one of the planet's settlements to secure replacement parts for their ship. They encountered junk dealer Watto and his young slave boy named Anakin Skywalker, who was already a gifted pilot, and also in the process of building his personal protocol droid, See-Threepio (though he was nothing but inner parts).

At this point, my brain sifted through the pieces (so far) that I imagined would piss off some die-hard *Star Wars* fans. Jar Jar Binks was an irritating creature. Anakin Skywalker, who'd one day become the infamous Darth Vader, was a sweet, innocent child, and I suppose *that* in itself was irritating. Natalie Portman was hardly a gifted actress. Finally, there was the acting and dialogue. Critics called it "wooden." That may have been an industry term I didn't fully understand, but for myself, I was merely trying to determine if it was all better or worse than the horrible acting and dialogue of *Jedi*. "Hang in there," I told myself. This is a *Star Wars* movie. There's always room for improvement."

Qui-Gon sensed the Force was unusually strong with Anakin, and was convinced he may be the one prophesied as "the Chosen One," destined to bring balance to the Force. Meanwhile, Watto refused to accept Republic Credits as payment for his replacement parts. Qui-Gon wagered the parts he needed, as well as Anakin's freedom from slavery, in an upcoming pod race in which Anakin would pilot his own racing speeder. The racing sequence was long and tiresome, but it was clearly Lucas's personal homage to the famous chariot race in *Ben-Hur*. Seriously? That masterful sequence with Charlton Heston could hardly be compared to this sci-fi mock-up. In the end, Anakin won the race and his freedom, though he faced the pain of leaving his mother behind. After a brief lightsaber duel between Qui-Gon and Darth Maul (Darth Sidious's Sith apprentice), the group escaped aboard the starship, bound for Coruscant, a planet that was one huge city.

Once arrived, Queen Amidala pleaded her suffering people's case to Chancellor Valorum (played by Terrance Stamp) and the Galactic Senate. Qui-Gon requested permission from the Jedi Council to train Anakin as his new Jedi Padawan learner, which was denied. The Council, including Yoda and Mace Windu (played by Samuel L. Jackson), believed that Anakin was too old and that his future was clouded and vulnerable to the dark side of the Force. Refusing to give up, Qui-Gon declared Obi-Wan ready for the trials as a Jedi Knight, and that he'd train Anakin, nonetheless. During a meeting of the Senate, Senator Palpatine (who'd one day become the Emperor of the galaxy, and played again by Ian McDiarmid) persuaded Amidala to call for a vote of no confidence in Chancellor Valorum, and to elect a stronger leader who would resolve the current crisis amidst a corrupt Senate. Her vote was pushed and Palpatine was named the new Chancellor in Valorum's place. Feeling she could do nothing more, she returned with her companions to her home planet Naboo.

While pleading for help from the Gungans, Padmé revealed herself as Naboo's true queen to gain their trust, and persuaded them to aid against the oncoming Trade Federation invasion. Jar Jar, despite his clumsiness, was promoted to combat general and joined his tribe in the battle against the droid army. During a battle to locate the Viceroy, Qui-Gon ordered Anakin to remain safe inside the cockpit of a Starfighter, but Anakin accidentally triggered its autopilot and ended up in a great space battle above the planet. With R2-D2's help, Anakin used his piloting skills to destroy the Federation droid control ship, and the droids themselves. Elsewhere, Qui-Gon and Obi-Wan were in a spectacular lightsaber duel with Darth Maul, who surprised us with his newly designed lightsaber with beams at both ends. Qui-Gon was mortally wounded, but then Obi-Wan took over and severed Darth Maul in half. Before Qui-Gon died, Obi-Wan promised to train Anakin as a Jedi.

The battles over, Palpatine took his place as the new Chancellor, Yoda promoted Obi-Wan to the rank of Jedi Knight, and reluctantly agreed to allow him to train Anakin. During Qui-Gon's funeral (his body burned just like Darth Vader's at the end of *Jedi*), Yoda and Mace Windu agreed there was still one Sith remaining after the death of Darth Maul because there was always two—a master and an apprentice. During a massive celebration parade, Padmé presented a gift of thanks to the Gungans to establish a world of peace between them…and then, the end credits, and the return of John Williams's classic closing score. There it was—the first *Star Wars* movie in sixteen years was over, and although I'd kept that mile-wide smile on my face the entire time, I knew I had a lot to think about and to contemplate amidst a world of harsh criticism from those who possibly expected more from Lucas than what they ultimately got.

I'll start by saying that despite its reputation in the *Star Wars* film world, I *don't* think *The Phantom Menace* sucked. In fact, I saw it three times that summer. Since its release, though, I've tried to figure out why it's hated so much. I suppose there are obvious and understandable reasons, the most significant being what a horrible annoyance a comic relief like Jar Jar Binks is. To have to listen to his distorted speech patterns, as well as his fellow Gungan mates, is an exercise in true patience and tolerance. However, I find him easier to tolerate than the Ewoks of *Jedi*, which are nothing better than a cross between the common Teddy bear and the Munchkins of *The Wizard of Oz*. In the end, I'm left with only the question of why comic reliefs are considered a necessary element in *any Star Wars* movie?

There's also the plot element of Anakin Skywalker as a young boy (whom many insist on calling "Annie"), which left many fans feeling as if the film was specifically created for ten year-old boys only (many criticized the original 1977 film of the same thing). Then there's the pod race famously paying homage to *Ben-Hur*. I certainly have no problem with paying homage to such a classic film, but there's the matter of execution and the race's failure to achieve any credible excitement beyond common speed and mayhem. Finally, there's the poor casting choice of Natalie Portman (in all three films), whom I've been knocking as an actress ever since her debut in the 1994 thriller *The Professional* because of her childish, whining and often somber demeanor in everything she's done on screen (she's the single reason I couldn't sit through all of Kenneth Branagh's *Thor*). Put simply—*the girl cannot act* (regardless of her Oscar for Best Actress of 2010 for *Black Swan*).

In all fairness, though, here's why I defend *The Phantom Menace* against those who condemn it. One of its strongest points is its political theme. Remember that we're in a galactic period before the rise of the Empire, and with that comes the necessary story of *how* and *why* it originally rose. The rise of any political power often begins with a single political crisis, in this case the blockade by the Trade Federation upsetting the galactic order. Senator Palpatine (aka Darth Sidious) plays both sides, outwardly seeking to resolve the crisis for the good of the Republic while secretly plotting to rise as the Emperor of what shall one day be known as the Empire. We know this from the original trilogy, and we're now in the midst of crisis that inevitably leads to an uprising of power that will bring (unwanted) order to the galaxy.

Watching any *Star Wars* movie means the excitement of laser fire, spectacular battles and the climactic lightsaber duel that's become tradition since '77. In fact, I think *The Phantom Menace* offers one of the best and most original duels since *The Empire Strikes Back*, particularly in the use of Darth Maul's double lightsaber. I also appreciate the original design of the battle droids, which may be a precursor to the future Stormtroopers. While *Menace* may never be as fresh or original as *Star Wars* and *Empire* (I think it's impractical to make any fair comparisons between them), it does have the gift of fine British and Scottish actors like Liam Neeson, Ewan McGregor and Ian McDiarmid. In fact, it's the diabolical scheming and plotting of McDiarmid as Palpatine that's most enjoyable in the entire prequel trilogy, the character so well-commanded in its dark intensity. And while we already know the fate of young Anakin Skywalker, having to sit through the likes of Jake Lloyd is, like Binks, an exercise in patience and tolerance. Samuel L. Jackson is a welcome addition to the cast, echoing the same joy we felt when we first met Billy Dee Williams in *Empire*, and it's also good to see Yoda (and his puppeteer commander Frank Oz) alive and well again.

I'll briefly give you my feelings toward the two films that followed in the prequel trilogy. Much like *Empire*, *Attack of the Clones* doesn't so much continue a saga debut, but rather gives it a fresh start ten years later with established characters. While it offers many improvements over its predecessor (less Jar Jar Binks, for starters), it continues to suffer from the same wooden acting and dialogue, and an older version of Anakin Skywalker played by Hayden Christensen doesn't necessarily improve things, as he's constantly whining about how unfair his life is. Still, things continue toward the fall of the Republic and the rise of the Empire we all know is coming, and we get to enjoy two and a half hours of serious fun along the way. For myself, *Clones* was a revelation because until this film clearly spelled things out, I had no idea the Empire actually rose out of the Republic as political corruption and fear spread throughout the galaxy (amazing, the things you learn, even in the world of *Star Wars*).

By the time *Revenge of the Sith* brought things to a full circle in 2005, George Lucas was perhaps listening to the disappointment of many fans and turned up the heat on Anakin's ultimate fate and the rise of Emperor Palpatine. This was a much darker film (the first *Star Wars* film to receive a PG-13 rating), and although Natalie Portman continued to be her usual annoying self, she surprised me by delivering the most thought-provoking and important line in the movie when she declared during the emergency meeting of the Senate, *"So this is how liberty dies, with thunderous applause,"* echoing our own post 9/11, George W. Bush era when America was deep into its own political turmoil overseas in Iraq. *Sith* not only improved the entire prequel package, but it brought a better understanding of the saga's entire tale (still only six movies back then). Hell, it even made *Jedi* look better. It was a personal conclusion to a saga I'd devoted my life to since I was ten years old, during the last summer of my freedom and independence before the new fears and responsibilities of fatherhood came one year later

So while *The Phantom Menace* many never find its way into the *Star Wars* hearts of millions the way the three films before it and after it have, let's all try to at least be *fair* with it, shall we? If absolutely nothing else, it's a shining example of Hollywood movie mediocrity—in other words, it ain't the worst and it ain't the best.

Summer of Sam

Directed by Spike Lee
(July 2, 1999, U.S. Release Date)

When you're a ten-year-old kid, the world exists only within what matters to you, leaving the outside realities a distant mystery. In July 1977, my family and I lived in the luxurious apartment complex known as North Shore Towers in the town of Floral Park, Long Island, and we'd rented a small beach house in Westhampton Beach (one year before we bought our own home). Life was a day at the beach, and even my soon-to-be obsession with *Star Wars* was still a month away. My only summer screen interests were attached to the new *Bad News Bears* movie and a giant killer whale called *Orca*. It's safe to say I lived a very sheltered life that summer away from the hell taking place in New York City.

Still, I wasn't completely oblivious to what was happening outside the safety of my four walls. Thanks to the local TV news, I couldn't avoid being aware of the Son of Sam (aka the .44 Caliber Killer) murders taking place all over the city. In fact, I felt anxious every time my mother went into Manhattan for the day (though I had no idea the murders took place only at night). I was also well aware of the infamous blackout that affected most of New York City on July 13 and 14 of '77, though the lights at North Shore Towers stayed on thanks to a self-generating power plant independent of local power companies which fed our complex. The crimes and looting that took place during the blackout, I'd learn about later on the news. Disco was king, the New York Yankees had a winning season that summer, and men like Reggie Jackson and Thurman Munson were my baseball heroes.

Despite my detailed childhood memory, sometimes it still takes a history-based crime thriller like Spike Lee's *Summer of Sam* to jump-start things in my brain after a long period of dormancy. It was that strong childhood memory that allowed me to approach this new film with great enthusiasm, though Beth being eight years younger than I, approached the film as only the girlfriend being dragged to something she had little interest in. At the film's start, American journalist Jimmy Breslin himself told us there were many New York stories that fateful summer, and what we were about to see was just one of them.

It was the summer of '77. The heat was stifling, and the city was living in fear of the Son of Sam. The man systematically shot his victims over a period of nearly a year. He lived alone in squalor, and was consistently driven mad by what he interpreted as a nonstop barking dog directing him to kill. Elsewhere, in a small Italian American neighborhood in the Bronx, local hairdresser Vinny and his beautiful wife Dionna (played by John Leguizamo and Mira Sorvino, respectively) were out for another hot night of disco dancing at a local club. They were happily married, but that didn't stop Vinny from cheating on his wife every chance he got, including doing her hot cousin in the car. Unbeknownst to them, the Son of Sam was watching them have sex in the car, but was scared off when the car horn honked. Instead, he killed another couple parked nearby. Vinny later discovered police activity near the spot where he and Dionna's cousin had previously parked, and was witness to the bloodied bodies of the slain couple. Realizing he could've been the killer's next victim, Vinny concluded that God had spared his life, and vowed to stop cheating on his wife. Their married sex life was hardly exciting, partly because Vinny believed his kinky urges weren't something to practice with his own wife (despite her willingness to please him in bed), hence his cheating to live out his fantasies with other women (including his own female boss).

Hanging out with his Italian buddies, Vinny's old friend Richie (played by Adrien Brody) returned to the neighborhood sporting a punk spiked hairdo, punk fashion, and fake British accent. While

Vinny was a man of the disco era, Richie implied "death to Disco" by embracing punk music and declaring The Who as his favorite band (a band I'd personally classify as *classic rock*, even back in the '70s). He was considered an unwelcomed and disgusting freak of the neighborhood by everyone in the neighborhood, except for the local sexually promiscuous girl Ruby (a girl Dionna later sought advice from on how to properly fuck her husband), who found his new look attractive (eventually sporting the punk look herself). Unlike the other guys of the neighborhood, Richie was interested in her as a person, and not just an object of sex. But his sexual orientation was in question, because he secretly earned money as an erotic dancer and male prostitute at a gay theater.

Tensions in the neighborhood rose as the Son of Sam killings continued. Local police detectives sought help from the local mob boss to find the killer, and a list of possible suspects was made by the local boys, Richie being at the top, being the misunderstood freak that he was. Richie and Ruby invited Vinny and Dionna to see their new punk band perform at the Manhattan music club CBGB, but when they arrived, Vinny and Dionna were intimidated and disgusted by the punk crowd, refusing to go inside the club. Instead, they drove to the famous Studio 54. Unable to gain entry, they ended up at the swinger's sex club Plato's Retreat, where they took drugs and participated in a kinky orgy. Despite *both* of them participating in sex acts with other partners, Vinny had the audacity to be upset and jealous with his wife for having appeared to enjoy the experience of sex with other men. They viciously berated each other during the drive home (while Swedish pop group ABBA gleefully sang "*Dancing Queen*"), eventually splitting up later.

Reaching their breaking point of tension and paranoia, the neighborhood gang of Italian hoods concluded that the latest Daily News sketch of the Son of Sam suspect greatly resembled Richie. They went after Richie as Vinny lured him out of his home and into the hands of the lynch mob ready to crucify him as the Son of Sam. It was at the precise moment of Richie's beating in the street (orchestrated to The Who's "*Won't Get Fooled Again*") that they learned the actual killer, David Berkowitz, was apprehended by police in

Yonkers, though it hardly resolved the darkness Vinny and the rest of the neighborhood had finally sunk to. Jimmy Breslin returned to remind us of the New York City story we'd just witnessed, one story among many.

Leaving the theater that night, I immediately regretted seeing *Summer of Sam* with Beth. She neither cared for the film, nor could she relate to its content of the past (she was only *two* in the summer of '77). I'd have been happier seeing this with someone my own age whom I could engage in thought-provoking conversation with about the era. Still, my personal thoughts remained my own, and nothing stopped them from reflecting and interpreting that time of my childhood when a small portion of the world outside of my own protected one was going to hell. Even if you don't personally remember the summer of '77, it's impossible not to bear witness to its events through Spike Lee's eyes, and feel its era-defining impact of drugs, music and sexual freedom. At its darker side, Lee employs weapons of lust, guilt, fear and betrayal to hit us hard, even when we choose to put aside the element of the prowling serial killer aside for a moment. In this film, the so-called "innocent victims" of the neighborhood can be uglier than the killer, which only shows us the state of human nature in the '70s (or any other decade, for that matter).

Summer of Sam may be Lee's personal tribute to a man like Martin Scorsese, his 1973 film *Mean Streets* in particular, with its visual neighborhood relations, tensions and even its trash. It's depiction of '70's pornography, perversions, pervasive language, and unflattering, defamatory representations of Italian American ethnic culture is powerfully and harshly realistic, if not offensive to some. At the same time, perhaps that harshness doesn't go far enough. This is hardly a serious piece of history, though it had the potential to be. Lee's intense visual storytelling is often overambitious with multiple periods of fantasy and delusion, particularly on the part of David Berkowitz, who despite being insane, is often laughable, rather than someone the film focusses on as a story subject matter. While it's certainly the summer of Sam, this is more a film about the victims. Not the victims who are brutally shot to death, but those victims suffering from overthought, overheated imagination and paranoia, and the need to ultimately find someone to blame for the crisis, and that someone most often turns out to be the one person who's different from the rest of us.

I was an innocent kid playing on the beach in the Hamptons in the summer of '77. Knowing what I know now of that summer, from *Summer of Sam* and real life, I think I'll keep it that way. My memories drift even further to the month of October, when the New York Yankees beat the Los Angeles Dodgers in the '77 World Series, and the legendary Reggie Jackson (*"REG-GIE, REG-GIE, REG-GIE!"*) became the first to hit three home runs in a World Series since Babe Ruth.

Thank you, "Mr. October," and thank you for that chocolaty-covered caramel and peanuts Reggie candy bar.

Eyes Wide Shut
Directed by Stanley Kubrick
(July 16, 1999, U.S. Release Date)

I've never gotten overly emotional about celebrity deaths (though the year 2016 was particularly harsh, including David Bowie, Prince, Muhammad Ali, and Carrie Fisher). In my entire life, I've only gotten really sad about *five* celebrity deaths. They include the late Farrah Fawcett, Robin Williams, Neil Peart of Rush, Eddie Van Halen, and *Stanley Kubrick.*

When the final year of the twentieth century began, I had only two forthcoming films on my mind. The first was (of course) *The Phantom Menace.* The second was *Eyes Wide Shut,* Kubrick's first film since *Full Metal Jacket* twelve years prior. However, on March 7, 1999, Kubrick died suddenly at the age of seventy, suffering a heart attack in his sleep. Upon hearing the news from Beth, I was stunned, sad, and heartbroken. His new film would be his *last* film—his swan song. It wasn't until I finally saw the film's trailer that I knew just even a little bit of what was coming, and that was barely anything. It offered nothing more than the names of Cruise, Kidman, Kubrick and a haunting song by Chris Isaak I'd never heard before. I remember cringing at the thought of Tom Cruise and Nicole Kidman teaming up again (wasn't Ron Howard's *Far and Away* enough of a disaster?). Still, this was a film by the immortal Stanley Kubrick, so I knew I had to see it, no matter what.

This was a group outing to the Hampton Arts Theater in Westhampton Beach. Beth, myself, and my cousin *Jill Z.* and her husband were eager to see what an artist like Kubrick had to offer us. Even as we sat down with our popcorn and sodas, we verbally contemplated the pros and cons of a Kubrick film with the likes of Cruise and Kidman. The first thing I found hard to swallow was Cruise playing a rich doctor, the role hardly fitting with his pretty boy persona. Dr. Bill Harford (Cruise) and his wife Alice (Kidman) lived in a luxury Manhattan apartment building on the Upper West Side with their seven-year-old daughter, Helena. While attending a Christmas party hosted by Victor (played by director Sydney Pollack), a wealthy patient of Bill's, Bill was reunited with an old friend from medical school (a drop out), professional piano player Nick Nightingale. Throughout the night, both Bill and Alice each had their opportunities to cheat on one another; Bill with a couple of hot, young models, and Alice with a suave and debonair older Hungarian gentleman. Alice resisted, citing her marital status, while Bill avoided his temptations when he was called to address a medical matter of a naked girl who nearly overdosed on a speedball.

The next night, while smoking a joint together, Bill and Alice got into an intense discussion about sexual temptations. Bill said he wasn't jealous of other men being attracted to her because he believed that women (in general) weren't drawn to infidelity. Alice defiantly protested and declared, *"Millions of years of evolution, right? Right? Men have to stick it in every place they can, but for women…women it is just about security and commitment and whatever the fuck else!"* and concluded by telling her husband (and perhaps all men in the theater) *"If you men only* knew." She then confessed that during their vacation at Cape Cod, she noticed an attractive naval officer and couldn't stop fantasizing about him for the rest of their trip. Bill was disturbed by this and frequently obsessed over the idea of his wife in the arms of this man with repeated visual images of the two of them in bed together. Before the conversation escalated further, Bill was called away to the house of an elderly patient who'd just died.

In the course of that one night away from his home and marriage, Bill was (unsuccessfully) seduced by the dead patient's daughter and would've ended up in bed with a prostitute named Domino had it not been for a sudden phone call from Alice. Later, he stumbled upon the jazz nightclub Nick Nightingale was playing at. Nick described another playing engagement he was scheduled for that same night—a gig on Long Island where he'd be required to play blindfolded amidst a costume gathering featuring beautiful women. Intrigued, Bill convinced Nick to share the address of where this all was, but Bill would need a costume, mask, and password to gain entrance. He managed to get all of them, though not without stumbling onto a bizarre sexual situation involving the underage daughter of the costume shop's owner, in which she was involved with two Asian businessmen.

Taking a taxi to a country mansion, Bill gave the password of *Fidelio* and entered the house. Inside was a bizarre sexual ritual accompanied by some of the most twisted and freakish music I'd ever heard, with all its participants wearing masks. The women were naked, and there was sex going on everywhere. It was then I realized I was watching this debauchery with my cousin Jill only two seats away from me. We hadn't been to the movies together much before, and what we'd seen was pretty harmless. Watching *this*, however, seemed something better suited between just me and the girl I was actually sleeping with (I can only imagine what Beth and Jill, the more conservative types, were thinking at that moment). Anyway, one of the masked women warned Bill that he was in great danger, and that he should leave immediately. Instead, he was escorted to a crowded room of masked people waiting to face him. He was unmasked and ordered to remove his clothes. But the woman who'd warned him intervened and insisted on redeeming him. Bill was permitted to leave, but warned never to speak to anyone of what he'd witnessed.

Bill went home that night feeling confused and guilty. He found Alice laughing in her sleep. When she awoke, she tearfully described her dream in which she had sex with many men and laughing at Bill as he watched her. The next morning, Bill was unable to find Nick and also discovered his mask was missing when he returned the costume. When he tried to see Domino again, he learned from her roommate that she'd just been diagnosed as HIV positive. Saying nothing, Bill realized he'd dodged a dangerous bullet by not sleeping with Domino. When he was summoned to Victor's home, Victor revealed that he was one of the masked guests at the bizarre sexual ritual the night before and was able to identify Bill through his connection with Nick. Victor claimed the secret society's warning were staged only to scare Bill from speaking of their existence.

Returning home to Alice, Bill discovered the misplaced rented mask on the pillow next to his sleeping wife. He broke down in tears and told Alice he'd tell her everything. While Christmas shopping with Helena the next day, they discussed their future following the events of the past two days. Alice believed they were awake now from what may have been a dream and that they should be grateful that their love and marriage was strong enough to survive it. She also said they needed to do something as soon as possible, and that was, *"Fuck."*

Stunned. That's the best word I can use to describe how the four of us felt at the close of *Eyes Wide Shut*. I can't speak for Beth, but Jill, myself and her husband felt fairly confident in our understanding of Stanley Kubrick and his films. But there was no real way of understanding what we'd just watched for more than two and a half hours. For the moment, I had to contend with the fact that the final word uttered in the final motion picture of Kubrick's spectacular film career was, *"Fuck."* I then had to comprehend the incomprehensible content of whatever the hell it was we'd just watched. Was this really what Kubrick waited twelve long years to give us? Maybe it wasn't exactly. He died before he could involve himself in the editing process. Maybe it was his *editors* I needed to direct my blame at. Whatever the situation was, I had a serious dilemma in trying not to hate a Stanley Kubrick film.

Calm down. Remember what Steven Spielberg reminded us of in an interview following Kubrick's death—you can't watch a Kubrick film just once to fully understand it. He was right, and it was months later when I rented the film on video, that I tried to look at things differently and ask myself some serious questions. Was *Eyes Wide Shut* a misfire or a masterpiece? Was it a film only a true "Kubrickian" could love? Would it have been better had he not died before its completion? Would it have been better if its stars hadn't previously made *Days of Thunder* and *Far and Away*? Are Nicole Kidman's firm tits and perfectly sculpted ass enough of a reason to sit through what on the surface is incomprehensible trash? These are questions without answers, except that time and repeated viewings are inevitably our friends when trying to understand the difficulties of cinema.

Kubrick was clearly attracted to the erotic mystery and psychological drama of Arthur Schnitzler 1926 novella of early twentieth-century Vienna *Traumnovelle* (Dream Story) to want to translate it into 1990's New York City (though it was mostly filmed in London). His pacing is considerably slow (but then so was *2001: A Space Odyssey*). This may be intended to convey the film's concept of the dream state (take note of the ongoing background of hazy Christmas lights in people's homes and the city streets) within the lives of Bill and Alice, and the variety of people they encounter. We're never given a clear definition of what is their reality and what is their dream. Is it only within a dream what we as human beings have the potential (or the stupidity) to seek out sexual pleasures and deviances that may likely get us into serious trouble? Is it only within a dream that nearly every character in the film, especially Bill, insists on annoyingly repeating the same piece of dialogue just spoken to them or did Kubrick intentionally write the screenplay that way?

It should be noticed that nearly every time Bill is on the brink of a new sexual discovery, he's conveniently (or miraculously) interrupted before anything bad can happen (including contracting AIDS). This may be interpreted as a sign that we should all keep our "feet on the ground" when it comes to commitment issues of intimacy and marriage because the concept of sexual misguidance outside the bonds of marriage is very clear, as are its regrets and consequences. In the end, though, and in an almost cliché-like tone, it appears the marriage of Bill and Alice will survive now that they're both "awake" from their dream…and apparently a good fuck won't hurt them, either.

Misfire or masterpiece? We'll never know. *Eyes Wide Shut* isn't a perfect film or the director's s best work. Nonetheless, I'm thankful to Stanley Kubrick for everything he gave us, and I wish I could tell him how much his films mean to me and my life. I miss you, Stanley, and I'll never forget you.

The Sixth Sense

Directed by M. Night Shyamalan
(August 6, 1999, U.S. Release Date)

It was Labor Day weekend 1999, and the beach house was filled with friends. We went dancing Saturday night, got drunk, ate too much food when we got home, and felt sick the next morning. It wasn't until the late afternoon that we were ready to leave the house and face the world. Stomachs settled, hunger returned, and we all drove to the nearest Taco Bell in Hampton Bays, right near the town multiplex. Although Beth had already seen it, the movie of choice for the group was *The Sixth Sense*. My own interest was mild. I'd seen the trailer, and the concept of Bruce Willis helping a child who saw dead people was hardly intriguing to me. Perhaps it was because I hadn't embraced too many scary movies since their glory days of the early 1980s.

From the start, though, I could see my reservations were premature and perhaps unfair. Tough guy Bruce Willis was immediately convincing as sensitive Philadelphia child psychologist Malcom Crowe. During a romantic evening with his wife to celebrate his recognized achievements for his honored work, a young man named Vincent broke into their house. He hid in the bathroom and accused Malcom of failing to help him overcome his hallucinations as a boy, and then shot Malcom before turning the gun on himself.

The camera faded to black and then it was the following fall. Malcom was beginning his work with a nine-year-old boy named Cole Sear (played by Haley Joel Osment, whom I recognized from his brief performance in *Forrest Gump*), whom he was determined to help to absolve his own guilt for failing Vincent, and to try and reconcile with his wife, who had become cold and distant. Cole's mother was concerned about his lack of social interaction, and left him and Malcom alone to conduct their sessions. Together, Cole and Malcom tried to get to the bottom of Cole's fears and anxieties, without luck. It was at a birthday party that Cole was locked in a closet and screamed for his life. He emerged unconscious and with strange bruises on his body.

In the hospital, Cole confessed his secret to Malcom—he said the words, *"I see dead people"*—people who walked around like everybody else, believing they were still alive and seeing what they wanted to see. Malcom believed Cole to be delusional and considered dropping him as a patient, though Cole begged him not to give up on him. It was later in his office that Malcom listened to an old audio tape of a session with Vincent when he was a boy, and heard a crying man begging for help in another language, thus believing Cole's story. He suggested that Cole put aside his fears and try listening to the ghosts to try and help them resolve their unfinished business.

During the night, Cole awakened to discover a sick (and recently dead) girl in his house. She discovered who she was and went with Malcom to her wake at her parent's home. The dead girl directed Cole to a hidden videotape, which he presented to the girl's father. The tape secretly showed the girl's mother poisoning her daughter's bowl of soup. This convicted the mother in everyone's eyes, but it also saved the dead girl's younger sister from potentially meeting the same horrible fate. Having helped the dead girl, Cole could learn to live with the ghosts in his life, and also overcome his inability to fit in at school. Before he and Malcom parted ways, Cole suggested that Malcom could learn to talk to his wife again by speaking to her while she slept.

Later while Cole and his mother were stuck in traffic, Cole confessed his secret to her too, revealing the traffic was due to a fatal accident down the road, and that the dead person was standing next to him outside the car. She couldn't believe such a story, but changed her mind when Cole told her of his grandmother visiting him and describing how she once saw his mother in a dance recital when she was a child, giving details that Cole couldn't have known about.

That night, Malcom returned home to find his wife asleep and their wedding video playing on the TV. Talking in her sleep, she asked Malcom why he left her, and dropped his wedding ring to the floor. Confused, Malcom suddenly recalled Cole's words of the dead not realizing they were dead and seeing only what they wanted to see. Malcom suddenly realized things he hadn't earlier. He remembered being shot by Vincent and discovered his fatal bloody gunshot wound. Turns out Malcom was *dead* the entire time he worked with Cole, fulfilling every detail Cole revealed earlier about the dead people he saw. With that, Malcom concluded his unfinished business, and his spirit departed from this world in a flash of light.

Okay, I'll admit it—I didn't read the clues carefully and was shocked to learn the truth, as were many moviegoers that summer, and in as much as I loved the film, I couldn't fathom how director M. Night Shyamalan pulled off this surprising final resolution, which I can hardly claim as totally original or groundbreaking. The shock of "they were dead the whole time" *has* been done before. Here are some examples:

> *The Twilight Zone,* season 1, episode 16, "The Hitch-Hiker" (1960)—Nan Adams, while driving alone on a country road trip, is in an auto accident and seemingly survives without a scratch. Along her journey, she's haunted by an old man hitchhiker who awaits her at every step of her trip. We learn at the end the old man is the personification of death, and that Nan did, in fact, die in the accident and was dead the whole time.

> *Carnival of Souls (1962)*—Mary Henry survives an auto accident after a drag race. Traveling to Utah, she repeatedly experiences terrifying visions and personifications when she gradually

becomes invisible and inaudible to the rest of the world around her, as if she weren't there. She's *not* there. We learn at the end that she didn't survive the accident and was dead the whole time.

Jacob's Ladder (1990)—Jacob Singer returns home from Vietnam only to be plagued by demons tearing his life apart. Blah, blah, blah, yadda, yadda, yadda…we learn at the end that he actually died in Vietnam under the influence of a mind-altering experimental drug and was dead the whole time.

You see what I'm getting at, don't you? Exactly *why* were we so shocked and astonished when we learned that Bruce Willis was dead the whole time? It wasn't anything new…yet there was something oddly refreshing about it, and that was probably because there were no *obvious* clues along the way. From everything we witnessed, Bruce was alive and well and helping to ease little Haley Joel Osment's suffering from seeing dead people. But even *that* claim isn't without challenge, because the clues *were* there—we just didn't know how to look for them. Many of these clues were small enough to be easily missed (like Bruce wearing the *same* shirt throughout the movie), but perhaps the most obvious clue is that when Cole describes the dead as those walking around like everybody else, not knowing they're dead and seeing what they want to see, the camera stays on Bruce's face. That should've been a dead (pun totally intended) giveaway, but we were all fooled, nonetheless. Still, like the final resolution of any Agatha Christie film, there's something deliciously decadent about not only realizing we were "victims" of a twisty plot scam the entire time, but in also being let in on the whole thing in the end.

By the way, as careful and precise as the filmmakers were in making sure they properly covered their tracks in hiding Bruce's true existence (or lack thereof), there's one moment in the film where I'd swear they screwed up. Watch the restaurant scene when Malcom seemingly shows up late to his anniversary dinner and sits across the table from his wife and you'll see there *is* a quick moment when she makes direct eye contact with him, as if clearly acknowledging his presence in that chair (sorry M. Night, but you're *busted*).

As for the famed director himself, I must confess that I pity the poor man, as he's never truly scored a solid movie hit since *The Sixth Sense*, the proverbial "one hit wonder," as I've come to define it. It seems he's had to pay a hard price ever since with crap like *The Village*, *The Happening*, *The Last Airbender*, and *After Earth*. Even his *Unbreakable* trilogy, while possessing some good moments here and there, failed to live up to any high expectations it tried to sell me at the time of their releases. Perhaps I place too high a price on the big, surprise ending and how it will ultimately affect me. Perhaps I'm just too damn hard on the guy.

Again, M. Night, sorry.

American Beauty

Directed by Sam Mendes
(September 15, 1999, U.S. Release Date)

So you think *your* family is dysfunctional?

If you've followed my stories from the beginning, you've shared with me the many movie-related and strictly personal accounts of how my family's quirks and dysfunctions was often directly tied to either the movie stories themselves, or simply the timing of their releases. *Kramer vs Kramer* was ill-timed with my parents' second split in 1979. *The War of the Roses* was ill-timed with my parents' third and final split ten years later. For those who weren't personally affected by these films, they and others like *Ordinary People* still challenged audiences to take a closer look at the typical American family. Subjects like divorce, legal custody, maternal disconnection and teenage suicide made us laugh, cry, and think (two of the films I mention won the Oscar for best picture of their respective year).

By 1999, I was beyond any personal impact from such films. I was a grown man in a new relationship, and in love for the second time in my life, with only the thought of my own marital future in mind rather than my parents' marriage of the past. *American Beauty* was, if nothing else, an opportunity to "look closer" from the outside and witness how a dysfunctional marriage between the likes of gifted actors like Kevin Spacey and Annette Bening would ultimately play out. Spacy played Lester Burnham, a confused, middle-aged magazine executive who hated his job and suffered an unhappy marriage to Carolyn (Bening), an ambitious and highly neurotic real estate broker. Jane, their sixteen-year-old daughter with a low self-esteem, despised both her parents. Their immediate neighbors were a male gay couple and a newly arrived family of U.S. Marine colonel Frank Fitts (played by Chris Cooper), his lifeless wife and their teenage son Ricky (played by Wes Bentley). Ricky was obsessed with his camcorder and often filmed his surroundings and the people in them, collecting hundreds of taped recordings that filled the shelves of his room. He was also a marijuana dealer, and Lester would eventually become one of his best customers.

Frank was a father like no other: a strict disciplinarian, homophobic and a collector of guns and Nazi-related chinaware. He subjected his son to periodic urine tests after having discovered his son's drug use at a younger age. That discovery landed Ricky into a military academy and then later into a mental hospital after he almost killed another kid over a disparaging remark. Still, Ricky didn't hate his father or consider him a bad man. He loved life, and had the spirit to appreciate all forms of beauty, even a paper bag blowing in the wind. He confessed as much to Jane as they were drawn to each other's idiosyncrasies, despite living in a world where it seemed one had to be "perfect" to be considered normal. Such was the case with Jane's conceited best friend Angela, who believed herself to be one of those perfect people and had no problem with openly discussing her apparently uninhibited sex life with multiple men.

It was during a high school basketball game that Lester discovered his infatuation with Angela (his sexual fantasies about her often oddly accompanied by images of red rose pedals). Lester was finally awakened from what he believed was a twenty-year deprivation of the spirit of his life. In short, he wasn't going to take it anymore. He quit his pointless job, told his boss to go fuck himself, and successfully blackmailed him for a year's salary (Spacey had just become my personal hero). He started working out and was looking good to Angela, though it disgusted Jane to no end. And in what I considered his best move, he bought the car he'd always dreamed of having without his wife's approval—a 1970 Pontiac Firebird (he ruled!). As a husband, he was finally standing up to his controlling, and sometimes ridiculing wife, even confronting her inabilities (or unwillingness) to engage in any sex with him, she believing it was more important not to spill beer on the couch rather than rekindle any lost love between them. Even when Lester discovered Carolyn was having an affair with her business competition, he expressed indifference. Lester became a better man while Carolyn slowly deteriorated into a lower fraction of what she used to be.

Meanwhile, Frank suspected Ricky's friendship with Lester might be homosexual. After spying on a drug transaction between them, Frank wrongly concluded that Ricky was giving sexual services to Lester. He violently confronted Ricky about it, hit him, and ordered him out of the house. Ricky falsely admitted his homosexuality, allowing him to finally be free of his abusive father. He asked Jane to leave with him to go to New York, even as she was ending her friendship with Angela over the flirtation between her and Lester. It was a verbal triumph when Ricky confronted Angela and accused her of being ugly, boring and ordinary.

When Frank approached Lester in the garage, he broke down in tears, hugged him, and then tried to kiss him. Lester gently resisted, and Frank left in humiliation. In the kitchen, Lester and Angela confessed their sexual attraction to each other and it looked like by the time they made it to the sofa, they were finally going to have sex. At that moment, we learned that Angela was a fraud in never having had sex before, and Lester's conscience was confronted with the immoral and illegal act of what he was about to do. He redeemed himself by not having sex with Angela, but instead comforting her in a shared bond of their frustrated lives. Left alone in the kitchen, Lester picked up an old picture of his family and smiled at the fascination of a better life in the past, while seemingly coming to terms with his mid-life crisis. It was then that a gun appeared behind his head and fired a bullet into Lester's head.

From multiple points of view, the gunshot was repeated, and we witnessed Ricky's fascination at the beauty of the look of contentment on Lester's face as he lay there dead. Back at Frank's house, he returned home bloodied and the camera turned to a space on the wall where a gun was missing from his collection. In the film's closing narration, Lester described the meaningful experiences of his past life which he was happy to have lived through, despite his own death, and acknowledging all of the beauty in the world.

It was, and still is, impossible for me to fully understand the meaning of *American Beauty* in my personal life without reflecting on the film from *three* different perspectives. There was the first time I saw it in the theater with Beth and walked away from it feeling its powerful impact as both drama and comedy, though not having any conceivable notion of what its story of Lester Burnham might mean to me personally because I was years away from becoming a married man myself. Unlike the films that coincided with my own parents' breakups, this was one that hit us in the face and gut with a sledge-hammer and declared, "This is what it's like, and fuck you if you can't handle it! You think your family is dysfunctional—take a look at these people!" Seriously, if I thought I had any preconceived notions of what social conformity, family imprisonment, sexual repression, illegal drug use, homosexuality, child abuse and pedophilia could be like, this film opened my eyes to its possibilities. Throw a man like Kevin Spacey into the mix, and it certainly makes my family look more like the Brady Bunch.

The second time I saw this film on screen was with my father and, in a way, looked at it from the perspective of the married man. Through the shared eyes of my father, who'd experienced his own version of marital hell with my mother, Lester Burnham was a funnier man in a more heroic light, particularly in his personal uprising against his domineering wife. It was easier to comprehend being trapped in a miserable and joyless marriage. Watching the Burnham's marriage deteriorate into an almost farcical situation seemed so beyond what one might consider suburban family reality, that it was impossible for me and my father not to laugh with joy as we silently recalled some of the ridiculous situations we both lived through at different ends. A man like my father could easily cheer for a man like Lester, and he laughed during the scene when he was driving and rocking out to the words of the Guess Who's *"American Woman"* on the radio. My father could also take comfort in the fact that Lester redeemed himself in the end by *not* trying to fuck his daughter's underage friend.

Finally, there's the way I perceive *American Beauty* now as a man who's been married to the same woman for more than twenty years. An ongoing joyous picnic, it has *not* been. There have been issues and frustrations of daily routine, communication, friendship, support, child raising and sexual repression that only other married men can talk about openly. There are moments when I watch the film today that I can truly call Lester Burnham my hero. Not only because he has the balls to stand up for what he believes is *his* in life, but to also get away with it (at least up until the moment he's shot in the head and dies) and walk away feeling good about himself and his life. Such rebellion is surely possible, but not without compromise, regrets and even consequences. Our real-life consequences may not necessarily be death, but ones we have to live with in return for whatever personal freedom we achieve in a marriage that's less than perfect.

Lester says it himself at the end of the film, *"You have no idea what I'm talking about, I'm sure. But don't worry…someday you will."* Perhaps over the last twenty-plus years, I *have*.

The Straight Story
Directed by David Lynch
(October 15, 1999, U.S. Release Date)

A G-rated Disney film by David Lynch (yeah, right, and monkeys may come flying out of my ass)? Never in the history of cinema could I imagine something so ridiculous, not from the genius who gave us *Blue Velvet, Twin Peaks,* and *Lost Highway.* Yet there it was—a movie promo ad in the New York Times of a film called *The Straight Story* by David Lynch. According to the media press, it was a simple tale (based on a true story) of an elderly farmer's journey across Iowa and Wisconsin riding on a lawn mower to see his estranged brother Lyle who'd suffered a stroke. On paper, it sounded curious, but hardly anything that would have me racing to the nearest movie theater. But Lynch's name attached to it had me doing just that. I had to see this thing for myself. My head was filled with many questions and expectations, while to Beth, who had no real knowledge of David Lynch, it simply sounded like a nice story.

When the film opened in a small town in Iowa, there was a familiar feeling I'd had before with a Lynch film—similarities between the feeling and flavor of this simple mid-western community and its people, and the same opening montage in *Blue Velvet.* This could've easily been the same town of Lumberton, North Carolina as in that infamous 1986 film. As for Alvin Straight (played by Richard Farnsworth, whom I only really knew from Rob Reiner's *Misery*), he was a stubborn man who refused to quit smoking and use a walker. When he heard that his brother Lyle suffered a stroke, he longed to visit him to repair the damage of their estranged relationship before he (Alvin) died. Determined to make the journey himself, but unable to drive because of his bad eyes, he formed a plan to drive to Wisconsin riding his lawn mower while towing a small, homemade travel-trailer. This drive aboard such a vehicle would have a maximum speed of no more than about five miles per hour, and his destination was 240 miles away. This drive also stirred worry and doubt in the minds of his daughter Rose (played by Sissy Spacek) and his neighboring friends.

His journey's first attempt failed because his old mower's motor died before he got very far. Returning home, he put the old mower out of its misery by shooting it. At the John Deere dealership, he purchased a used 1966 lawn tractor, thus allowing him to restart his journey. Along the way, we witnessed some of the American landscape's true beauty, and it was during these moments when we could truly appreciate the soul behind this undertaking by simply watching the look of peace and contentment on Alvin's face.

His journey wasn't without human interaction, though. He first shared his campfire and words of wisdom with a young, female hitchhiker who was pregnant and running away from home, stressing the importance of family by comparing it to a bundle of sticks that couldn't be broken. Later, a large convoy of cyclists raced past him, and when he arrived at their camp later, he was greeted with applause. The next day, he stopped and listened to a woman angrily rant about always hitting deer in the road, despite taking numerous precautions (including playing Public Enemy real loud from her car). When the mower's brakes failed while traveling down a steep hill, he also discovered the vehicle had transmission problems and would need fixing. A kind man named Danny offered Alvin the use of his property to sleep on while he awaited repairs.

During his short hiatus, Alvin met another elderly World War II veteran, and the two shared war stories in the neighborhood bar. It was during these traumatic stories of combat and loss while fighting the Germans that we learned of the pain and anguish Alvin experienced in his past life. This seemed a necessary plot point to remind us that Alvin's life wasn't mundane, and that his personal journey wasn't merely to see his brother, but to bring closure to a life spent, both good and bad. When Alvin's tractor was repaired, he was presented with an excessive bill for parts and labor. He reminded us that even an old man such as he wasn't short of brains and cleverness, as he effectively stood up for himself by negotiating the final price down to a fair number, while also describing his journey and the importance of having a brother to the twin brothers who repaired his vehicle, who appeared to relate to Alvin's personal struggle.

After crossing the Mississippi River, Alvin made camp in a cemetery, and chatted with the Catholic priest who knew of Lyle's name, but didn't know that Lyle had a brother. Alvin told him that all he wanted now was to make peace with Lyle after failing to talk to each other for the past ten years. Finally arriving in Mount Zion, Wisconsin, Alvin treated himself to his first beer in years, while getting directions to Lyle's house from the bartender. After some engine trouble, Alvin finally arrived to Lyle's dilapidated, old house. Lyle (played by Harry Dean Stanton, previously of Lynch's *Wild at Heart* and *Twin Peaks: Fire Walk with Me*) tearfully gazed at his brother's tractor and asked Alvin if he'd ridden it just to see him. Alvin simply responded, *"I did."* Nothing else was said, as there appeared to be peace and understanding in this simple reunion. The two brothers sat there silently, gazing up at the stars.

So many thoughts and emotions went through my mind when the film ended. I was touched at the film's simplicity and beauty, but more than that, I was overcome with disbelief that this rare gem came from a man like David Lynch. But as time passes and my thoughts become clearer on *The Straight Story's* content, my disbelief is less. Watch *Blue Velvet* and *Twin Peaks* again and you'll see that Lynch has a strong appreciation for capturing pieces of celestial Americana on film, and with *Straight*, he offers us the simple beauty of the rural American Midwestern landscaping without getting unnecessarily sentimental about it. His characterization of America is a warm and straightforward approach, and not simply because of its physical beauty. Lynch reminds us that this isn't just a story about Alvin Straight and his life-defining journey through quiet, rural towns, but also of the people who live there. These are kind people who embrace

Alvin's presence, and are willing to talk to him and listen to his story. In short, they *care*.

I've used the word *simple* and its variations often, but I think it's the best word to describe everything about *The Straight Story* and its surrounding landscapes. Using alternate words would be a wasted use of adjectives, serving no additional purpose. But simple is also a word I can attribute to how the film makes me feel: in a life filled with stress and cynicism, it's the simplicity of reminding myself that there *are* kind people in the world willing to take a sincere interest in others, that may relieve me of the burdens on my shoulders, and take a *simpler* approach to life's challenges. Maybe these are false hopes, and maybe I take the movies a little too much to heart without realizing the self-delusions they bring to one's mind. Nonetheless, I won't deny that after I watch *The Straight Story*, I'm always smiling, and smiling is never a bad thing.

The Insider

Directed by Michael Mann
(November 5, 1999, U.S. Release Date)

When I was twelve years old in December 1979, I went to a double-feature of *The China Syndrome* and *And Justice For All*. As I previously described in *It's Strictly Personal*, both films were dark eye-openers to a young boy who had, prior to these films, no real knowledge or understanding behind the fears, dangers and corruption of real-life issues as nuclear power and criminal law. That young boy left the movie theater a little older and wiser, and even a little scared. Not to suggest that twenty years later, at the age of thirty-two, I was naïve to the dark ways of the world. It's just that even as I got older, the power of the movies to open my eyes a little wider never failed to have its effect.

Although I only watch CBS's *60 Minutes* on occasion, I have nothing but respect for this show as perhaps the last surviving example of a news program with some balls and integrity in a perverted world of media diseased with outrageous sensationalism. As a spectator, though, I can only watch and appreciate the "big news story" from the outside of the TV screen. It rarely occurs to me to consider the process and the risks involved from the origin of the story to the legal and bureaucratic bullshit involved before it sees the light of day on the air for us to watch on TV. Along the way, films like *All the President's Men* and *Broadcast News* offer additional insight to help me think outside my own box, and consider alternate possibilities of how things get done.

The Insider seemed like another film opportunity to teach me a few things about the television news business. I knew I had to see it to once again experience the dynamic chemistry, and thrilling and dramatic style that Al Pacino and director Michael Mann had successfully delivered four years prior in *Heat*. Throw Russell Crowe (an actor I long admired since *L.A. Confidential*) and Christopher Plummer into the mix, and I knew there was potential for something very special. I also knew this sort of film might be best experienced by seeing it with my father, who felt the same affection for Pacino as I did.

Prior to this film, I had only a vague memory of the actual tobacco industry whistleblower Jeffrey Wigand (Crowe) who went on *60 Minutes* in 1995 with American journalist Mike Wallace (Plummer) to reveal that tobacco giant Brown & Williamson intentionally manipulated the tobacco blend to increase the amount of nicotine in cigarette smoke, thereby increasing the impact of the addiction to the smoker, and of course, increasing their sales. He also revealed that the seven CEOs of "Big Tobacco" perjured themselves to the United States Congress about their awareness of nicotine's addictiveness (wait a second—big tobacco companies *lying* to increase sales and get rich? Nah).

Even as important as the whistleblowing and the big story were to this film, it focused less on the actual television interview, and instead paid necessary attention to the relationship between Jeffrey Wigand and CBS producer Lowell Bergman (Pacino). Their meeting was by pure chance, but it was immediately apparent to Lowell that Jeffrey had something important he wanted to say. Jeffrey was unjustly fired from Brown & Williamson and he was disgruntled. But he was also bound to a signed legal confidentiality agreement, stressing that he couldn't discuss or reveal anything about his former position with the company. It was an agreement Jeffrey had every intention of honoring until the big "powers that be" threatened his life and his family's. While anger, emotion and even vengeance dictated Jeffrey's actions, it was also clear to him and Lowell that he had threatening information that the American viewing public had a right to know about. So as cliché of good and bad, right and wrong, risk and sacrifice dictated, the big news story would be revealed to the world, and justice would supposedly be done, though not without the price of Jeffrey losing his marriage.

His marriage was an interesting point I couldn't overlook, specifically his wife (played by Diane Venora, who bore a striking resemblance to Jessica Lange). It reminded me that a film, accurate or not, can only give a dramatic version of what may or may not be the facts of a real marriage. If Venora's portrait of Jeffrey's real-life wife was accurate, then I was disgusted to see what a pathetic excuse for strength and support she truly was. She irritatingly went to pieces when she learned Jeffrey had been fired, and that their precious car and house payments were now at risk. These were surely upsetting events, but this woman clearly chose not to abide by those famous words sung by Tammy Wynette in "*Stand by Your Man*."

My practices as a writer and an architect have never been risky. That's not the sort of business I'm in. And yet while I'm not oblivious that truth brings great risk by those who stand to lose from it, not only those doing the wrong, but also those who stand to get sued for telling the truth, it's still sometimes a great piece of movie dialogue that further exploits that which we already think we know, and when a man like the great Al Pacino says it, it somehow hits harder:

> *You pay me to go get guys like Wigand, to draw him out. To get him to trust us, to get him to go on television. I do. I deliver him. He sits. He talks. He violates his own fucking confidentiality agreement. And he's only the key witness in the biggest public health reform issue, maybe the biggest, most-expensive corporate-malfeasance case in U.S. history. And Jeffrey Wigand, who's out on a limb, does he go on television and tell the truth? Yes. Is it newsworthy? Yes. Are we gonna air it? Of course not. Why? Because he's not telling the truth? No. Because he is telling the truth. That's why we're not going to air it. And the more truth he tells, the worse it gets!*

This was one of Pacino's great monologues that easily rivaled his sensational verbal antics in *And Justice for All* and *The Devil's Advocate*. He spoke, I listened, and maybe I understood the bullshit of the world a little more. After his fight with CBS, Lowell was ordered to take a vacation and was forced to tell Jeffrey that it looked like the story wouldn't air. Furious and dejected, Jeffrey accused Lowell of manipulating him, and Lowell defended himself while continuing to praise Jeffrey's testimonies. Still refusing to lose the big fight, Lowell contacted an editor at the New York Times and disclosed the full story and events that took place at CBS. The Times printed the story on the front page and condemned CBS in their negative editorial. Although accused of betraying the network, Lowell and Mike Wallace still believed that bowing to corporate and legal pressure was a mistake against *60 Minutes'* credibility and integrity. Jeffrey's interview finally aired, though Lowell resigned his position anyway, believing the reputation of the network's news show was permanently stained.

This is where I separate fiction from real life. In fiction, the good fight was fought, the story broke to a shocked nation, whistleblower Jeffrey Wigand was a hero and Brown & Williamson seemingly paid the price for their crimes. In real life, all that is probably bullshit because in the end, what did it ultimately change? Yes, forty-six states filed a Medicaid suit against Brown & Williamson leading to a $368 billion settlement in health-related damages (the company was defunct in 2004), but that hardly solved the ongoing health-related issues tied to nicotine addiction. The tobacco industry still exists today and people continue to smoke to no end despite all of its dangers. So in the end, what does the so-called "power of the press" really accomplish? We're given the facts, the cover-ups and those responsible for them, and ultimately too many people choose the attitude of "So what?" and continue to do damage to themselves. *That's* the nature of human logic for you.

For myself, though, *The Insider* continues what *All the President's Men* and *Broadcast News* started in its nature to further educate me in what the purpose of the press *can* be, or at least, *used* to be in a pre-Donald Trump world. Michael Mann's film doesn't fail to entertain, absorb and even anger us when we see how far a powerful corporation like Brown & Williamson goes to threaten and discredit the life of one man willing to stand up against them. Men like Al Pacino and Russell Crowe command the screen in their immovable stand to protect truth-telling in America. Such a stand looks great on screen, and it's also good to know it can sometimes happen in real life too. It happened for Jeffrey Wigand, but what did the rest of us learn from it? Perhaps nothing. Maybe that's why we still need movies like *The Insider* to remind us to keep trying to learn new lessons.

Cradle Will Rock

Directed by Tim Robbins
(December 10, 1999, U.S. Release Date)

I've always personally believed that history and the movies represents a double-edged sword. On the one hand, movies offer us an opportunity to experience history through the eyes and minds of the artists responsible for bringing it to the big screen. On the other hand, I hate admitting that I've learned about history through the movies and not through the more traditional format of books and educations. Nonetheless, I confess that I wouldn't have learned about periods of our own American history if not for films like *All the President's Men, The Right Stuff,* and *JFK,* just to name some. That in mind, it's remarkable what you'll discover at the movies when you're not searching for it in the first place.

Tim Robbins's *Cradle Will Rock* was a surprise. I had no idea the director of *Dead Man Walking* had another film coming out, and knew nothing of it other than the movie poster outside the multiplex. The poster gave me no clue to its subject, but I was intrigued at its array of stars, including Susan Sarandon, Bill Murray, Hank Azaria, John Turturro, Emily Watson, and John and Joan Cusack. It was one of those movie situations with little planning, in which you're simply standing in front of the theater box office and you mutually decide that the film looks good, and why not take a chance in seeing it?

The Great Depression and the movies have always fascinated me. America was at its financial lowest, and yet box office receipts didn't suffer because people still sacrificed the ten cent ticket price to forget their troubles for a period of time. That single dime bought you a cartoon, a newsreel, a film short and the main feature. What I knew virtually nothing about, however, was how *theater* fit into the era. Surely, tickets to a Broadway show didn't cost a mere dime, so how could those other than the financially well-off afford to go to the theater? How could those working in theater remain employed if there was no audience? I'd soon learn of the Federal Theater Project (FTP), a theater program established in the United States as part of FDR's New Deal to fund live artistic performances, entertainment programs, and to provide a relief measure employing artists, writers, directors and backstage theater workers. It lasted only four years (1935–1939), its funding cancelled by Congress after responding to accusations of Communist infiltration and racial integration.

In the film, at the height of the Depression, homeless and aspiring singer Olive Stanton's (Watson) luck turned when she got a job as a backstage hand with the FTP. Aspiring playwright Marc Blitzstein (Azaria) was working on a new musical, but lacked the proper inspiration to finish it. While sitting among those at a political protest, he experiences visions of two imaginary figures representing his deceased wife and famed German playwright Bertolt Brecht (never heard of him) who encouraged him to develop the play as a more relevant vehicle to the modern times rather than his previous abstract concept of musical performance.

Meanwhile, famed Mexican painter Diego Rivera (played by Rubén Blades) was commissioned by Nelson Rockefeller (Cusack) to paint what would become known as the mural *Man at the Crossroads* in the lobby of 30 Rockefeller Plaza at Rockefeller Center. The mural's original concept (which Rockefeller approved) featured a contrast of capitalism as an opposition to communism. However, repeated complaints about the piece's representation of "anticapitalist propaganda" caused an ongoing dispute between Rockefeller and Rivera, until it was finally ordered destroyed before it was completed.

The FTP faced increased pressure from the federal government, which had already begun their investigations into alleged left-wing infiltration of our American way of life through the House Committee on Un-American Activities. The Works Progress Administration

(WPA) was threatened with losing its budget and cut funding for all FTP productions, resulting in layoffs of thousands of theater workers, and ordered all ongoing projects, including what turned out to be Blitzstein's new politically motivated musical *Cradle Will Rock* to cease immediately. Because actors and musicians involved with the show were denied the right to work by their local unions unless they had federal approval, the show was forced to close. But rather than give in to political pressure, the show's director, the great Orson Welles (pre-*Citizen Kane* and played by Angus Macfadyen) and producer John Houseman (played by Cary Elwes) secured an alternate shuttered theater and established an improvised performance with Blitzstein acting as both the entire cast and the musical orchestra.

In an act of government defiance, the theater was packed with not only those who wanted to see the show, but also the cast forbidden to perform in it. As Blitzstein sang his first song, it was Olive Stanton who summoned the courage to defy her injustice by rising from her seat and singing her song. It took the act of just one to inspire the others to stand and perform their portion of the show without setting foot on the stage. As the show progressed, the cast and audience broke into a state of jubilance and celebration. Outside the theater, a group of former FTP performers staged a mock funeral for the ventriloquist dummy previously belonging to Bill Murray's sad and defeated character, representing what would be the eventual downfall of the FTP. As the procession moved through the streets of Manhattan, it inevitably walked into the present-day Times Square of 1999, lined with all its glorious billboards and Broadway show advertisements. A rather original and ingenious way to conclude this film, I thought.

Beth being the Broadway guru she was (and still is) loved it instantly. I loved it too, but I needed time to fully gather my thoughts on its subject. My first thought was that the talents of Vanessa Redgrave and Paul Giamatti were completely wasted, as she played only a dimwitted wife and he a total buffoon. My next thought was that while I loved theater, it was only "within the box" of the average run-of-the-mill Broadway production of the modern shows of the '80s and '90s like *Cats*, *Les Misérables*, *Phantom of the Opera*, and *Miss*

Saigon (just to name some). Never had it occurred to me to step outside those tourist attraction features to truly understand and appreciate how theater fell into the realms of our own American history, particularly during its harshest period of communist paranoia when anything and everything considered subversive could be attacked and destroyed by our own government.

However, there's real-life history and there's the version of history Tim Robbins chooses to show us. It may not matter because the point is successful in showing us the themes and dangers of artistic censorship, and the hard truth of the relationship between life and art. Lovers of art, be it on the canvas, the screen, or the stage are likely also lovers of freedom: freedom of expression without persecution. *Cradle Will Rock* reminds us of the struggles of the past and the importance of making sure those struggles don't ever return in our free society. I'm reminded, and I'll try never to forget.

The Green Mile
Directed by Frank Darabont
(December 10, 1999, U.S. Release Date)

It was late December 1999, and it was the day before Beth and I flew to Dallas, Texas to welcome the new Millennium with her family. We were already packed and there was time enough for one more movie...one *final* movie to close out the twentieth century. What would it be? The new Oliver Stone football movie with Al Pacino? The new all-star cast psychological drama by the guy who directed *Boogie Nights*? Or would it be the new thriller with Matt Damon who played a talented guy named Mr. Ripley? All of these were good options, but if I had to choose the *last film* I'd see before ushering in the new century, it had to be the new pairing of Frank Darabont with another story by Stephen King. After all, Darabont's *The Shawshank Redemption* was one of my top ten favorite films of the '90s, so who else could do justice to King's other great prison story (which I hadn't actually read)? No one, in my opinion...and clearly, this was something that perhaps only *I* gave a damn about.

The film began in the present day at an assisted living facility with an elderly patient named Paul Edgecomb who became tearfully emotional while watching the movie *Top Hat* on TV because it reminded him of events he experienced as a young man when he was a prison guard on death row (nicknamed "The Green Mile") at Cold Mountain Penitentiary. He then told his story to his female companion Elaine.

The year was 1935. Paul (played by Tom Hanks) was head supervisor over other death row guards (he also suffered from a severe bladder infection). One day, they were introduced to John Coffey, a physically large, but gentle-mannered black man convicted and sentenced to death for the rape and murder of two little white girls. One of the guards, Percy, was an obnoxious little creep who was also the nephew of the state governor's wife, and he wasted no time in abusing the privilege by demonstrating his sadistic personality toward the inmates, knowing full well he'd never be held accountable for his actions.

The somber mood of "the Mile" was softened when they discovered a spirited little mouse (one of the inmates named him Mr. Jingles) that could be trained to do circus-like tricks. When Mr. Jingles was killed by Percy, we learned of John Coffey's extraordinary powers when he took the mouse in his large hands and breathed life back into him. He also healed Paul's bladder infection by simply touching his infected area. Who was John Coffey? A mutant? An aberration? A miracle? Or was he an angel sent from heaven? Over time, Paul realized what sort of supernatural and magical power John possessed to heal others, and therefore couldn't believe that John was guilty of the crimes he was convicted for.

Meanwhile, the guards were now forced to deal with a new psychotic convict called "Wild Bill" Wharton (played by Sam Rockwell) who frequently started trouble by assaulting the guards, often forcing them to restrain him and throw him into the block's padded cell room. Though, admittedly, it was hard to sympathize with Percy when "Wild Bill" attacked him because that little prick certainly deserved it. Percy's sadistic streak even grew to a new level when in exchange for reassignment to another facility, he insisted on being allowed to oversee the execution of the next convict set to die. But at that execution, Percy deliberately skipped soaking the sponge used to conduct the electricity to the convict's head, thus causing an agonizing and visually gruesome death. As punishment for his actions, Percy was bound and gagged, and forced to spend a night in the padded cell.

While Percy was locked away, Paul and the other guards secretly smuggled John out of the prison so that he could (successfully) use his miraculous powers to heal the warden's wife of her fatal brain tumor. When Percy was finally released, he was warned that if he continued his spoiled and sadistic attitude, the others would report him for his various acts of professional misconduct, their jobs be damned. But it was John who sealed Percy's fate when he used his powers to "release" the affliction of the warden's wife into Percy's brain, thus throwing him into silence and eventually shooting "Wild Bill" to death (an act which landed Percy in the same mental asylum he'd planned to be transferred to). John also used his powers to show Paul that it was actually "Wild Bill" who raped and murdered the two little girls, the crime for which John was wrongfully condemned, and also releasing his supernatural energy into Paul in the process.

Concluding that John was an innocent man, Paul suffered the thought of allowing him to be executed, and even contemplated allowing John to run free. John, however, despite his innocence, was willing to die as he viewed the world as a cruel place (I agree) and was in pain from all the suffering people inflicted upon each other. When asked about his final request, John confessed to never having seen a *"flicker show"* before. The movie he watched was *Top Hat* (a new feature at the time). As Paul looked on, John cried as he watched the beauty and magic on the screen. This sadness continued when John was finally executed and all the guards were in tears.

Returning to the present day, Paul told Elaine that John Coffey's was the last execution he ever presided over. He resigned his prison job and worked in the juvenile system instead. He concluded his story by taking Elaine for a long walk and revealing that Mr. Jingles was still alive, having been blessed with a supernatural long life from John's healing powers. Paul also revealed that because of those same powers, he himself was 108 years old. He didn't consider this a miracle, but rather a divine punishment to linger through life longer than those he loved for his crime of having allowed an innocent man of miracles to die.

I'm an atheist. This is an important fact for my interpretation and perspective of *The Green Mile*, because despite this personal life choice, there are two moments of religious faith and contemplation that truly catch my attention in this film. The first is spoken by actor Graham Greene as a death row inmate, when he asks, *"Do you believe that if a man repents enough for what he done wrong, then he'll get to go back to the time that was happiest for him and live there forever? Could that be what heaven's like?"* and Paul responds, *"I just about believe that very thing."*

The second occurs when Paul faces John shortly before his execution and asks, *"On the day of my judgment, when I stand before God, and He asks me why did I kill one of his true miracles, what am I gonna say? That it was my job?"*

As an atheist, what do these questions mean to me? On paper, nothing. Yet I'm haunted by their deeper meanings. Despite not believing in God, perhaps there's something to consider about the possibilities of heaven (which Jews are *not* supposed to believe in, by the way. Why, I cannot say). Is it a place with pearly white gates so comically depicted in various fictional scenarios? Or on a simpler lever, is it a frame of mind and soul created by our own lives after death? If I take Graham Greene's question to heart, could I easily transport myself to the happiest time and place of my former life and live there for all of eternity? I can't help but hope that such a possibility exists. As for Tom Hank's question of judgment, I can only contemplate a decent man's struggle between his own beliefs of faith, what he knows to be the right thing to do, and simply what his job requires in allowing another decent man to die for all the wrong reasons because the law says so.

Let's talk about the word *decent* for a moment. It's key here because as prison films go, *The Green Mile* is perhaps the only one of its genre that really grabs the heart because we come to care about every decent character on screen. Not only the decent correction officers on death row, but the inmates themselves. These men live what lives they have left as calmly and peacefully as possible while waiting for their day of execution in the electric chair. Except for John Coffey, we don't even know what crimes these other men committed, and perhaps we don't care. Convicted criminals or not, the film portrays them as men with souls filled with regret and penance.

Yet even as we recognize decency in this film, we're just as capable of hating and despising men like Percy Wetmore (*Wet more*—that's funny considering Percy pisses himself after being attacked) and "Wild Bill" Wharton, whom we're more than happy to watch suffer in their respective ways. This may not be Stephen King's story intention, but it can clearly bring out both sides of love and hate from us, nonetheless.

John Coffey has often been referred to as a "magic Negro figure"—a term coined by director Spike Lee to describe a stereotypical fictional black person depicted as a *"saintly, nonthreatening person whose purpose in life is to solve a problem for, or otherwise further the happiness of a white person."* Whether or not you agree with his allegation is entirely up to you, but perhaps you'll also recall Robert Redford's 2000 film *The Legend of Bagger Vance*, also featuring a black man in a similar position of almost angelic, sound judgment who's meant to serve the problems of a white man. That being the case, do we assume that one race is wiser than the other? I don't. Personally, I think we're each just about as smart and as stupid as the next person.

As a story teller, Stephen King never ceases to amaze me in that he can write bone-chilling horror like *Carrie*, *Salem's Lot*, *The Shining*, *It*, and *Pet Sematary*, and yet he can also tug at our hearts with stories like *Stand by Me* (written as *The Body*), *The Shawshank Redemption* (written as *Rita Hayworth and Shawshank Redemption*), and *The Green Mile*. Even his epic story of time travel in *11/22/63* manages to not only think outside the box of traditional terror, but also explores the possibilities of love and devotion across the boundaries of time and fate. Again, another example of the artist's versatilities within the realms of providing an emotionally absorbing experience.

It was late December 1999, and it was time for one final movie to close out the twentieth century. I'm deeply grateful that movie was *The Green Mile*—something that perhaps only *I* gave a damn about.

*****

This is the last film of 1999 I shall discuss in any great detail, and subsequently, the end of the last year of this book.

Like my first two books in the *It's Strictly Personal* trilogy, I once again invite you to go back in time to the beginning. Not necessarily the beginning of *this* book, which began with the sci-fi thriller *The Lawnmower Man*, but rather the beginning of the first book which introduced readers to an eight-year-old boy who experienced the 1975 Walt Disney fantasy film *Escape to Witch Mountain*. Even *I'm* astonished at how far one's life can travel in twenty-five years, as the innocence of childhood evolves into the preadolescence of boyhood, into the hormonal rages of a teenager and college student, and finally into a (supposedly) mature adult—and all through the eyes and experiences of the movies. So many movies, so many time periods, and so many people. How many of those people still exist in my life today, and how many of them faded to black just like the end of a movie?

The twentieth century ended for me and Beth not with a bang, but with a soft whimper in Dallas, Texas, and a New Year's Eve spent in front of the TV watching different locales of the globe usher in the new millennium in their own celebratory fashion. I don't even recall watching the infamous ball drop in Manhattan's Times Square to the voice of Dick Clark. In all likelihood, Beth fell asleep before midnight and I decided to pop a movie into my in-laws' VCR instead.

Returning home to New York in those first few days of January 2000, the world was unchanged. The paranoid fears of Y2K didn't come to pass, and it was life as usual. Work continued, love and relationships continued, and the movies continued. Leftover from '99, *The Talented Mr. Ripley* was first on my list of movies to see. When it was over, I was deeply inspired to visit its filming locations in Rome and Venice as soon as possible (as of this writing, I *still* haven't been to Italy). I also fully expected (and hoped for) a theatrical sequel to pick up where Matt Damon's Tom Ripley left off after having strangled his male lover. Such a sequel (to this day) was never released in the United States.

The start of the 2000s at the movies would be a mediocre one, as I didn't see anything that peaked my interest until the summer blockbuster season with *Gladiator*, *Mission: Impossible 2*, and *X-Men*. Interestingly, even the screen disappointments didn't seem all that terrible because next to me was Beth to share it all. This was the optimistic side of me acknowledging that in the end, good or bad, time at the movies with the woman I loved never felt wasted. Everything in that light was filled with the possibility of potential, even the not-so-great movies.

The new and glorious century had begun. Work was good, economic times were good, my love life and the future it held was good, the family beach house in Westhampton Beach was open again, the new *Star Wars* prequel trilogy was alive and underway, we still had a Democrat in the White House, and there seemed every reason to believe the party would continue come the next Presidential election in November 2000.

What could possibly go wrong?

And that, my friends, was the year 1999 for me.

Before We Say Goodbye (For the Last Time)

Once again, we ask the big question: *Why stop now?* Actually, it's easier to answer this time—nothing makes a better stopping point than the end of the century. Not to suggest that life, love and the movies stop at the end of the century, but rather they take an alternate turn by this particular point in my life.

While the year 2000 brought a very optimistic view of the future for me, it also marked a period of my life where everything plateaued to a steady level, offering little change or inspiration. Work was good, but it was routine. My relationship with Beth was good, but after more than a year together, it had settled into its own form of routine. I knew I wanted to marry her someday (we married on September 30, 2001) and I knew we'd have a future together (our son Sam was born on February 4, 2006), but for the time being, we lived a routine of work, apartment living, restaurant dining, and moviegoing.

I suppose what I'm saying is that at this settled point of my settled life, the movies too, felt *settled*, and that meant they often left me less impressionable. When that happens, the whole thing feels less *strictly personal*. And when *that* happens, it's time for me to stop. Not to suggest the new century was an end to the movies in my world. While I can't imagine my adulthood being what it was without brave and bold new experiments in moviemaking and storytelling like *Memento, A.I. Artificial Intelligence, Mulholland Drive, The Eternal Sunshine of the Spotless Mind,* and *Sideways,* the motion picture business of the twenty-first century has, in my opinion, experienced a severe shift in what people want to see and what Hollywood wants to give them, and it (unfortunately) all started with a movie I love, Brian Singer's first *X-Men* in 2000.

I had no interest in *X-Men* because I knew nothing of them. It was Beth who dragged me to see it in the middle of an afternoon together in East Hampton. I was pleasantly surprised at not only experiencing a solid adventure film with exceptional performances, but also a story that went beyond its surface of a fantasy tale of superheroes with extraordinary mutant powers doing battle with evil beings of more sinister mutant power. At a deeper level, the film offers more socially relevant messages of isolation, racial intolerance, social paranoia and social acceptance. From its inception in 1944 Nazi Poland, we're reminded of how history was greatly impacted by an evil race who feared what they didn't understand, or what they chose not to accept. In the present day, many of the "good" mutants who join forces as the collective "X-Men" are, nonetheless, feared by the general public because of the powers they possess and the inability of others to understand these powers.

The entire political issue behind the mutant's existence and forced registration serves as a throwback to Nazi Germany when Jews and others outside the social norm were forced to register themselves and carry their proper papers with them. In the world of *X-Men*, social class and struggle exists not only between humans and mutants, but between all mutants, as well. By the film's end, even when our heroes have saved Manhattan and its political foreign visitors at Ellis Island, we depart from the story unsure of what will become of the human race, and how we'll relate to each other. The fact that Ellis Island is part of this sequence serves as a reminder of history's immigrants who once came to America seeking freedom from the oppression left behind in their old countries.

There may also be a reflection of society's traditional and unacceptable attitude towards the gay community (perhaps it's a direct message from Bryan Singer himself, who is openly bisexual), or towards the issues of illegal immigration, or variations in religious beliefs, or simply the fact that some people exist in the world who are different from others. Whatever the choice, the film asks us to think about who we are in real life, what we choose to accept and not accept, and with time and patience, realize the potential that we *can* behave better towards each other. I saw this potential when watching *X-Men*, the first superhero movie of the new century by a director trying to also make a valid social statement, and it seemed like things were off to a good and intelligent start for this genre of moviemaking.

I think I was very wrong. Not only did *X-Men* inevitably lead itself into an overblown film franchise (thirteen films total, so far), but it also kick-started a new-century overrun with endless comic-book action films and the inevitable (and sometimes unfortunate) sequels they generate. This makes my son and his generation of preteens and teens happy and enthusiastic, but for me personally, it makes my head spin. For every one of these spectacles I may find exceptionally good like *The Dark Knight* and the first *Avengers* film, there's the onslaught of many others whose story not only encompasses our world, but alternate worlds of the past, future, and who knows what else. My son may follow all of it intelligently, but it's impossible for me to express any interest between multiple *Avengers*, *Spider-Man*, *Guardians of the Galaxy*, and *Suicide Squad* films.

Director Martin Scorsese personally claims these movies are *"not cinema"* and further adds, *"Honestly, the closest I can think of them, as well made as they are, with actors doing the best they can under the circumstances, is* theme parks. *It isn't the cinema of human beings trying to convey emotional, psychological experiences to another human being."* Such a critical statement may piss off a lot of comic-book fanboys, but I consider the man's statements dead on.

This is our world of movies now, but I didn't see it turning out that way when the new century began. Besides *X-Men* and some of the exceptional titles I previously mentioned, there was also the events of September 11, 2001. That may sound odd to you, but bear with me for a moment and I'll try to express myself in my own fashion on this day of remembrance and reflection.

It's impossible for me to discuss that tragic Tuesday more than twenty years ago without telling you where I was that morning. I was on my way to work in Greenwich Village when the subway train stopped at Christopher Street. The train doors failed to close and we didn't move for some time. Impatient, I left the train and walked the rest of the way to my office. As I made my way to Varick Street, I saw people gathered in large masses. I looked around and couldn't account for a reason for this. I didn't see a traffic accident, a fight between people, or anything unusual. It didn't occur to me to raise my head and look *up* for several minutes. When I did, I was shocked to see the huge plume of smoke smoldering from the first tower hit by the plane at the World Trade Center. From my street perspective, though I could see only *one* tower, as the other one was directly behind it, hidden from my view.

A short time later, I witnessed the great ball of fire that was the explosion of the second plane hitting the second tower, though I didn't know this yet. From my perspective, it appeared as if the explosion stemmed from the first building—a result of the raging fire, I imagined. By the time I got to my office and turned on the radio, I learned, like every other American that day, what was happening to our country. A short time later, I and other colleagues stood in the conference room facing the burning towers. Try to imagine a roomful of architects discussing whether or not the steel structures of the 110-story towers will hold, when all of a sudden they each collapse within a time period of one hour and forty-two minutes. When I finally got home that night to Eighty-Sixth Street after a long walk from the Village, Beth and I held each other like never before.

Let me now tell you of the feelings I experienced through the movies and how they impacted my life following that horrifying day. Because downtown Manhattan was closed below Fourteenth Street for several days, I was home glued to the TV news like many others. When I felt I could no longer tolerate the stories and the images anymore, I switched channels and was consoled by an airing of *Close Encounters of the Third Kind*. Suddenly, I was an innocent ten-year-old boy again seeing the film for the first time at the Zeigfeld Theatre in 1977, and a sense of calming peace filled my soul (I even took to writing a personal letter to Steven Spielberg himself, which he, of course, never answered. You can read it for yourself in *It's Strictly Personal*).

No longer able to withstand the confinements of my apartment, the movies played a huge role in trying to slowly recover. The first movie I went to see just days after 9/11 was *The Others*. Hardly an uplifting film, but a good, solid ghost story that helped take my mind off of things. That weekend, Beth and I went to see an outrageous French comedy with Gérard Depardieu and Daniel Auteuil called *The Closet*. The following weekend, when we were back at the beach house, we went to laugh at *Shrek* on screen for the second time. I was already anticipating *Star Wars: Episode II—Attack of the Clones* the following summer, and thinking to myself, "George Lucas, we need you now more than ever. Please don't let us down."

In such a short time following 9/11, the movies helped to save my fragile state of mind. But there was also something about the motion picture industry and how movies were handled and marketed in the wake of the attacks. Hollywood displayed a very rare (and very *temporary*) shift in sensitivity toward violence and destruction on screen and attempted to raise the spirits of the American people. They started by immediately pushing back the release of the Arnold Schwarzenegger terrorist-action vehicle *Collateral Damage* to spring 2002. This was a good start. The Gene Hackman/Owen Wilson film *Behind Enemy Lines*, released a month and a half after 9/11, while receiving mostly negative reviews, was a considerable box office success because of its patriotic subject matter during a time when American patriotism was at a new high level. A scheduled TV airing of the 1992 Wesley Snipes thriller *Passenger 57* on Cinemax was cancelled (for obvious reasons) and even an NBC airing of *Back to the Future* was sensitive to the use of the word "terrorist" and deleted it from the film's dialogue (that may have taken things too far, but there you have it). Hollywood even surprised me by simultaneously rereleasing every screen comedy from the previous summer of 2001 because they knew as I did, that nothing heals like the power of laughter.

It appeared as if the insensitive money-whoring pigs who run "Tinsel town" were actually capable of acting like human beings when national tragedy demanded it. But like I said, it was very temporary. Before we knew it, movie makers were up-and-running again in an effort to destroy as many of our American cities as box office tickets would allow—whether through natural causes as in *The Day After Tomorrow*, invading aliens in Spielberg's remake of *War of the Worlds*, giant robots in Michael Bay's *Transformers* movies, a videotaped monster in *Cloverfield*, and Earth's destruction in films like *2012* and *Battle: Los Angeles*. Shit, I hadn't seen that much destruction on screen since the summer of 1998 when New York City was clobbered by a giant comet, an asteroid the size of Texas, and Godzilla himself. Clearly, nothing sells movie tickets to the common multiplex movie-goer like good 'ol fashioned self-destruction.

Take a moment now to think back to the state and mood of our county immediately following the attack on Pearl Harbor in 1941, and remember the war films released only months afterward. American heroes like John Wayne lit up the black-and-white screen to fight for our country. Sure, there was violence and destruction, but it was targeted at our *enemies* overseas and not our own cities at home. Why is it so impossible to think this sort of patriotic film formula wouldn't work today? I mean, if there *had* to be two more John Rambo films since the '80s, would it not have been exciting to see Sylvester Stallone kick some royal Al Qaeda ass? Maybe it's just me, but not only would I have paid good money to see this kind of sequel, but I would've cheered my damn American ass off.

Let me ask *this* question—is it going to take another fatal trag-edy on American soil before the powers-that-be of the motion picture industry realize that movies *can* serve a higher purpose and respon-sibility than merely creating yet another globally destructive enemy force that the heroes of the DC and Marvel world need to save us from in this world or an alternate one? I've said this before and I'll gladly repeat it now—movies, when done with a certain degree of intelligence and sensitivity, have the power to reach us, teach us, and perhaps every so often, give us some positive meaning and inspiration in our lives. Even if I'm occasionally impressed by some of today's modern releases like *Blade Runner 2049*, *A Quiet Place*, *Bohemian Rhapsody*, *1917*, and *Tenet*, I still ask where that meaning and inspi-ration lies today. *Some* may find it in the endless superhero sequels of our time, but they'll never inspire anything in *me* (and others, I'm sure).

Perhaps the big question isn't so much, why stop now, but rather do the movies have any future? Will they ever be great again? Will they ever "save" our lives again? If you read David Denby's 2013 book *Do the Movies Have a Future*, he believes with his own sense of hope and passion, that they *do* have a future. For myself, I don't know what the answers are. Perhaps the answers depend on *us*, and how we choose to embrace the films out there today, and those to come. The recent COVID-19 pandemic took away many of our options with the closing of movie theaters, while at the same time, enhanced our possibilities with subscription video on-demand streaming services like HBO Max, Hulu and Netflix. But if we choose *not* to invest our time, money and minds on the crap that's out there, then perhaps Hollywood will get the message and use their imaginations of originality again, and treat its audience with a little more respect and a little less insult.

That's unrealistic thinking on my part, I'm sure. But still, I believe the change can happen with anyone who has the passion of keeping the movies *strictly personal*. It's that passion that *can* and *will* bring the movies back to life again.

It starts with *me*.

CPSIA information can be obtained
at www.ICGtesting.com
Printed in the USA
BVHW041250230323
661009BV00001B/50